The Offshore Advantage

Terry Neal

The
Offshore
Advantage

Privacy, Asset Protection, Tax Shelters
Offshore Banking & Investing

MasterMedia Publishing Corp.

Contact:
MasterMedia Publishing Corp.
515 NW Saltzman Rd, Suite 752
Portland, OR 97229
Tel: 800-334-8232 Fax: 503-668-0494

Library of Congress Cataloging-in-Publication Data:
Neal, Terry, 1946-
    The offshore advantage : privacy, asset protection, tax shelters,
offshore banking & investing / Terry Neal.
    p. : cm.
    ISBN 1-57101-331-8
    1. Tax shelters — Law and legislation — United States — Popular
works. 2. Tax havens — United States   I. Title
Kf6297.5.Z9N43   1998
343.7305' 2044 — dc21   98-40732
                                                                                    CIP

Manufactured in the United States of America

Table of Contents

Foreword

For over twenty years I have helped people to achieve their financial objectives by "going offshore" with their money. What did these people hope to achieve?

Many wanted financial privacy, realizing that their affairs were an open book here in the United States. Others desired solid legal protection for their wealth, a financial fortress against lawsuits, ex-spouses, governmental confiscation's and many other growing threats to their financial security. Undoubtedly, many were looking to save or defer taxes, admittedly a goal that is increasingly difficult to legitimately achieve offshore, but nevertheless one that beckons those seeking the few remaining loopholes. Lastly, we have seen a growing number of Americans and other nationals who rightly believe they must globally diversify their investments and who happily discovered a cornucopia of good investment opportunities.

These underscore a few of the many reasons there is such a massive outflow of money to safer havens. Unfortunately, it also highlights the fact that while the U.S. may still be a premier nation amongst nations, it is simply no longer the safest place for your wealth.

Whatever your reasons for exploring the world of offshore finance, it can indeed be tricky terrain for the uninitiated. That's why I am thrilled that Terry Neal has written *The Offshore Advantage*. No one knows the ropes better than Terry Neal. Terry Neal brings to this book almost 25 years of experience in the offshore arena. His firm Offshore Corporate Services has provided efficient, knowledgeable fiduciary services to so many of my offshore clients that I can confidently say that he is truly a master of the "ins and outs" of the offshore world. *The Offshore Advantage* shares these secrets in a most informative and interesting way.

This is a book that should be read by anyone with concerns about money. If you have never journeyed abroad with your money, you will learn how to take those important first steps. If you are a seasoned foreign investor, you will find many new and better ways to maximize the offshore advantage. If you are a professional or financial advisor, you will have at your fingertips precisely the information your clients want and need – and expect you to have.

Even if you have read a score of books on offshore finance, you will want to read *The Offshore Advantage*. Offshore strategies are ever changing. The laws, economic trends and opportunities change with time, as will the conditions of your life. This book, with its many sound ideas can be your blueprint for a more financially secure future now and in the new millenium.

Arnold S Goldstein, JD, LLM, Ph.D.
Author of *Offshore Havens* and
    How to Protect Your Money Offshore

Preface

Independence Day 1998 my family and I watched the largest July 4th fire works display on the U.S. West Coast from the motor yacht Zarahemla anchored in the Columbia River between Portland, Oregon and Vancouver, Washington. Three generations of Americans on board thrilled to the magnificent aerial display that has come to commemorate our country's birthday. Sunday morning July 5th our church service began with the singing of "God Bless America." It ended as we stood and sang our national anthem "The Star Spangled Banner." These were passionate events that brought tears to our eyes and made us feel ever so blessed to have been born in the greatest nation on earth and to be a part of this very special country which was founded on a freedom formed by a visionary people to ensure the inalienable right of liberty for all.

Notwithstanding my love and passion for this great country I fear for its future. We are no longer what we were. I have discovered first hand that information and education can be easily manipulated to achieve the objectives of those in power. Our free press, the cornerstone and guardian of our liberty, has largely become a tool of the elite. Greed and power have made the "Spinmeister" the ultimate professional for the overlords of America.

Perhaps some of the information we will cover together may be familiar to you. For most, the truth comes as a shock. You may wonder why this information is not common knowledge or why it isn't highlighted in the media. The fact is that the truth is frequently overshadowed by rhetoric. And it would appear that the major benefactors of both of America's political partys' interests would not be well served were some of these truths openly and honestly reviewed.

As to those in the media, it is best one keep in mind that they are driven by advertisers. Over a portion of my life I have been involved in this industry and I write from some experience. Perhaps a small example may help to illustrate. I once had a discussion with a rather famous producer of the investigative television program known as "20-20." He was in hot pursuit of scandalous information for a program he was then producing. When discovering some really positive information about the industry he was preparing to trash, and in response to my question as to whether or not he would include it in his programming, he said, —"If you want good news buy advertising; scandal generates ratings, good news is boring."

That comment speaks volumes, but let me pose a question — Do you think for, even an instant, that "20-20" or any other investigative program would be allowed to trash the advertisers that keep them on the air? The reason for their concentration on scandal is largely an issue of ratings. Higher ratings mean advertisers pay more to get their message out to viewers. Programming is ratings and advertising driven.

Much of what you're going to read in this book is not taught in school, but it should be. Government must approve educational curriculum, and instruction in truth, outside the sciences, is not always helpful to those in power. There are few sources you can consult to learn what is offered in these pages. My objective is that you gain new insights, understand what's going on, and use this information to your considerable benefit.

You may want to internalize a number of facts before your mind will even begin to allow you to implement the critical strategies necessary for you to secure your future in these tumultuous times. There is good news in this book, but I would first like to present a summary of some negative information for you to consider:

Regarding Predatory Litigation

70% of the world's lawyers reside in the U.S.

94% of the world's lawsuits are in the U.S.

Litigation on commission is illegal virtually everywhere in the world except the U.S.

The US is graduating record numbers of lawyers and there are now more law students in school than in actual practice.

If you earn $50,000 or more per annum your chances are one in four of being caught up in adversarial litigation next year.

Regarding Your Rights To Privacy

Privacy rights are virtually gone in the US. Your private bank statements, phone logs, credit card purchases, brokerage statements, and so forth, are largely available to those who might want to do you harm. And, of course, any information about your property holdings, leases, credit financing, credit information and the like, is readily available. Predatory lawyers and government employees are free to draw adverse conclusions from these records as they build a profile on you.

Regarding US Tax Revenues

25% of wage earners in the US carry 80% of the tax load.
The top 10% of income earners pay 58.2% of total taxes.
The bottom 50% of income earners contribute only 4.8% of America's tax receipts.

The Internal Revenue

The IRS is more cloaked in secrecy than the CIA.
The US General Accounting Office calls the IRS "not auditable for the fourth straight year in a row.
We don't know how the IRS works, and it operates with impunity because we don't know.
Without court authority, the IRS can seize your assets.
Without a warrant, IRS can obtain information on you from banks, credit card companies, and numerous other sources.

Regarding the US Constitution

The American bureaucracy has made a clear mockery of the greatest document ever written by the hand of man — the Constitution of the United States.

The separation of powers deemed critical by our forefathers has been thoroughly abandoned in light of bureaucratic r u l - ings. Agencies of the federal government have combined the legislative, judicial, and executive powers of government unto themselves, in clear violation of the Constitution.

The Post Office, IRS, DEA, SEC, ATF, FBI, and other monolithic bureaucratic institutions can seize your assets and deem you guilty of crimes against the state, (victimless crimes) without due process, and it becomes your responsibility to prove your innocence. The concept "innocent until proven guilty" now only seems to apply to crimes of violence.

Elsewhere, within the pages that follow, I argue briefly that we are in the midst of a class revolution. This revolution is not about blood and bullets. It is about education and economics. Those who take the time to learn something beyond the party line and carefully and prudently act upon their newly-found knowledge, move rapidly beyond the rank and file. They literally become members of a new class of enlightened, self-directed, financially solvent, independent, free citizens.

Terry L. Neal

Acknowledgements

Many individuals have contributed to the writing of this book, and the author is honored to express appreciation to: Lee Morgan and Aaron Young, my associates and men of particular insight and integrity; Neal Toutant whose intelligence and background have added depth to the text, Felix Reuben, a constant inspiration and close confident, Kirk Koskella, a client and friend who has developed a considerable depth of knowledge in some of the more complex offshore strategies; and Dr Sherry L Meinberg, my sister and an author herself, who patiently read the entire manuscript and provided comments and grammatical corrections.

Michael Potter, Arnold Goldstein, Arnold Cornez, Larry Turpin, and Michael Brette have all written books on asset protection and the offshore world. Their influence, friendship, and business relationships I acknowledge and appreciate. A special thanks goes to the law firm of Potter & Day for providing the working draft for the chapter on Fraudulent Transfers. Many thanks to Albert Yokum, editor and publishing consultant, who personally converted the manuscript into a book and who has provided invaluable expertise in this publication and a prior book entitled *Barter & The Future of Money*. There are many more that have directly or indirectly contributed and I thank them all, and hope that my efforts measure up to the invaluable contributions they have so freely given.

Introduction

This book is not for everyone. This book is directed to what I call the *Upward Mobile, Middle Class*. These are they who have family incomes of $40,000 and up, or have committed themselves to be there.

This is a book about **Privacy** and the lack of it. This is a book about **Asset Protection**, the need for it and how to do it. This is a book about **Tax Havens**, why they exist and how they work. And, this is a book about **Offshore Investing**, and what you don't know about it.

What is it about the word "*offshore*" that stirs the emotions of almost anyone who hears it? Isn't it amazing that almost everyone has an opinion about offshore banking, for example, and few know anything about it? Incredibly, and notwithstanding the glamour associated with international travel, the percentage of people who have a working knowledge of Offshore Financial Centers is small, particularly when contrasted with the huge amount of misinformation on the subject. This book is designed to clear up the mystery.

Why another book on Asset Protection? Is there really more to be said about the loss of privacy in America? Does anyone out there really care about the erosion of personal rights, given the current financial strength of the U.S. economy? Do reasonable people concern themselves with the run-amok government of America, or is it only a cause for nutcase right wing radicals?

This book began several years ago when the overwhelming evidence of government by the government became the basic principal overarching multiple pieces of legislation and executive rulings. The incredibly bold precepts promulgated by the founding fathers of America called for a government "by the people, for the people." That day is past. According to an ever-growing number of professionals within the legal industry, the U.S. Constitution is simply a relic of history. The greatest document ever struck off by the mind and hand of man, (President George Washington's theme), has become window dressing for a burgeoning, out-of-control bureaucracy that has spawned some fifteen million laws, and rulings, that have the effect of law.

The evil empire, (President Reagan's name for the former Soviet Union), lies in waste. The rising sun of Japan and the setting sun on America, (President Carter's repeated theme), has been reversed. The U.S. dollar has regained it's prominence as the world's most important currency. Even gold, the money of last resort that has served world civilizations for over 5,000 years, has lost it's current bout with the U.S. dollar. The United States Federal Reserve System underwrites the world. And, so it goes. So why would anyone want to go offshore, out there where the drug dealers hang out and nothing is really safe?

Contrary to public opinion, the offshore industry and it's correlative, offshore banking, is legal, safe, and can provide many benefits that are no longer available in America. This should sadden us all, but to ignore these realities is to do so at your financial peril.

As radical as it may sound, I am personally convinced that America is once again in the midst of a revolution. This revolution is not about blood and bullets, it's about education and economics. And, when I say education, I mean what it used to mean – clear knowledge about a subject, not the confusion we so frequently encounter today.

If after you've read this book you're not motivated to talk about it with friends, and you don't believe it's really necessary to reorganize your affairs, it means only one of two things:

1. I've failed to put across the need and urgency for you to take action
2. You are not apart of the upward mobile middle class

Please devour this book. Read it with colored pencils and scribble all over it. New information will be coming at you at a remarkable rate, mark it as you read. I hope you enjoy reading it as much as I have writing it.

Terry L. Neal

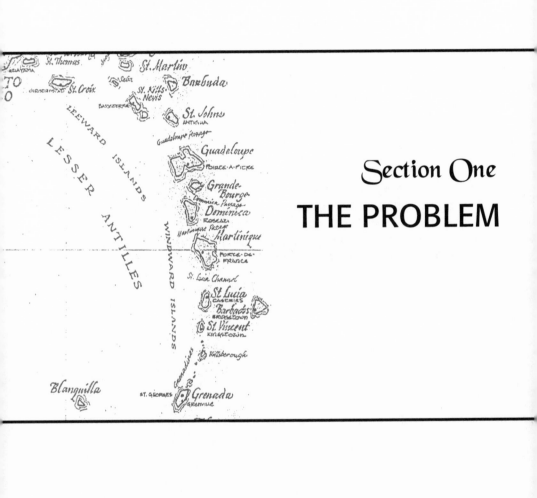

Section One

THE PROBLEM

A Word of Caution

There are many advantages to offshore strategies, including guaranteed privacy, premier asset protection, various tax shelter options, and higher and safer investment returns. But before you launch into the offshore world, I recommend you access consultation services. You may want to call us for a referral at 604-684-2622 in Vancouver, Canada; 503-645-9553 in Portland, Oregon; or 869-469-1606 in Nevis, West Indies.

∞ Chapter 1 ∞

GLOBAL THINKING

"People find new information distinctly threatening, because if they incorporate it they will have to do a good deal of work to revise their maps of reality, and they instinctively seek to avoid that work. Consequently, more often than not they will fight against the new information rather than for its assimilation."

M. Scott Peck
"The Road Less Traveled"

GLOBAL THINKING

If you've ever seen the aftermath of a tidal wave, you cannot help be moved by its devastating power. Boats smashed to pieces and scattered on the shore, buildings collapsed -- a vast scene of destruction and disarray. And yet, if you have boating experience and are out to sea, you know that a tidal wave can move right beneath your hull and you might never know the difference.

That's the way it is with the truly massive changes in the world. They seem to happen with sudden fury, but in reality the big transformations move beneath us so silently we rarely know what is happening.

CLAIMING PERSONAL SOVEREIGNTY

A tidal wave is sweeping under us today. Money has burst through the floodwalls of national borders and now flows freely wherever it will. People with money recognize that no single country is a safe haven for their wealth and now send it wherever they get the best return.

This change is part of the process that is causing the death of national governments. A change that is inevitable if governments can't control the exodus of money. Feeling the threat, the bureaucracy reacts with ever-harsher means of exacting wealth from the people whom government was created to protect. Later chapters deal with the forces that are transforming the US government and the subsequent pressures which US citizens will encounter.

The nation state is being superseded by a host of overlapping quasi-governmental bodies while at the same time national borders are uncontrollable -- open to a flow of drugs, illegal immigrants and cash. Nationality has more meaning now as an ethnic preference than a political persuasion.

The alert individual is claiming personal sovereignty as nation states lose their authority. Slowly, quietly, as if waking from a dream, we take control of our lives and make the decisions that are best for us. Governments can no longer deliver what they promise -- protection and security. It is the task of the sovereign individual to assume those responsibilities.

GO WITH THE FLOW

There are three kinds of people in the world: those who make things happen; those who watch things happen; and those who wonder what happened. The people who steer their ships safely to harbor are those who "make things happen;" those who never get off the dock are the ones who "watch what happened;" and those whose ships get dashed on the rocks are the ones who simply "wonder what happened."

By understanding the processes that are in play, the individual who makes things happen has the opportunity to place assets in secure locations and watch them grow. These pages tell how to chart that course. The other two types may as well close this book now.

We are concerned in this chapter with global change as it affects the flow of money. Therefore, consider these pieces of information:

1. Personal income in the U.S. in 1994 was $5.6 trillion.
2. The most widely used figure for the amount of money held by offshore tax free jurisdictions is $5 trillion.
3. By 1995, the total value of the world's equities was $18 trillion.
4. From 1980 to 1994 the movement of U.S. wealth into stocks in foreign lands increased by a factor of 16, to $1.5 trillion.
5. The richest country in the world per capita in 1992 was Liechtenstein, a tax haven in Europe where the average per capita GNP was $54,070, more than double the figure for the U.S. It is thought that this number has climbed every year through 1998.

6. The difference in income per head of household
   between Switzerland and Mozambique, is about 400
   to 1. Two hundred and fifty years ago, the gap between
   the richest and poorest nation was perhaps only 5 to 1.

Why are these numbers significant? Because they show the dramatic flow of money and the shift in wealth. This is the tide one either rides toward riches, or misses, and then spends the rest of existence wallowing in the shallows.

THE NEW NATURAL RESOURCE

The most sought-after natural resource in the world today is not oil, natural gas, timber or even gold. It is people with assets — the ones I call the Upward Mobile Middle Class. These people are those that either have combined family incomes of $40,000 or more, or, they are one's that have committed themselves to be there. These are those that comprise the top 25% of the wage earners in America. These are the productive in society, those committed to thinking smart and working hard.

Many of the Upward Mobile Middle Class have incomes well in excess of $250,000 per year, but taken as a group these are the people to whom this book is written. The vast majority of the Upward Mobile Middle Class would be described as educated (no diplomas required), resourceful, believers in personal freedom, honest, fair, and responsible.

Nations now compete with one another to bestow citizenship, tax incentives -- even status as diplomats -- on individuals who have money and who are willing to either reside in their country or at least to deposit their cash there. Elsewhere in this book you will read about the advantages many countries offer.

Hong Kong Chinese are a case in point. For years wealthy Chinese business people worried what the Communists would do when they reclaimed the crown colony from the British in 1997. To protect themselves and their assets, many of them put their apartments up for sale. With the million dollars or more even small units sold for, they became instantly wealthy by Western standards, and looked for a haven for their money.

More than 100,000 of them were attracted to Vancouver, British Columbia. At the time, Canada did not require immigrants to declare the wealth they held outside the country. The Chinese saw this as an opportunity to spread out their money in a variety of safe places.

Many of them obtained Canadian passports -- just in case -- and put money in Canada and elsewhere while continuing to live or do business in Hong Kong. In one Canadian government program, all they had to do to gain citizenship was to create at least one job. In another program they had to have more than $350,000 in assets and invest at least $245,000 in a business that creates jobs before they arrived.

Many have settled into life in Canada. But others see themselves as stateless -- their ancestry in China, their residence and passport in Canada, and their wealth wherever they please. These people are called "astronauts" because they rocket back and forth across the Pacific between Vancouver, where their wives and money are, and Hong Kong, where they still run businesses.

The world is awash in anecdotes about the stateless elite -- people with money who have divorced themselves from affiliation with any but the most convenient country. One individual is reported to have come up with the money required to buy citizenship in a Central American nation, and added enough to become an ambassador from that country to the U.S. He renounced his U.S. citizenship but continued to live in his home in Florida, driving about with his diplomatic license plates, immune not only from paying U.S. taxes, but also parking tickets.

The statistics about Liechtenstein and Switzerland are of particular interest because for years they have been tax havens within Europe and have become prosperous because they attract the wealth of that continent's elite. The same is true of many Caribbean nations that have become prosperous as banking centers for the wealthy.

Not everyone is in a position to become part of the stateless elite. But practically everyone is able to send at least part of his or her wealth offshore to a safe location.

STATELESS WEALTH

You are probably an overseas investor already and are not aware of it. Chances are if you own mutual funds, part of your investment is now abroad, invested in a foreign company. Pension and mutual funds, insurance companies, universities, foundations and big-time investors have been downsizing their investments in the U.S. economy for years and redirecting greater amounts to quality offshore jurisdictions. The reasoning is that the U.S. stock markets have grown so far so fast that eventually they are headed for a crash or at least a significant downturn, as evidenced by the events of August and September of 1998. Since the U.S. market can't grow so fast forever, why not seek sanctuary in markets that are not yet overheated?

The effect is like a stone thrown into a still pond, causing ripples to wash up on many shores. The exodus of U.S. cash has literally created stock markets around the world, and made many people wealthy. In the formerly Communist countries of Eastern Europe, for example, equities are booming. The value of Poland's stock market rose 77 percent in a year.

There was a sixteen-fold increase in the amount of U.S. money invested in foreign stocks from 1980 to 1994 -- up to $1.5 trillion. Overseas investments account for one eighth of all money invested by U.S. mutual funds and pensions. Pensions alone have about $400 billion invested in foreign securities and are expected to add $150 billion to that total over the next three years.

Most of the money goes into either "global funds," which can buy equities anywhere in the world, or "international funds," that buy only abroad. In the 1970s, only 30 percent of the stocks available for investment were in foreign countries. Now, 60 percent of all stocks available are from foreign lands and that number is growing fast. Many of them are improbable mixes: for example, to invest in the Middle East you are likely to get a basket of stocks including companies from both Israel and Arab nations.

In the mid 1980s there were 29 global and international funds, but little more than a decade later there were 658. The assets of these funds grew from $5.2 billion to $264 billion. Much of that investment in foreign mutual funds was drawn out of investments in U.S. companies, U.S. bonds and U.S. money market accounts.

EMERGING MARKETS

The axiom that a "rising tide raises all boats" could not be truer than in the "emerging markets." The upwelling of value in the U.S. stock exchanges has overflowed into other countries, creating wealth and opportunities previously unknown. Emerging markets" is a marketing euphemism devised in 1981 by Antoine van Agtmael, a World Bank official, to put a better face on developing Third World economies. World Bank president Robert McNamara was then moving to launch stock exchanges in these countries.

Emerging markets consist of thirty-nine nations in Latin America, Eastern Europe and Asia, with the exception of Japan. These have been profitable avenues for investment. The average diversified fund in such countries rose 38 percent in 1993. In 1994, nineteen out of twenty of the best-performing stock markets in the world were in such countries. South African stocks, for example, have outperformed the Dow Jones Industrial Average by 25 percent over several years.

By the twenty-first century the economic output of these developing nations will account for 60 percent of the world's production. China alone will overtake the United States as the world's largest economy by 2020. That country has shown economic growth of 4 percent to 14 percent yearly throughout a decade.

South Korea will be a bigger economy than Great Britain soon, notwithstanding the currency crisis and resultant recession in 1998. They have built manufacturing facilities to take advantage of cheap labor and raw materials everywhere from Oregon to Central and South America -- more than 200 plants in Latin America alone. These Korean enterprises account for half the clothing industry in Guatemala as well as Honduras. That means the Koreans can produce goods with wages as low as 11 cents per hour with practically no unions, and then export into the lucrative U.S. market through the North Atlantic Free Trade Agreement.

National governments can no longer shield weak industries. Governments now yield to pressure for "free trade" or risk being sidelined and impoverished, like North Korea or Cuba. The World Trade Organization serves as the battering ram to demolish protectionist barriers to competition. Telephone systems around the world have traditionally been a preserve of national companies and protected monopolies. Yet these, too, are destined to become things of the past in sixty-seven nations in Asia, Latin America and elsewhere.

Ratepayers are likely to save as much as $1 trillion as international long distance rates plummet. But it was either lower the rates or die, because international telephone calls are about to be superseded by Internet telephony. Through the Internet it is possible to talk anywhere in the world for no incremental cost beyond a monthly access fee.

The world is opening up to U.S. investors who are willing to think globally, notwithstanding governmental initiatives to discourage external investment.

EUROPE

Will Europe challenge U.S. hegemony, or is the continent destined to sink into a dreamless sleep? The European community's forthcoming joint currency -- the European Monetary Unit (Euro) -- may exact a price Europe can ill afford to pay. To be considered stable and responsible enough to take part, participating governments must limit national debt to 60 percent of Gross Domestic Product. At the same time, annual budget deficits cannot be more than 3 percent of GDP.

For the Euro to work, it is important that each participating country tow the line with these standards. Otherwise, why would the thrifty Germans give up their perfectly good Deutschmark or the Swiss their Frank if the Portuguese, Italians or some other country lacking discipline ran up huge deficits and debased the currency for the others?

Many European countries cannot meet these exacting standards. France, for example, is having difficulty getting its house in order. And Britain will not be ready to take part when the Euro is launched. The value of currency now becomes a function of government discipline and management. It is a standard which European governments will feel compelled to meet. If the British Pound or the French Franc try to stand apart from the Euro, it is certain those currencies will become deeply discounted and their citizens will not be able to compete in the European marketplace.

Meeting the criteria has put Italy between a rock and a hard place. The Italian government's budget must meet the accepted standards or Italy will not be accepted in the European Monetary Union by target date 1999. But Italy is also under pressure to provide services and incentives for young families to have children. At this writing, Italy has the world's lowest fertility rate -- 1.17 children per couple. At that rate, the average age of Italy's workers will be close to 70 in 2050, and Italians could become extinct in 200 years.

There are now more Italians over 60 years old than there are under 20. This is known as the "cross over" phenomenon and is unlikely to be reversed. The United States will experience this as well, but not until 2035.

Other countries in Europe, such as Germany, France, and Sweden, are also experiencing population decline. Productivity is bound to fall in these countries as more resources go toward pensions and medical bills and less toward investment and production. Europe may be a short-term challenge to the United States, but on the long term is likely headed for an era of quiet and rest.

WEALTH SEEKS SAFETY

The U.S. dollar has been the standard for international transactions for decades -- but will it remain so with a solid Euro on the horizon? Although the dollar seems impregnable at this writing, remember that it was not too long ago that the Pound Sterling was the monetary measure of the world.

If the dollar is ever dethroned, it will have disastrous consequences for those whose wealth is stored in this currency. The U.S. economy is able to function as well as it does because hundreds of billions of dollars in U.S. cash leaves the country every year to become the monetary unit for the world's underground economy. Indeed, at this writing approximately two out of every three dollars are abroad. Can you imagine what would happen if all those dollars came back to America? How about run away inflation?

In Russia, for example, the U.S. $100 bill is the standard unit of exchange and many businesses will not accept the Russian Ruble. When drug dealers tote suitcases of currency across borders, it is in the U.S. dollar. When billions of barrels of oil are bought and sold, the currency it is evaluated in is the U.S dollar. Serving as the world's standard for international monetary exchanges has given the U.S. dollar great stability. It is in every other country's interest to preserve and defend the value of the dollar because they need it themselves for international exchange. When the dollar is weak relative to other currencies, other countries prop it up.

There is something dreamlike and artificial about the value of the dollar -- almost the way there was about the Ruble under the Communists. The government there set an artificial value for their currency, which worked well enough within its borders, but it was not accepted at the government-fixed rate outside. Eventually, the country could not trade because few would accept their currency at its posted rate. The Soviet Union had to barter hard goods for hard goods.

What would happen to the U.S. dollar -- indeed to the U.S. economy -- if the dollar were displaced by the Euro as the international currency standard? Although the German economy is well managed and so is the Swiss, neither the Deutschmark nor the Swiss Franc could ever be a serious threat to the dollar because their economies are relatively too small. But a unified European currency representing the productive capacity of that entire continent can and may supplant the dollar.

THE OFFSHORE IMPERATIVE

Why is that important to the individual investor? Because if your wealth is measured in dollars and the dollar loses it's vaunted status, your wealth will wither as a result. The only way to protect yourself is to trim your sails to the prevailing winds and have a substantial portion of your wealth aloof from any single currency, ready to flow in any direction.

North Americans have long ignored overseas investments because of fears of the risks. What about runaway inflation, what about sudden devaluation and economic turmoil? Europe has the potential to become a far more secure place to invest than the U.S. The change in Europe is like the tidal wave running under our decks. We have not yet felt the impact -- but we will.

The governments of Europe will have to exercise self-discipline in their welfare state mentality in order to take part in the EMU. Imagine the competition for the U.S. Imagine the opportunity for investors.

When Communism failed, the veil of secrecy about its incompetence and ineptitude was swept away. Now revealed is a continent of poorly constructed buildings, roads, and factories -- you name it -- all needing to be replaced. In addition, there are hundreds of millions of people with a newly acquired taste for the good life. They have whetted this appetite with a surge of purchases from the West. But better still, they also want to participate in our brand of capitalism by producing their own goods and services.

That means there is a universe of opportunity for building new enterprises and generating wealth. That's going to require capital -- hundreds of billions worth -- and the potential rewards for these kinds of investment are great.

WHERE TO GO

The $5 trillion invested offshore in tax free jurisdictions is a very big indication of how attractive these opportunities are. To take advantage of them -- as you will see elsewhere in this book -- it is important to establish part of your own fortune offshore.

The countries that seem to do best in this business are those that have been part of the British Commonwealth. One obvious reason they work well for Americans is that, whether it is Gibraltar, the British Virgin Islands, or Nevis, they all speak English. That simplifies life when conducting banking transactions.

The other reasons these are good sanctuaries for your wealth is that most of them have a history of stable financial conditions where foreign exchange controls have not been repeatedly applied. This is the reason many investors stay away from countries like Brazil and Spanish-speaking Latin American countries. Although it is possible to earn phenomenal interest rates on bank accounts there, inflation is so high that by the time you try to exchange the local currency for U.S. dollars you may wind up behind. Furthermore, many of these countries' central banks have no independence and therefore cannot protect their economies.

Appropriate countries to consider are those that have privacy laws to protect you from governmental interference. Additional details on tax havens are offered elsewhere in this book.

SUMMARY

The world changes at ever increasing speed. With these changes come dangers for the ill-informed, but great opportunities for those who are aware of the way the wind is blowing. This is especially important for people with money who seek to preserve it for themselves and their heirs. For this reason, it is critical to look beyond the borders of the United States for investment opportunities.

There are other, equally compelling reasons to shift at least some of your wealth from any given nation. The picture of investment opportunities abroad may look attractive, but the problems at home may alone be the most significant motivator for moving money offshore. We deal with one of the worst problems in the next chapter.

∞ Chapter 2 ∞

THE LEGAL THREAT TO YOUR ASSETS

*"...the foundation of the destruction of this people is
beginning to be laid by the unrighteousness of your lawyers
and your judges"*

Alma the Younger
Circa 82 BC

THE STATISTICS TELL THE STORY
5% or less of the world's population reside in the U.S.
20% or thereabouts, of the world economy is U.S.
70% of the world's lawyers reside in the U.S.
94% of the world's lawsuits are in the U.S.

Interesting statistics, aren't they? Two questions come immediately to mind: why is this, and how does it affect us?

As to why, there are two possible answers: There are too many lawyers, or Americans are simply too greedy. Are there too many lawyers? Well, consider this:

In the United States there are over 700,000 practicing lawyers.

In the United States there are more students in law school
than there are in practice.

A society with a large quantity of lawyers is oriented towards litigation. Legal confrontation, handled on a contingency or commission basis, is focused on the transferring of wealth through disputes. This is what I call Predatory Litigation.

With so many lawyers chasing work, it is no wonder the U.S. is the most litigious society the world has ever seen. All those lawyers seeking revenue means everyone's assets have become a target. Incredibly, **if your income is $50,000 per year or greater, you have a one in four chance to be involved in a lawsuit this year.**

> Q: Why do so many lawyers have broken noses?
> A: From running into parked ambulances.

It may be a bad joke, but it illustrates the pressure toward litigation that is natural in a society so professionally weighted toward lawyers. And if it's a bad joke, there are plenty more as bad. Just go on the Internet and search for lawyer jokes. There are tens of thousands listed.

You can pretty much tell where a person -- or a society -- is conflicted by the object of its jokes. We joke about sex, spouses, money, ethnic groups -- and lawyers. I have yet to see a lawyer joke that is not hostile, and perhaps that says more about non-lawyers than it does about lawyers. After all, we're the ones who keep them in business.

It may be a cheap shot to blame lawyers for lawsuits. It could be argued that there would be no prostitutes, for example, were there no johns to patronize them. I agree with Walt Kelly, creator of Pogo Possum, whose character said: "We have met the enemy and they is us."

Today's society is the problem, lawsuits are the symptom and lawyers are the facilitators. Lawyers are in business because of simple human greed. For a nostalgic treat, rent the 1960's movie "A New Leaf," with Walter Matthau. He plays a spoiled rich guy who squanders his fortune and then can't pay his bills. Matthau's butler advised him to marry, " . . . because marriage is the only way to acquire assets without working."

Ah, what naive and simple times those were; today the quick path to riches is litigation.

> Q: Why don't sharks eat lawyers?
> A: Professional courtesy.

Do Americans look for something for nothing more than some other nationalities? Maybe so. After all, most of our families came here in search of opportunity -- whether it was the chance to operate a hot dog stand in Brooklyn or homestead free farmland in the Dakotas or strike it rich in the gold fields of California -- they all came here looking for something.

When the free stuff all got taken up with the closing of the American frontier, we kept the get-rich-quick spirit alive through Hollywood, where there was the chance to make it big as a movie star with not much more than a cute figure, good connections, and a flashy smile.

Something-for-nothing is also enshrined in Las Vegas. There, even in the airport is the sound of the slot machine plinking out unearned winnings. This city is the Mecca where pilgrims come with hearts full of hope seeking adrenal kick and the fast buck.

I'd like to believe that my mental musings are just a negative take on a lousy situation, but a recent national survey revealed the following mind-set held by a majority of those supposedly seeking wealth:

SURVEY OF A U.S. BELIEF SYSTEM

Recently a close friend of mine, a prior CIA Ph.D. in Russian studies who now heads up an investment firm, shared with me the results of a U.S. study where those surveyed ranked their opportunities for achieving wealth. The following reveals the unfortunate results:

1. Win the lottery
2. Win a civil lawsuit
3. Receive an inheritance

What does this tell you about the mind set of a growing number of people? What does this say about modern morality, self-reliance, and personal self-discipline?

It takes hard work to develop a business or invest wisely. It takes hard work to build assets and diligently accumulate them into an estate for your own security, your retirement, or as an inheritance for your heirs. Apparently the majority of Americans now believe it's a easier to put a buck into a slot, pull the lever and hope to get a cascade of free money. But what's worse is that a majority of people evidently also consider it perfectly acceptable to find a reason to sue someone in order to make their fortune.

Is it really okay to exploit a real or imagined basis, find a lawyer who'll take a suit on commission, and take a shot at getting into the pockets of a successful person who has spent the time to accumulate assets? Unfortunately it is easier and quicker to sue someone than it is to commit oneself to worthwhile goals, hard work, long hours, and ethical conduct.

THE THREAT TO BUSINESS

Everyone who has anything is vulnerable. But professionals and business owners, large and small, are prime targets for lawsuits. After all, other than rock stars and athletes, who has more wealth to plunder?

In Europe and Latin America, business people are often kidnapped for ransom. But in the U.S. the shakedown comes through lawsuits. Of entrepreneurial companies going public between 1986 and 1993, 62 percent had been sued, according to a survey by the National Venture Capital Association as cited in *Investors Business Daily*. In that same period of time, 19 of the 30 largest companies in Silicon Valley were hit with lawsuits -- totaling half a billion dollars.

"Joint and several liability" or the "deep pockets" approach is an open door for assaults on business assets. Through joint and several liability, if a firm so much as does business with another company that is the target of a lawsuit, it can be dragged in as a defendant to pay damages. It's called the "tort tax," and it cost business owners in America $132.2 billion in 1991 and was estimated to grow by 12 percent per year since 1980, according to Tillinghast, an insurance consulting unit of Towers Perrin.

Some parts of the country are worse than others. Alabama is known to be the best place in the country for plaintiffs seeking damages in product liability cases. Juries there have made some of the highest awards anywhere in the country. The situation is so bad the U.S. Supreme Court in 1996 actually struck down several Alabama laws that required high damage awards and declared them unconstitutional.

Few reasonable people would suggest that companies should not be held liable for defective or dangerous products. But it is also true that product liability lawsuits have stifled entire industries, from breast implants to water slides. There have been Congressional efforts to limit punitive damage awards to $250,000 or three times the compensatory damage, whichever is greater. But there are powerful forces at work against such limitations. One obvious reason is that class action lawsuits for product liability amounts to a $250 million per year income for plaintiff's attorneys, plus all the legal fees the defendants must pay their lawyers.

THE FUTURE

What's the future of lawsuits in America? There will be a lot more of them if the lawyers have their way. Take California, for example, where practically every tenth person you see is a lawyer. The state has prided itself on being the leader in so many things -- and now in law-suits as well. Attorneys and their clients have become increasingly creative in their reasons for suing. As a matter of fact, the trial lawyers there were the largest financial backers of a ballot measure that can be seen as a model of what may be in store for the entire country some day.

California lawyers sponsored Prop 211, which may not have passed but is the legal profession's "wish list." The ballot measure would have made it even easier for stockholders to sue if they lost money on a stock. "Strike suits" are those that target a company when its stock prices drop. There are people whose sole business directive is to buy stock they think will lose value. Then they sue.

The idea was to protect the savings of retirees by giving them greater power against securities fraud. But the biggest winner would have been the state government and the lawyers. The measure would have allowed "punitive damages" against a defendant found guilty of "willful, outrageous or despicable conduct" in stock manipulation. But the people who lost money in such stock frauds would not benefit -- such awards would have gone to the state!

Punitive damages have not been previously allowed as blunder for state or the federal government security suits. If the measure had passed, there is no telling what heights governments may have, or may yet reach with the "punitive damages" concept.

California also toyed with the idea of allowing plaintiffs to collect 100% of damages from deep-pocket defendants. This means that all expenses of a lawsuit could wind up the liability of someone only marginally involved. Even companies headquartered outside California could be dragged into their lawsuits. Several large accounting firms sponsored a study to learn the consequences of such laws, among their findings:

1. a large increase in legal staffs
2. the huge payoff for frivolous lawsuits would result in the equivalent of a 1.6% increase in California State income tax on business, an estimated $1.5 billion per year from the beginning
3. a large exodus of businesses from California

The estimated job loss was such that almost 300,000 people would lose their employment over the next decade as businesses fled such an oppressive atmosphere. And it's not just companies that would suffer: the loss of business would cost every household in the state as much as

$235 per year. Eventually state tax revenues would drop by almost $5 billion over a ten-year period.

The rest of us would be dragged into this lawyer's feast whether we wanted to be or not. The Economic Strategy Institute of Washington, D.C. estimated that such a law in California would cause a drop in U.S. GNP of from $48 billion to $102 billion, and that eventually almost 2 million Americans could lose their jobs.

Whether or not such a law passed in California this time is not the issue; the point is that creative trial lawyers are seeking ever-broadening avenues toward even more lawsuits. And although they may not achieve their goal today or tomorrow, they are going to continue in that direction until they reach the Promised Land of your assets.

AND NOW THE GOVERNMENT

The government has also gotten into lawsuits. Take the experience of James L. Fisher, for example. Since 1972 he had been president of Towson State University and had served on the board of directors of Baltimore Federal Savings & Loan, a solid pillar of the community.

But when the S&L failed in 1988, the federal government slapped him with a $32 million lawsuit charging him with gross negligence. He couldn't afford the legal fees of $14,000 per month, so at the age of 61 he spent his time researching his own defense.

"I had read materials, listened to experts, participated in discussions, and attended monthly meetings in good faith," he wrote to the Baltimore Evening Sun. "And so at the age of 61 and after a lifetime laced with volunteer public service, I am disillusioned, my life threatened by an irrational creature of government that may not be checked in time to save me."

For such exposure, most bank directors are paid the princely sum of $2,000 to $6,000 per year -- plus a checking account without fees.

He's not the only one to suffer under strange, government-sponsored negligence lawsuits. Lawrence Brown, who appraised real estate for Pacific Savings Bank, was sued for negligence for $28 million. The only problems in the case against him was that four of the six alleged negligent appraisals were made after the loans, so they had nothing to do with the decision to lend. Nor was there evidence that Brown had even made the appraisals -- he died before he could testify.

I think it is ironic that the government now sues former directors of banks and savings and loans which failed when it was the very same government that created the conditions that undermined their stability. In 1981 the Democratic dominated Congress passed new rules about real estate that made lenders take notice of deals they would have shrugged off in the past. The next year banks were allowed to double the loan size for commercial real estate and to make them on much looser terms.

Banks and S&Ls financed considerable new developments across the country in the early 80s. But when Congress overhauled the tax laws in 1986 the real estate market collapsed taking the banks right along with them. The government was always the real culprit.

FACING THE LEGAL REALITY

We have a judicial system where a lady spilling coffee on herself after leaving a drive-through restaurant sues because the coffee was hotter than industry standards, and is awarded 2.8 million dollars in damages. Hasn't our judicial system lost touch with reality? Do you suppose it is safe to assume that much of the judgement was earmarked for the lawyers who dreamed up the suit in the first place? Typically, a law firm working on a "contingency basis", a legal term meaning essentially that the firm is working on a commission basis, collects all of its expenses directly off the top of settlement or judgement receipts. It then takes a third to one half of any balance that is left. Contingency resolutions frequently end up with from 75% to 100% of actual receipts, thence comes the conventional wisdom: "In civil litigation, only the lawyers win."

According to U.S. News & World Report, August 24, 1998, in an article entitled "It's a tort world after all," coverage was given to some interesting recent contingency litigation. In a suit over faulty plastic plumbing installed in Sun Belt homes, lawyer George Fleming won a settlement of $170 million in cash, plus costs for reinstalling pipe. From the total award he demanded $108 million in cash, nearly two-thirds of the cash portion of the settlement. (I wonder how that computes on an hourly basis.)

A Minnesota bank teller, pressed by her employer to take a lie detector test when she was questioned about missing funds, sued for emotional damages and won $60,000.

A Hindu plaintiff mistakenly bit into a beef burrito and sued claiming he had clearly ordered a bean burrito and suffered emotional damage because beef is forbidden in his religion. (Unearned income from lawsuits evidently is not.)

A 56 year old Texan got $1.8 million when a dog scared him by darting in front of his bicycle, his wife got another $50,000 for loss of household help, companionship, and sexual affection. (I wonder if Monica could hold Bill up on this one.)

The New York subways are a prime target for contingency litigation with lawyers winning between $40 to $50 million a year. One couple sued for $10 million for injuries received when they were hit by a train while having sex on the tracks. In another case, one homeless man on heroin and another who had a bottle of wine for breakfast loitered on the tracks and got $13 million for having got burned by the third rail. (They got another $9,000 for loss of income as squeegee men washing car windshields at corner stop lights.)

A New York drunk lost an arm when he fell in front of an oncoming train and got $3.6 million.

An Illinois woman whose late husband, an immigrant from Korea, climbed down onto the New York subway tracks and urinated directly on the third rail, thus electrocuting himself. She was awarded $1.5 million because there were no signs in Korean warning against such behavior.

A fleeing mugger was shot after trying to rob a 71-year-old man and was awarded $4.3 million.

Recently a woman sued charging that her dog was killed by a neighbor's secondhand smoke. What do you think, are we getting carried away?

Given an out-of-control tort system where judges bend over backwards to help plaintiff's lawyers reach deep pockets, and in which the plaintiffs' bar is able to frustrate tort reform by purchasing decisive political influence through campaign contributions, what is your recourse?

If you have anything or have accomplished anything or have served anywhere -- from a school board to a Little League -- you may be the object of a lawsuit and your assets may be seized.

CONCLUSION

Most lawsuits get settled out of court, but you still have to pay an attorney and often sometimes thousands of dollars in "walking away money." It's common knowledge among professional "suers" that most people and companies will pay what equates to a "ransom" just to make the suit go away. And you would likely do it too. Because once a case comes before court, especially if before a jury, you can have no idea what the outcome will be. Your assets are literally dangling in the wind.

One of life's most unpleasant experiences is receiving legal service. This is especially true if you pride yourself on personal honesty and integrity. You must now live with the stress and uneasiness of having litigation pending against you. It works on you; it disrupts your life, it interrupts your social relationships, it puts a cloud over your activities for the foreseeable future. And, you must deal with this, all the time knowing that the outcome is uncertain. Even if the litigation is frivolous, it will be vexatious, and there is always the chance that the presiding judge or jury might not agree with your view of matters.

Its common knowledge that juries tend to give awards to those they consider financially less fortunate, particularly if they are attractive or present themselves well. This appears to have more to do with whom jurors identify as opposed to any form of reasonableness. If a Plaintiff's lawyer were to paint you as one who has "deep pockets" that may be all it takes for you to find yourself with a legal judgment to pay.

Unfortunately our legal system is not about discovering truth, it's very much more about who presents the best case and, all too frequently, who the jury feels can afford to lose the most. As a result of this reality, and other pressures that may be unique to your situation, such as your status in the community, the risk of a "finding" of negligence and how that effects your professional career or business, the anticipated trial tactics that may expose your personal history, business secrets or confidential family matters, you will surely find yourself under huge pressure to settle.

Is anyone surprised that it's the upward mobile middle class and the wealthy that get sued. People who do not have readily available resources to seize, or are considered "judgment proof" rarely find themselves a target of predatory litigation. It's simple economics. If lawyers don't believe you've got access to a large pool of assets, their primary negotiating leverage is gone. (Not to mention their anticipated paycheck.)

Lawsuits -- perhaps the fear of them as much as the reality -- are one very good reason to move a portion of your assets to a safe haven.

∞ Chapter 3 ∞

FADING PRIVACY

*"The freedom and happiness of man...are the sole
objects of all legitimate government." "Oppose with manly
firmness any invasions on the rights of the people"*
Thomas Jefferson

YOUR DUTY TO PROTECT PRIVACY

As an American, you have more than a right to privacy; you have
a duty to protect it. What does it mean, after all, to be an American? As
we have moved toward a multicultural/multiracial society, we have come
to learn that to be an American has nothing to do with the color of our
skins. As we have moved into an international economy and Americans
have taken up residency in many countries of the world, even your residence does not make you an American or not an American.

America has become a bundle of rights and expectations -- primarily freedom, and its corollary, privacy. To be an American, it seems to
me, is to be an individual who protects those rights and expectations,
whether on the battlefield, in the courtroom, or in financial institutions.

In this chapter I present the view that it is not only your right to
sequester some or all of your assets offshore, it is your duty as an American, because that is the only way to protect your privacy, and therefore
your freedom. It is the only way to remain a spiritual American.

According to Richard A. Spinellow, associate dean of faculties at
Boston College, who foretold "The End of Privacy" in *America* maga-
zine:

> A world where privacy is in such short supply will undermine our
> freedom and dignity and pose a grave threat to our security and
> well-being."

Spinello is one of many scholars and observers who report on the
loss of privacy in America -- and the consequent loss of freedom. He
said that many Americans feel that their financial life has become public record as a consequence of the "Information Age," and he suggests
many of us feel like "the powerless victims of technology that has stripped
away our privacy without our ability to recognize what has happened."

Information about you has become a commodity. Purchases you make, from visits to abortion clinics to Club Med, give information about you. This information becomes part of data bases that flows from hand to hand without your knowledge or consent. Why do you think you continue to get phone calls from telemarketers? They know more about you than you wish they did.

Major credit bureaus such as Equifax, TRW and TransUnion have information about anyone who has taken out a car loan or borrowed money for a home or who uses a credit card. For one buck major customers of Equifax can learn your Social Security number and birth date, the balance of your mortgage, other bank loan information, student loans, bill payments, credit card accounts and limits, where you have lived and who you work for.

Until the advent of the computer age, individuals took for granted privacy in their personal affairs. But now, through data brokers such as Information America, Inc., information hunters can track you down anywhere -- can get on-line access to county and state records from many states, business records, bankruptcy records, lawsuits and property records.

Much of the privacy debate on the Internet relates to tiny files of specific information called "cookies," that allow companies to keep track of what you do when you visit their web sites. In essence, cookies brand your computer so the retailer's site can determine if you visit again and what interests you there. Part of the problem is that companies are collecting, sharing, and selling detailed information on web travelers gained from their cookies. Cookies can contain information such as your age, income, gender, as well as a list of the things that you've purchased online and the other sites you visit regularly.

SPIES ARE US

I received a bulk e-mail the other day from Spies-R-Us, a company that for less than $20 will sell what it calls its SNOOP COLLECTION, "300 giant resources to look up people, credit, social security numbers, current or past employment, mail order purchases, addresses, phone numbers."

The promotion says: "The Internet is a powerful mega-source of information, if you only know where to look. I tell you how to find out nearly ANYTHING about anybody, and tell you exactly where to find it." For example, you can "find out a juicy tidbit about a co-worker," or "check out your daughter's new boyfriend."

The promotion advises you to "Research yourself first! You'll be horrified, as I was, at how much data has been accumulated about you." And now, for twenty bucks, any yahoo with a computer can find it out as well.

That's not even the worst of it. A company called International Intelligence Network Corp. conducts "Public Information and Asset Tracking" seminars, through which anyone can learn how to get more than 50 pieces of financial information on anyone through public records.

People are buying and selling such information about you, combining it with information from other sources and creating profiles about you. Most of this is for commercial purposes -- they want to sell you something. But this information is available to anyone who might spend the money to buy it -- former spouses, suers, kidnappers.

Other information seekers are legitimate, though still invaders of privacy. The Marriott Hotel, for example, puts the names of its guests together with records of the vehicles they drive and the property they own to find out who is most likely to respond to their mailings.

Even as you read this, somebody with $20 worth of software may be ransacking databases about you -- finding out what you have and where you have it. And it's all perfectly legal! Contrast what's going on with Justice Brandeis' quote:

"The right to be left alone is the most comprehensive of rights, and the right most valued by civilized men."

Justice Louis Brandeis
U.S. Supreme Court - 1928

TECHNOLOGY'S THREAT TO PRIVACY

The controversy over privacy is an unwelcome outgrowth of the Space Race -- and the microchip and computer that were its offspring. With them came a Pandora's Box of electronic devices that have made information about you readily available.

Electronics made it possible, for example, to tap telephone lines -- to listen in to private conversations. Other devices made it possible to eavesdrop on things going on inside your home. Radio transmitters are now small enough to be hidden inside cardboard or behind wallpaper. The judicial system had made such evidence inadmissible in court, and in 1967, in Katz v. United States, the Supreme Court broadened this prohibition to make wiretapping and other electronic surveillance illegal without a valid warrant.

The next year saw the Crime Control Act, which sets up a system through which courts can approve wiretapping. But the Supreme Court ruled that even in cases involving national security, there must be a court order for wiretapping.

But government and private organizations both are in the business of gathering information about you. For most of history, it was simply physically impossible to gather, assemble, distribute and update information about everyone. Imagine all the typewriters, mimeographs, manila folders, card files and file cabinets it would take. The sheer cost and volume of work it would take to keep track of you protected your privacy.

But computers have changed all that -- powerful information management tools are within the reach of virtually everyone. Government agencies such as law enforcement and taxation, private groups such as banks, credit, insurance, employment, medical and merchandisers now have reams of information about you. And they share it, and use it in ways you have neither knowledge nor control, under existing U.S. law.

There are rules that give you some rights -- "fair informational practices" laws. These were enacted in the 1980s when it became clear the safeguards to protect privacy were not sufficient for the computer age. These rules cover federal and some state agencies, credit, insurance, banking and law enforcement. You have the right to know what's on these organizations' databases about you and to have them corrected -- even if you have to sue to do it.

Americans, unfortunately, do not have the same protection as citizens of Sweden, France, Germany or other countries. Those countries have national data protection or privacy protection commissions that license computer data banks, receive complaints from citizens and enforce the rules. In the U.S., you're on your own.

A Louis Harris survey in 1994 showed that 84 percent of Americans were "concerned" about threats to their privacy, and 51 percent of those were "very concerned." Some are concerned enough to do something about it. They have chosen to make sure that at least some of their assets are protected from prying eyes by sequestering them offshore.

"The chilling effect of the loss of privacy is an undesirable incentive to conform to societal norms rather than assert one's individuality. Ultimately, what is lost is not only the private emotional releases we all need but, most importantly, the creativity that leads to human achievement.

Privacy makes possible individuality, and thus freedom. It allows us to cope with the larger world, knowing there is a place where we can be by ourselves, doing as we please without recrimination."

Robert S. Peck

In late June of 1998 I received a forwarded email from a VP of Tektronics that had originated with Bill Gates of Microsoft. Microsoft was then testing new software that tracked emails copied out through the Internet, which was designed to gather and report back the identity, address, and other private marketing information resident on every computer receiving a given email. The implications of this one piece of seemingly benign software should scare the britches off of all of us.

The Federal Communications Commission has ordered cellular companies to install tracking technology by 2001. This means that government will have, and to some extent already does have, access to tracking your every whereabouts whenever you're carrying a cellular or digital phone. Law officers would be allowed to obtain the exact location of a cellular telephone customer without a court order and without advance approval under a proposal the FBI is now circulating on Capital Hill. According to FCC rules, the technology must pinpoint within 125 meters any cellular phone that is turned on, whether a call is in progress or not.

In a full-page newspaper article entitled *PRIVACY? NOT IN AMERICA,* published 29 July 1998 in the *Oregonian* comes this: "... the Clinton administration, following a 1996 congressional mandate, is considering assigning every American a health care identification number. It could be used to create a giant electronic database capable of tracking everyone's medical records from cradle to grave. Privacy experts argue that the unique health identifier would make an already bad problem worse, marking the final step in what has been a long march from privacy to a virtual information free-for-all. Just how this information is used, and who has access to it, is anybody's guess."

PRIVACY: YOUR RIGHT — GOVERNMENT'S DILEMMA

The U.S. Constitution guarantees you many things -- such as the right to free speech, freedom of religion and assembly -- even the right to keep and bear arms. But the "right to privacy" is not guaranteed in the Constitution. What you do have is a tradition of Supreme Court rulings and interpretations of various Amendments to the Constitution -- primarily the Fourth and Fourteenth.

The Fourth Amendment shields you from "unreasonable search and seizure" and other law enforcement arrest and pre-arrest techniques. The Fourth Amendment is part of the Bill of Rights -- a sacrosanct element of the protection we have extended to ourselves. Unreasonable search and seizure is so odious because the British used to enter colonial homes, ransack the dwelling and take things without probable cause that a crime had been committed. The British had only meaningless, easy-to-get writs and pieces of paper to justify their intrusions. Often enough, these unacceptable violations of privacy came because the Crown wanted to extract more taxes.

The Fourth Amendment is the one that prevents officials from searching your person, your automobile or your home without "probable cause" or a valid search warrant. But this is a Constitutional Amendment protecting you from the government -- not from other private citizens. As we noted, other individuals are probably executing an electronic search of your possessions right now.

The gap in protection of your "right to privacy" in the Constitution has been noted and -- short of adding an Amendment -- the judicial system has gone a long way toward guaranteeing your rights. Other Amendments to the Constitution have been broadly interpreted so as to protect you.

For example, the Fourteenth Amendment has been used by the U.S. Supreme Court in 1961 (Mapp v. Ohio) to, in effect, prevent police from using in court against you any evidence they gathered through an illegal search. The Court said you were being forced to testify against yourself with such evidence -- a violation of the Fifth Amendment protection against self-incrimination.

The Fourth Amendment is not enough to protect your privacy today because it was written in the Eighteen Century after the American Revolution -- long before either the Electronic or Information Revolutions. Who could have imagined in the days when information traveled at the speed of a horse or a ship with a stout wind in its sails, when it took days or even weeks to find out important news, that information about private citizens would someday be bought and sold?

Do you have the right to keep your affairs to yourself -- the "right to privacy?" The answer is "yes and no." As noted earlier, there is no Constitutional protection of your right to privacy, but the legal system has rallied to interpret many Amendments.

The First, for example, guarantees your right to associate with whomever you wish. The Third and Fourth protect you from unlawful searches and seizures. The Fifth defends against self-incrimination. And the Ninth says that the rights enumerated in the Constitution "shall not be construed to deny or disparage others retained by the people." These Amendments have been woven together into a broad tapestry that includes your privacy -- whatever that is. There is no single definition of privacy that everyone accepts.

According to Justice William O. Douglas, the "right to privacy is older than the Bill of Rights." He made that decision in the case of Griswold v. Connecticut (1965) that had to do with privacy and the use of contraceptives. Douglas said privacy was protected under the "penumbra" or shadow of other constitutional guarantees. Earlier, in 1928, Justice Louis Brandeis said privacy is the "right to be let alone."

A political scientist, Alan Westin, in his book *Privacy and Freedom* (1967), said we ought to define privacy as the right of persons to control the distribution of information about themselves. His definition does not have the force of law, but it is a valuable thought. If we use his concept, then privacy is invaded when someone gathers information about you and perhaps makes public what only you should have the right to disclose.

A PERSONAL EXAMPLE

In 1995-96 in the days before shredders had become popular, I experienced something that only happens in spy novels. A secret group of unscrupulous competitors began covert surveillance of a publicly traded company I had founded almost twenty years earlier. Their intentions were to destroy their major competition and their plan was quite simple. Secure information on the company, twist the information such that it would appear that the company was involved in underhanded dealings, make scandalous assertions about the company's integrity, remain absolutely anonymous.

It was eventually discovered that these criminals had been collecting the trash taken out by the office building's night janitors. Over time they amassed large amounts of important and confidential data and were eventually able to compile lists of thousands of the company's clients.

Employing KGB tactics, they launched a carefully orchestrated crusade to distribute twisted information — "disinformation" — via thousands of anonymous nighttime faxes sent to clients, shareholders, news services, and investment related people. The faxes were always sent in streams after midnight and were essentially untraceable. They gained access to the company's computer systems via Internet hacking and wreaked havoc wherever they attacked. Confidential client information was distorted.

Twisted documents and disinformation were also sent to the SEC, the NASD, the Justice Department, Internal Revenue, and a myriad of newspapers and radio and television stations. Company personnel were simply unable to deal with the quantity of incoming calls trying to establish the validity of the information. And, although the media was generally prudent about reprinting information for which they had no reliable source, one major newspaper did print unverified slanderous material on the front page of their Sunday business section. Their retraction the following week was small by comparison and missed by most readers.

It was probably naïve of me to not expect my home to also be a target. Frankly, nothing like this had ever happened to anyone I actually knew before. Further, I hadn't even been substantially affiliated with the company for many years. Nevertheless we were to eventually discover that our home telephone numbers had been tapped, including our home fax and Internet sources. Our household trash had been picked up at curbside and sorted off premises to see what confidential tidbits they could gain about my personal affairs. (We now shred virtually everything that goes in the trash, other than kitchen items, and have four units strategically located throughout our home to make sure we don't forget.)

THE GOVERNMENT RESPONDS

Mail began to disappear from our mailbox, some to be returned days later, other mail was to never arrive. The office in my home was broken into at 2 a.m. one morning while my wife and I were just fifty feet away down the hall. The police could do nothing. The post office expressed concern but no action. The federal communication commission gave us copies of laws that made wire taps illegal but admitted that virtually no one was ever caught and if they were they rarely were made to pay damages.

The SEC and two other agencies finally decided to respond. They began an investigation, not of the criminal culprits, but of the company itself on the basis that "where there was smoke there must be fire." The cost of these investigations for lawyers, accountants, detectives, and lost employee time is now in the multiple millions. It has been estimated that the cost to those who orchestrated the project was a small fraction of that amount. Unfortunately in today's upside down world, crime frequently does pay.

As I have learned from numerous very expensive lawyers that work in Washington, former executives with various government agencies, once a government investigation is underway the bureaucracy is passionate about declaring they have won. There is no higher priority. Truth is essentially unimportant, only the truth as they wish it to be. **Without exception, bureaucracy's truth is how it's spun, not what it really is**. The counsel I have heard repeatedly in our nation's capital —— and that rings most loudly in my ears is:

> "Never confuse yourself with the belief that they care about
> the truth...or doing what's right. They only care about
> winning."
> Name Withheld
> SEC Enforcement Section

A quote from Thomas Jefferson sums up my previous belief system about our bureaucracy.

> "The policy of the American government is to leave their
> citizens free, neither restraining nor aiding them in their
> pursuits."

Now, I find myself favoring Thomas Jefferson's even more famous quote, that says,
> "God prevent we should ever be twenty years without a
> revolution."

And forgive me one more quotation, which comes from Brigham Young, the great 19th century colonizer of over 100 towns and cities in the American West, when he said:

"I love the Constitution and the government of this land, but I hate the damned rascals that administer the government."

THE HEART OF THE PROBLEM

The reason "privacy" is such a problematic "right" is that it runs counter to government's interests. On the level of national security, for example, an absolute protection of your right to privacy means assassins, criminals, drug dealers, revolutionaries, saboteurs, spies, terrorists and other troublemakers could hatch their plots behind the cover of their "right to privacy."

The FBI has been pressing the telecommunications industry to help it through the bewildering maze of technological innovations so it can wiretap more easily. The FBI claims to only conduct about 800 wiretaps per year out of 150 million telephone lines. Of course those are only the "legal" wire taps which as we've recently learned from former agent's ratting on the government, represent only the smallest fraction of the actual government wire taps. The FBI now claims they need the capacity to intercept 60,000 lines across the country at any given time. According to James X. Dempsey of the Center for National Security Studies, the FBI is actually asking for the ability to tap 1 percent of all lines in existence. Why? Is this about catching drug-dealers and kidnappers or about citizen control?

Barry Steinhardt, associate director of the ACLU, points out that: "The problem is that wiretapping is the worst kind of indiscriminate search. The FBI has to intercept thousands of innocent conversations every time they wiretap a suspect. I think it's time for us to reevaluate the use of wiretapping."

The courts will tell you your rights to privacy are not absolute -- government retains the right to invade it. Georgia's laws against sodomy were upheld in Bowers v. Hardwick in 1986, for example, even between consenting adults in private. Each of the 50 states has its own laws concerning privacy. The only universal standards are those inferred from the U.S. Constitution, and those apply only to government agencies.

The main reason the U.S. government is fighting against your rights to privacy is due to its own need for revenue -- the blood of its existence. The government has become the enemy. They are an enemy to your rights of privacy, liberty, and freedom, the very rights the government was created to protect in the first place.

The problem began in 1915 when the U.S. instituted an income tax. Prior to that, excise taxes and other taxes carried the burden. World War I and the huge cash drain it brought to this country meant the government needed a greater flow of revenue. The problem with an income tax is how does the government know how much you have earned? It relies for the most part on the honesty of its citizens. But let's face it: people lie, especially when it comes to paying out money they would prefer not to. Knowing that fact about human nature, government has taken action to pry into your affairs.

THE DILEMMA

These are the horns of government's dilemma: on the one point, government is instituted to protect its citizens and their rights -- including the right to privacy. On the other point, government must violate that privacy in order for it get the revenue it needs to exist. Given that choice -- between your rights and funding its expansion -- which do you think government chose?

For example, the Fifth Amendment protects you against self-incrimination, saying, "No citizen shall be compelled, in any criminal case, to bear witness against himself, nor be deprived of life, liberty or property, without due process of law." But tax investigators and the Securities and Exchange Commission and others can seize your financial and personal records to be used against you in a criminal case. These vulnerable records include those in the possession of U.S. banks, accountants, investment brokers and others.

Even your garbage can testify against you. The IRS and other law enforcement agencies are allowed to poke through your curbside trash for evidence without a search warrant. The Securities and Exchange Commission can enter your investment advisor's office and rummage through your files without a search warrant or the permission of the advisor.

The federal government admits having about 25 files on every American -- some have as many as 200. (Some recent authors claim the government has approximately 70 files on every adult in America.)

Whatever the number, these files are stored predominantly on computer, and they know loads about you.

The Privacy Act of 1974 is intended to protect citizens from federal invasions of privacy. It prohibits agencies from exchanging personal information they have on file about you. But the Paperwork Reduction Act (1980) had the effect of allowing any agency to have access to personal data any other agency had gathered about you. This makes it possible for their computers to cross check your activities -- the IRS checking with banking, for example. The Computer Safeguards Bill of 1988 set new limits on government's use of computer records, but agencies quickly found new ways to subvert the intentions of this bill. You are quite simply an easy target.

BANKS COLLABORATE

The biggest invasion of your privacy is the enlistment of banks to report your activities. You can't even open a bank account unless you tell the bank your Social Security number or taxpayer ID.

The "Bank Secrecy Act" of 1970 was actually Congress' way to eliminate bank secrecy. Only the government would have the gall to call this a bank secrecy act! Through it, banks are required to make a microfilm or other reproduction of both the front and back of each check, draft or similar instrument drawn upon it and presented to it for payment. Banks must also keep a record of each check, draft or similar instrument received by it for deposit or collection, together with an identification of the party for whose account it is to be deposited or collected.

Some people decided to just do without a checking account and use only a savings account. But the Bank Secrecy Act was amended later to close that loophole -- any account that pays $10 or more in interest per year must report it under the Act.

Since 1984 the IRS gets a "third party report," that gives your name, birth date, Social Security number and the amount of interest paid on everyone with a checking or savings account, stock brokerage account or mutual funds/money market funds. This third party report is matched to what you report as income on your taxes in April.

Don't think you'll get around it by going on a cash basis. Banks have to submit a third party report whenever there are transactions involving $3000 in cash or other non-revocable instruments of payment -- such as traveler's check, cashier's check or money order.

Banks must also maintain records on every check you write over $100 and cash transactions -- either deposits or withdrawals -- over $10,000, as well as credit transactions over $5,000.

Such a law was challenged, and wound up in the Supreme Court in U.S. v. Miller. The court upheld the government's right to nose through your bank records when it proclaimed that "bank customers whose records are sought by the government -- for whatever reason -- have no right to (expect) that access is controlled by an existing legal process." That means deposit slips, withdrawal forms and checks are considered to be public domain documents.

So, bank records are routinely subpoenaed -- even if they are not directly involved in a case. If a third party is thought to contain information possibly connected to an investigation, it can be dragged out into the open. You can be a completely disinterested and innocent bystander and have your personal records aired in the open for all to see.

The majority of Americans are essentially asleep at the switch. They do not know, or simply do not care, that their rights to privacy, liberty, and freedom have been taken away. Some argue that if they have nothing to hide what does it matter. I can assure you that it does matter and a great, great deal! I may have nothing criminal to hide, but I still close my drapes at night.

Each of us has the right to challenge the IRS in its effort to investigate our bank records through the Tax Reform Act of 1976. If you are suspected of a crime, however, you have no right to protest. And would they really be investigating you if you were not suspected of something? Cylindrical reasoning is it not?

With the Financial Privacy Act of 1978, the federal government must notify targets of an investigation so you can have a chance to challenge their seizure of your records at a bank, savings and loan or credit card company. To the best of my knowledge no one has recently prevented any government agency from gaining any information they have wanted. Their powers have been expanded upon, and your rights continue to be trod upon.

It could be argued that the Federal government has a right to keep tabs on your activities both for the sake of domestic security and to prevent tax evasion. But what about other snoops? There are private firms known as "asset locators" whose job it is to find out where your keep your stuff and how much stuff you have. Disgruntled employees or others often employ them with a lawsuit in mind, crooks, swindlers, gold-diggers, long-lost relatives and others who want what you have.

While waiting in the departure lounge in St. Kitts, West Indies, I met a divorce lawyer who specialized in high profile multi-million dollar cases. He told me that his initial client retainer was a million dollars. As it turned out we were both flying to San Juan and later on to Dallas. Later, in the Admiral's Club in Puerto Rico, we were to discover that our seat assignment to Dallas was next to one another. Subsequently we spent many hours together. In the course of conversation, he shared with me that he was presently working on a divorce pre-planning strategy, which included his firm having a detective agency collecting all the trash, every day for almost a year, for an entire thirteen story office building in Los Angeles. All of this effort to find any scrap of paper from one office on one floor that would help lead them to information that might put the unsuspecting husband in an indefensible position.

So, where is privacy in the United States? For the most part, your life is now an open book to anyone who, for any legitimate or illegitimate reason, wants to know what you have.

CONCLUSION

Imagine King Hezekiah's surprise when the prophet Isaiah told him he had cooked his own goose with his tendency to brag. (2 Kings 20:13-17)

King Hezekiah -- the Biblical figure who ruled Judah after David and Solomon but before Jesus -- committed the cardinal error of revealing his wealth to his enemies. The King of Babylon sent an envoy to visit with Hezekiah because it was common knowledge the old Hebrew king had been ill.

Instead of merely receiving the letters and gift from the Babylonian king and sending the messenger on his way, Hezekiah "showed him all that was in his storehouses -- the silver, the gold, the spices and the fine oil -- his armory and everything found among his treasures. There was nothing in his palace or in all his kingdom that Hezekiah did not show them."

When Isaiah the prophet learned that the king had showed his wealth to the envoy from Babylon, he warned Hezekiah: "The time will surely come when everything in your palace, and all that your fathers have stored up until this day, will be carried off to Babylon. Nothing will be left." And that, in fact, is exactly the way it happened.

Isaiah would not have needed a crystal ball to make such a prophecy. He could just imagine the envoy going back to the King of Babylon and telling him about all the goodies the sick old Judean king had stored up. And he could see the Babylonian king's eyes grow big with greed.

Wise people from the time of Hezekiah to today have learned from his example: Be careful to whom you display your wealth -- especially to greedy kings. Hezekiah's people lost both their wealth and their freedom.

Spinello tells us there is a direct link between privacy and freedom: "...those who violate our private space by acquiring confidential information without permission may use it to exercise control over our activities," he warns. "Thus, there is a close relationship between privacy and freedom."

This is why I advise all freedom-loving people to place at least some of their assets outside their country -- safe, beyond prying eyes and grasping hands. Ultimately, it is the only way to ensure you are able to gain, or retain, a measure of personal privacy and the attendant personal freedom it can provide.

∞ Chapter 4 ∞

THE U.S. CONSTITUTION

"The U.S. constitution is the most wonderful work ever struck off at a given time by the brain and purpose of man."

Gladstone

FREE AGENCY

Undergirding and overarching the entire framework of the Constitution of the United States is the absolute commitment to individual rights and personal liberty. Nothing about this amazing document could be clearer. The recognition that every individual has the right to personal liberty is the substance of its core. Liberty is all about the power of choice. The power to choose is guaranteed to all men and women. This speaks volumes about our species.

One of the most dramatic concepts expressed by ancient prophets and philosophers is the principle of free agency. The ancients argued quite convincingly that "imagination" or "creativity" and its correlative, the "power to choose," was in fact the single thing that separated man from animals. It seems that the incredible ability to imagine an outcome and then to consciously choose that result is only present in humankind. It is the greatest of all our capacities.

The book of Genesis taught that man and woman are God's children. Other parts of the Bible refer to God as "our Father," strongly inferring, or at least conveying the mental image that mankind is literally a part of God's family. (A belief once fervently affirmed, but not much in vogue today.) The extraordinary book of Genesis forms the foundation for both Judaism and Christianity. Contained within its pages is another important notion, a message which suggests that when individuals are able to discern the difference between good and evil and make thoughtful, independent choices between them, they are acting as gods. Sound like heresy?

And God said, Let <u>us</u> make man in <u>our</u> image, after <u>our</u> likeness:"

"So God created man in his own image, in the image of God
created he him; male and female created he them."

"For God doth know that in the day ye eat thereof, then
your eyes shall be opened, *and ye shall be as gods,*
knowing good and evil."

"And the eyes of them both were opened..."

"And the Lord God said, Behold, the man is become as
one of us, to know good and evil;"

THE POWER OF CHOICE

Simple observation would indicate that we appear to be the only living things on this planet that can imagine something clearly in our mind and then do it. For example, stop reading and look around. If you're indoors consider that everything in the room in which you are now sitting was first a thought in someone's mind. Slow down and reread that last sentence and think this concept through.

Everything created by man was first mentally considered, then a choice was made, and then it was constructed. What other living creature has imagined and chose to do something new, something none of their predecessors have done? What has a chipmunk, a whale, a dog, or an ape, done for this generation of chipmunks, whales, dogs, or apes? They live, and they have instinctive behavior, but they have been denied the power of true choice. In order to choose you must be able to imagine the effects of your choice and actions.

Our ability to imagine multiple outcomes and choose to pursue the one we feel is best suited to our situation, is the basis of true freedom. There is no greater power on earth. It is the source of all of our accomplishment it is the source of most of our misery. As far back as the beginning of civilized humankind we observe that thinking man concluded there was no greater gift.

Over the years it has been my pleasure to study and enjoy ancient history. It is something of a passion and I unabashedly dive into materials that deal with quite diverse societies and subjects that span the thousands of years of recorded history. Although I pretend to some knowledge about Meso American and Fertile Crescent archeology, the fact is I simply enjoy the attempt to understand the minds and hearts of those who have gone before.

Reviewing the sweep of history, it is fairly clear that personal freedom and true individual rights are a situation found infrequently, anywhere on the globe. The great breakthrough on the subject of personal liberty was, and still is, the Declaration of Independence and its attendant document the Constitution of the United States.

THE CONSTITUTION

The Constitution is truly a remarkable feat. Those that framed this phenomenal work believed they had been touched by deity. The second president of the United States and a participant in its drafting, said this:

"Our constitution, was made only for a moral and religious people. It is wholly inadequate to the government of any other."

Powerful words. Today this statement is politically incorrect. Today a person of education and substance would hardly dare to say such a thing. But, in the present age we do not appear to have the moral and religious people we once did. Decisions of law have replaced ethics and morality. I cannot help but wonder if the majority of people actually believe that just because something is legal, that it's therefore moral? And, in our heart of hearts, do we honestly believe that our society is balanced and on the right track?

Evidently the U.S. Congress and the expanding bureaucracy it has spawned no longer believe the constitution is adequate to the government of the people. To see how far we've come from its basic principles we need look no farther than the way Congress itself assesses its worthiness. How much new legislation was passed this year? How many new unknowable laws? How many volumes have been produced on the nuances of any given judge's thinking on some kind of legal technicality? How many new rulings, which have the effect of law, have been put in place through essentially secret committees?

Unfortunately these are the details on which the lives of real people hang. And, the result of this incessant tinkering with technicality and favor granting is that there are now approximately fifteen million laws, and rulings that have the effect of law, which have been enacted by Congress or the bureaucrats that control our lives.

It seems we've lost the point on which America was founded. The first and most basic principle of the Constitution and life itself is free agency – the right to choose. Each of us has the inalienable right to be just as wrong as we want to be, until that right impinges upon the rights of another. Years ago I recall a teacher telling a classroom of students that "Your rights end where my nose begins." The great American experiment was based on inalienable individual rights. It was created from something much finer, and better, than technical debate. James Madison, considered to be the "Father of the Constitution," had this to say:

"Whatever may be the judgment pronounced on the competency of the architects of the Constitution, or whatever may be the destiny of the edifice prepared by them, I feel it a duty to express my profound and solemn conviction, derived from my intimate opportunity of observing and appreciating the views of the Convention, collectively and individually, that there never was an assembly of men, charged with a great and arduous trust, who were more pure in their motives, or more exclusively or anxiously devoted to the object committed to them, than were the members of the Federal Convention of 1787."

The Constitution of the United States and its predecessor the Declaration of Independence make crystal clear that the most important single function of government is to secure the rights and freedoms of individual citizens. To think otherwise is to not understand the basic underlying principals on which our forefathers staked their lives. Thomas Paine said this:

"Rights are not gifts from one man to another, nor from one class of men to another.... it is impossible to discover any origin of rights otherwise than in the origin of man; it consequently follows that rights appertain to man in right of his existence, and must therefore be equal to every man."

Ezra Taft Benson, a fervent constitutionalist and former Secretary of Agriculture to President Eisenhower, made this important observation about personal rights:

"If we accept the premise that human rights are granted by government, then we must be willing to accept the corollary that they can be denied by government."

He goes on to say, "The important thing to keep in mind is that the people who have created their government can give to that government only such powers as they, themselves, have in the first place. Obviously, they cannot give that which they do not possess. So the question boils down to this: What powers properly belong to each and every person in the absence of and prior to the establishment of any organized form of government?" Very solid thinking.

In the Preamble to the Constitution the great purposes of this inspired document were set out:

"WE THE PEOPLE of the United States, in Order to form a more perfect Union, establish Justice, insure domestic Tranquility, provide for the common defense, promote the general Welfare, and secure the Blessings of Liberty to ourselves and our Posterity, do ordain and establish this CONSTITUTION for the United States of America."

Here the people were speaking as sovereign, not as a King or some self appointed elite. The people declared they were establishing government and that it existed to ensure the blessings of liberty to themselves. J Reuben Clark, Jr., former Under Secretary of State and Ambassador to Mexico, said this about the establishment of the government of the United States:

"Deeply read in history, steeped in the lore of the past in human government, and experienced in the approaches of despotism which they had, themselves, suffered at the hands of George the Third, these patriots, assembled in solemn convention, planned for the establishment of a government that would ensure to them the blessings they described in the Preamble. The people were setting up the government. They were bestowing power. They gave to the government the powers they wished to give. The residuum of power was in them. There was no emperor, no lex regia here."

In the inspired words of Thomas Jefferson, as found in the Declaration of Independence:

"We hold these truths to be self-evident, that all men are created equal, that they are endowed by their Creator with certain unalienable Rights, that among these are Life, Liberty and the pursuit of Happiness. That to secure these rights, governments are instituted among Men, deriving their just powers from the consent of the governed."

WHAT IS EQUALITY?

A word about equality. To say we are born equal does not mean we all come to earth with the same talents and abilities. Such a philosophy flies in the face of prudent observation. We are certainly not born with the same talents. Mozart was born with incredible musical talent. He composed his first symphony at five. Try as I might, and notwithstanding my appreciation for music, I cannot do likewise. But, the Constitution and the Declaration of Independence did inspire, and endeavor to secure, the equal right for any person to become as unequal as they want to become. This has everything to do with personal self-discipline; a subject much pooh-poohed, by the current intelligencia.

You see, if I really wanted to write a symphony, it may not be as good as Mozart's work, but it could be done, were I to make the personal investment in time and goal-directed energy. The decision then is mine, just as it should be. Mature, independent, well thinking, individuals should revel in their personal sovereignty. People are simply superior to governments. People form governments, not the other way around. In the words of Frederic Bastiat, the French political economist:

"Life, liberty, and property do not exist because men have made laws. On the contrary, it was the fact that life, liberty, and property existed beforehand that caused men to make laws in the first place."

The proper role of government should be restricted to those activities within which any individual citizen has the right to act. Proper government derives its power from the governed. Its responsibility is to protect its citizens from the loss of freedom, physical violence, theft, and other such matters. Ezra T Benson was right on target when he said:

"No individual possesses the power to take another's wealth or to force others to do good, so no government has the right to do such things either. The creature cannot exceed the creator."

The coercive and parasitic nature of the State was dramatically presented by the German sociologist, Franz Oppenheimer. He strongly set forth the premise that there were only two means by which man could obtain wealth, and that these two methods were mutually exclusive. The first method was simply production and voluntary exchange. The second method was robbery by the use of violence. He refers to the latter as "political means." Political means are clearly parasitic, for it requires previous production for the exploiters to confiscate, and it subtracts from, rather than adding to, the total production in society. Oppenheimer goes on to define the State as the "organization of the political means," or "the systematization of the predatory process over a given territorial area."

UNCONSTITUTIONAL

So what does all this mean? Big government has decided, and evidently a large number of U.S. citizens now agree, that the people who run the Post Office, the IRS, CIA, SEC, DEA, Department of Labor, etc., are better suited to making the majority of our important decisions for us, than are we. This philosophy requires that the individuals in the system give up personal rights in exchange for government coddling.

Are we not discouraging free agency? Are we not doing exactly what the Germans did prior to World War II and the Russians did immediately after? Have we not learned that when mankind gives up their rights "for the greater good," it's essentially a lie? Of course it may have some temporary advantages, but in the long run it always ends badly.

The oft-told story of the "frog in the pot" bears repeating because it speaks so loudly of our conditioning. It has been said by those who claim it's true, that if you drop a frog in a pot of boiling water it will immediately bounce out. But, if you place a frog in a pot of water and then turn up the heat the frog will boil to death. Because the heat rose slowly the frog was sapped of the energy to leap from the pot. Now consider that the rights that our forefathers fought so hard to preserve are rapidly eroding. Are we being gradually conditioned to the point we simply don't have the energy to resist, or do we simply not care?

Congress has proliferated numerous federal agencies; government expansion is exponential. Agency authority continues to grow. Totalitarianism is alive and well within the US bureaucratic establishment. Although some governmental agencies provide important services they also strip us of our liberty. Most, if not all, of these rapidly expanding fiefdoms encroach on our individual rights. Bureaucracy's mission is to regulate and control. And woe be it to the man or woman who stands in their way.

There is a story found in one of my favorite books that speaks of a band of robbers who formed a secret society to acquire wealth and gain control over the people. Eventually they penetrated the highest levels of government. They gained control because so few paid any attention. Prosperity was abundant, so why rock the boat?

Today many federal agencies are unconstitutional. They combine the legislative, executive, and judicial branches.

They have assumed the power to make rulings, rulings that
    have the force of law.
They have assumed the power to enforce their own rulings,
    a position taken by kings.
They have assumed the power to penalize when their rulings
    are violated, a power exercised by dictators.

But, no one rocks the boat. To do so would brand one as a radical or out of the main stream. Addressing this subject, Ezra Taft Benson states:

"They (federal agencies) are unconstitutional because they represent an assumption of power not delegated to the executive branch by the people. They are also unconstitutional because the people have no power to recall administrative agency personnel by their vote."

"To all who have discerning eyes, it is apparent that the republican form of government established by our noble forefathers cannot long endure once fundamental principles are abandoned. Momentum is gathering for another conflict — a repetition of the crisis of two hundred years ago."

And again from J. Reuben Clark, Jr:

"... in my opinion, built from observation over the years, when the true history of our detours from constitutional government is written, it will be found that they were largely put in motion...and aided and abetted by certain fellow travelling liberals, among them being those who have been trying to destroy the right and tradition of the Supreme Court of the United States to declare laws unconstitutional. They are gradually — not too gradually — trying on us all the tricks the Roman Emperors used in order to hold their autocratic power, in an effort to build here a lex regia concept either through a dictator or through a socialized, Sovietized government that will establish the same sort of society."

In the words attributed to John Adams by Daniel Webster, he sums up his commitment to the personal sovereignty of the individual when he says:

> "Sink or swim, live or die, survive or perish, I give my hand and my heart to this vote...It is my living sentiment, and by the blessing of God it shall be my dying sentiment. Independence now, and Independence forever."

Step up, become self-reliant, study and learn, set personally meaningful goals, answer to yourself and declare your personal sovereignty.

∞ Chapter 5 ∞

GOVERNMENT OUT OF CONTROL

> *"Condemning the righteous because of their righteous-*
> *ness; letting the guilty and the wicked go unpunished be-*
> *cause of their money; and moreover to be held in office at the*
> *head of government, to rule and do according to their wills,*
> *that they might the more easily commit adultery, and steal,*
> *and kill, and do according to their own wills—"*

> *Helaman*
> *Circa 20 BC*

This book began with the illustration of a tidal wave, the devastation it can reek and the huge changes it can effect in the lives of those living on the seashore. And yet, were you boating, and out to sea when the tidal wave passed under your hull, you would likely not recognize the life-threatening power moving beneath you. A sea change is sweeping under us today. We are living through the death-throes of over-ripe national governments and this has enormous significance in our lives.

Congress must share the blame for these failings. Because of changes it has made almost every other year for two decades, the tax code is out of control. What began in 1913 with a 14-page law and a one-page form, is now so complicated that the nation's 120 million-plus taxpayers spend $8 billion a year to get help preparing their returns. The tax code is 9,451 pages long, 820 pages of which were added because of 1997's tax bill. The IRS' simplest form, 1040 EZ, has a 28-page instruction book. According to Fortune April 13, 1998, "To complete the regular 1040, a taxpayer must spend an average of nearly ten hours. Own a small business? Add another ten hours for the dreaded Schedule C. Have investment income? Get ready for a blizzard of capital gains rates on Schedule D. If you have time to kill, you could settle down with the IRS's roughly 230 other forms."

THANKS BUT NO THANKS
French philosopher Bastiat once said,

"Government is the myth whereby half the
people try to live off the other half."

Another anonymous philosopher said,

"Government is the process of turning energy into
solid waste."

In the U.S. we've arrived at a point that even a budget calling for $1.6 trillion in taxes is not enough to fund our bloated bureaucracy. Though many Americans work half the year just to pay their share, the federal government still must borrow another $100 billion in order to operate.

The accumulated U.S. national debt exceeds $5 trillion, this is roughly equivalent to a year's personal income for all Americans combined. The U.S. national debt is comparable to half the combined net worth of the entire World War II and older generations. Annual interest payments on this debt cost Americans as much as they pay for the U.S. Army, Navy, and Air Force combined.

Imagine a household with an annual income of $100,000 and a debt load (exclusive of mortgage) of $300,000. Imagine that household paying $15,000 per year in interest only on that debt -- never even attempting to retire the obligation. Now try taking that balance sheet to the bank for a loan. Does this really make any sense at all?

The Boston Tea Party -- one of the first acts of armed opposition to British taxes and the action that ultimately led to outright rebellion against the crown -- erupted because of taxation only a tenth as heavy as the tax burden Americans shoulder today. It would be one thing if Americans could see light at the end of the tunnel, if they could even believe in some kind of plan to liquidate the national debt.

But as of this writing there hasn't been any governmental effort whatsoever to repay the national debt. What does the U.S. Congress and the Executive office debate? Simply whether or not the government should continue to overdraft it's operating account in the coming years. Yes, we got lucky in 1997, and notwithstanding government's tinkering, the private sector experienced a boom that in turn generated greater than expected governmental revenues. But can it last? Is it even possible to assume that 5,000 years of recorded history to the contrary, the United States will end run the consequences of fiat paper money, bureaucracy bloat, and an exponential growth in the laws and rules that regulate lives?

There is plenty of rhetoric to be sure, but government overspending continues. Sanity is gone, philosophy takes precedent over reality. Is it any wonder many Americans are saying: "Thanks but no thanks." James Bovard, in his publication "Lost Rights," sums it up:

"While courts have created new due process rights for welfare recipients, disruptive school children and criminal defendants, the rights of farmers, homeowners, parents, and businessmen have been shredded. The modern ideal of due process appears to be to permit citizens to exhaust their life savings fighting court battles against heavy-handed government agencies."

FEARS

North Americans have long ignored overseas investments because of fear of the risks. What about runaway inflation? What about sudden devaluation or economic turmoil? Europe may have the potential to become a more secure place to invest than the U.S. in the not too distant future. The sea change in Europe is like the tidal wave running under our decks. We have not yet felt the impact -- but we will.

With the collapse of Communism, the chances of an all-out war in Europe have faded dramatically. External violence is receding as a threat throughout the continent. Every European country is cutting back on defense. When the Germans closed military bases, they wanted to convert them to schools -- the next battlefield.

The U.S., on the other hand, sadly sees too many of its young people wasted by violence. American children are twelve times more likely to die of gunfire than children in the rest of the industrialized world. Whether through murder or suicide or by any other means, U.S. youngsters are five times more likely to die young than those in any other developed nation. And it is getting worse. From 1950 to 1993, murder rates have tripled and suicide has quadrupled in children younger than 15.

At a 1997 money conference attended by the author, a panel from Switzerland was addressing questions from the floor. One of the questions dealt directly with street violence in Europe, a concept virtually unknown to the Swiss. Representatives of a number of U.S. enforcement agencies were in attendance and they were disturbed that the Swiss were not enthusiastic about helping them track down American holdings in Switzerland; an act which would cause the Swiss to violate their country's privacy laws. From the Swiss perspective it would seem that whenever the U.S. government wants confidential financial information from Swiss bankers, they immediately allege that drug money or street violence is involved.

A U.S. law enforcement person speaking from the floor was quite outspoken in his opinion that citizen rights to privacy were the underpinnings of violent crime. It was quite dramatic when a spokesperson for the Swiss delegation pointed out that there were only five violent crimes that ended in the death of someone in Geneva during all of 1996, as compared with the daily violent murders in the greater Miami area where we were then meeting. And, this despite the fact that Switzerland had supported rights to privacy for the individual for over 700 years!

IRRELEVANT BORDERS

What we understand as "countries" or "nation states" today are relatively recent in human history -- the past 500 years or less. Newcomers as they are, they may already be on their way out the door.

We define a country by its borders; by a single secular authority in charge of the territory and representing it to the rest of the world. Countries also have an authority that is superseded by no other body. But the heart and soul of what makes a country is the power to tax. No matter what you call an area, if it does not have the right to demand money of its citizens and have the power to take it from them if they don't pay, you don't have a country.

For a number of reasons countries are not what they used to be, and that is an important thing to remember when deciding where to put your money. In one of those odd congruities of history, the things that separated countries disappeared at the same time the means to unite them appeared. Contending ideologies that divided the world into hostile camps ceased being an issue in the late 1980s and early 1990s. At that very moment in history, the Internet emerged as a fast, economic way to communicate and do business across borders.

The Internet poses a threat to national governments, as we know them because it facilitates trans-national loyalties and affiliations in a way that governments cannot control. The things that are important these days have a way of ignoring borders. Just ask the Laps in northern Scandinavia who could not eat their reindeer meat because a decade after the Chernobyl nuclear power plant meltdowns it was still contaminated with radiation. Or ask the parents of children hooked on cocaine-based drugs imported into the U.S. through any number of holes in the border. Or ask the residents of California, Texas or other border states where illegal aliens have come to roost. The same is true of Germany, the Netherlands, France and England, where immigrants have taken over whole neighborhoods.

Yet the main threat to national governments is the loss of control of money. It is now possible to conduct major transactions across borders using the Internet and offshore banking. And no government is in a position to get a piece of the action with a tax. That's the kind of thing governments are able to do well when goods or people or cash are passing through checkpoints at borders or ports or train stations or airports. But when deals are made for information or for goods already within the jurisdiction, how does government track and tax?

Governments already know the handwriting is on the wall. One of the great mysteries some future generation will try to resolve is why the Clinton-Gore administration pushed so hard to popularize a technology that will ultimately cut them off at the pockets – the Internet.

WHO NEEDS IT?

Why do we pay taxes? Most people would say because they feel they must. During times of national emergency such as natural disasters or wars, most citizens of a country acknowledge, if only grudgingly, that a government is necessary to protect them from the danger.

But the popularity of Libertarian, Survivalist and other anti-government groups widely considered at the fringe of society is merely the tip of the iceberg in the American public's apathy toward government. Many mainstream Americans consider themselves "Independent" when it comes to voting because they no longer feel an attachment to the two-party system.

A generation ago, Jimmy Carter called the IRS "a disgrace to the human race." The U.S. income tax is held in such low esteem that Congress' chief tax writer, chairman Bill Archer of the House Ways and

Means Committee, believes it should be "torn out by the roots."

By and large, much of what government offers in the way of services are things people would just as soon do without -- or they would rather have them provided by private industry on a voluntary basis. One reason Americans have this attitude of indifference toward government is the success we have seen from deregulation of monopoly industries. The telephone companies in particular lost their monopoly status, and notwithstanding the soothsayers, the result has been much lower costs and vastly improved service. Americans made careful note of this result, and many would like to see the same deregulation of other government-provided services, such as Social Security, Internal Revenue, and prisons.

Ever since the IRS established the withholding tax, the pubic and eventually the Congress have clamored for tax reform. After all it was instituted to pay for a war and it was supposed to end directly thereafter. From at least one point of view, we have already had tax reform. However, the tax reforms that have survived the legislative quagmire have, without exception, made the system more complex and dramatically increased the costs of compliance. The more complicated the tax structure becomes the more taxpayers complain and seek solutions. And yet complexity is exactly what the legislators find so advantageous.

The incredible, almost unknowable, intricacy of the U.S. federal tax system provides a forum for the professional legislator to pontificate upon. They can give speeches about its unfairness and promise that if they could just have expanded powers they will provide the needed tax cuts and make the system more fair. Unfortunately, attempts at reducing taxes seem to always result in an increase in tax revenues. Legislators don't really want to reduce taxes, they only want to *talk* about reducing taxes.

Governments are putting themselves out of business. The main thing we need from government is protection. Police protect us from one another at a local level, and armed forces protect us from one another at a national level. But internationally, the job is largely done. World War is not a likely event, the warfare of the future will likely emerge in a different form. There is no Evil Empire likely to stage an all-out attack on the United States. But there are a host of rogue states with the means to develop chemical or germ warfare or to smuggle a small nuclear device through our porous borders. It's still a dangerous world, but dangerous in a different way.

The point is that it is fair for national defense consumers to ask why money is being spent on multi-billion-dollar, missile-firing nuclear submarines capable of wiping out whole continents, when that tool is inappropriate to meet the threats of the day. Nationality does not have the emotional import it did when there was greater danger of war. There is no moral onus to looking elsewhere, to shopping for the best national domicile. Loyalty is not an issue when there is no threat.

The day is likely coming when governments will compete with each other for their revenue base. Competitive jurisdictions? You bet. The fact that you were born within the territory controlled by the United States will no more mean that you are a life time customer of this, and only this, government's services. You do have choices.

YOU BETTER SHOP AROUND

Computers and the Internet make it possible to do business from practically anywhere in the world. Why, then, operate out of a jurisdiction that taxes higher than others? It is possible today for an accounting firm in The Netherlands to handle the work for a company in Los Angeles. Through faxes and e-mail and Internet telephony, there is no cost advantage to doing business with the lawyer down the street. Every professional in the world has the opportunity to do business from wherever they wish.

The same is true of national governments. The U.S. national defense budget has averaged 3 percent of Gross National Product. That is expensive especially when citizens of countries the U.S. purports to protect, such as Germany, do not pay nearly as much. Americans who choose not to pay for this service to protect citizens of richer countries are no more to be criticized than residents of Seattle who buy goods in Portland. It's just the marketplace in action. That is why there is already the dollar equivalent of a full year's production of the American economy sequestered in offshore institutions.

A NEW APPROACH

Ironic, is it not, that the United States -- which was founded to guarantee freedoms to its citizens -- has become an oppressive regime for the sake of gathering taxes.

There was no income tax until 1915, when the government anticipated getting into World War I and needed more revenue to pay for the
fight. Preparing for war has been the rational for the income tax for the
rest of the twentieth century.

In 1916, one man, John D. Rockefeller, could have paid off the
entire U.S. national debt. In 1997, Warren Buffett and Bill Gates combined could not pay the interest on the national debt for a period of only
two months! The interest on the national debt for about two months
totals $50 billion.

To keep the cash flowing, the U.S. government has chiseled away
at the freedom of its own citizens. Huge bureaucracies, like the IRS,
FBI, ATF, SEC, NSA, CIA, DEA, and on and on, all have authority to
invade our privacy, our homes and even take our lives in the pursuit of
money to run our $1.6 trillion dollar government appetite.

Isn't that the tail wagging the dog? Would we rather have our freedoms or our government? Most of us would choose freedom. But it
doesn't have to be an either/or decision. Why not a reduced government and a means of support that does not violate our freedoms? Why
not a point-of-sale modified national sales tax? Paying when you buy
would eliminate the need for all those investigative and controlling agencies to know all about your private lives, your private banking activities, and so forth. By abolishing the income tax and therefore disbanding
the IRS, and eviscerating other oppressive secret three-letter agencies
(those that continually desecrate our rights as Americans), it is possible
to reclaim our heritage. In the meanwhile, it is no surprise that wealth
continues to flow overseas.

∞ Chapter 6 ∞

BANKING, MONEY, AND THE FEDERAL RESERVE

> *"To emit an unfunded paper as the sign of value ought not to continue a formal part of the Constitution, nor ever hereafter to be employed; being, in its nature, repugnant with abuses and liable to be made the engine of imposition and fraud."*
>
> *Alexander Hamilton*

MONEY

Money, we all need it, we all want it, and we all use it. It impacts much of what we do throughout the majority of our lives, it shapes a considerable amount of our thinking, and it sparks much of our action. But, oddly enough very few people really know how money is created and what that actually means to them. We tend to leave such weighty matters to those who seem to know more about these issues than do we. History teaches us that this is a very big mistake. When the people are not informed the privileged few have control. Study this chapter carefully, your improved understanding of the way things really are will better prepare you for the choices you'll want to make to secure your financial future.

OVERVIEW

It's like watching the weather during tornado season. Economists view actions of the Federal Reserve Board with a mixture of fear and wonder, because the Federal Reserve has the power to raise or lower interest rates, and therefore wield enormous power over the economy.

How much power? Consider this: Every time the Federal Reserve raises rates one quarter of a percentage point, about 50,000 home buyers are priced out of the market, according to economist David Lereah of the Mortgage Bankers Association.

68

Stock prices rise or fall according to how heavily dependent those companies are perceived to be on borrowings. And when rates are high, many investors switch from buying stocks in business to bonds from government.

Higher interest rates cause the dollar to rise against other currencies. A stronger dollar makes U.S. goods relatively more expensive in the international marketplace, and imports more accessible – thus potentially idling U.S. factories and accelerating an imbalance of payments. The ripple effect of all these changes is to act as a brake on the economy – companies slow down and lay off workers, who are out of work and cannot buy.

That's an enormous amount of power. What is this institution and who are the people who have such control over our lives? And, just how far does their power actually go?

THE FEDERAL RESERVE SYSTEM

The Federal Reserve System, sometimes referred to as the "FRS" or the "Fed" is not federal, and there are no reserves, at least not in any traditional sense of the term.

The Fed is a quasi-private company controlled by a select few. Stock shares of the Federal Reserve are issued to federally chartered commercial banks. However, the stock does not represent incremental ownership, the shares cannot be sold or pledged, and shares in the Federal Reserve do not provide for ordinary voting rights, as they normally do with other private corporations. The U.S. government does not own any stock in the Federal Reserve System, but the FRS has a TOTAL monopoly over government banking activities and its decisions literally effect the lives of virtually everyone on the planet.

The decisions made by the fed are rendered in secret meetings, weeks prior to the release of any information to public sources. All notes and transcripts of such meetings are destroyed prior to public announcements, so that no information will be available under the Freedom of Information Act. Neither the FBI nor the CIA enjoys such secrecy.

The Fed exists to ensure profits to a select few, and it is the single most important board piece in the game of world domination; not by the United States, as you might logically presume, but by influential bankers and power brokers.

The Federal Reserve System is the beating heart of a legalized cartel. It is the epitome of a secret combination designed to get gain at the ultimate expense of the uninformed public. This institution is the source from which fiat money flows; money backed by nothing. In its truest form, this is counterfeit money, which the current government requires that every American accept or suffer the consequences of the use by government of overwhelming force. In this, citizens are stripped of their fundamental rights and liberty.

The Constitution actually requires that money be only gold or silver. The founding fathers were historically informed. Gold and silver are the ONLY money that has stood the test of 5,000 years of recorded history. This requirement has been overruled by a compromised legislature, although a Constitutional amendment to validate this action has never been passed.

The Federal Reserve is the third resurrection of the centralized monopoly originally chartered by the Continental Congress in 1781. The same men, who initially chartered the private business that would gain an absolute monopoly over money, eventually realized the error of their ways and refused its renewal. When the Constitution was first drafted it included the language from the former "Articles of Confederation" which said:

> "The legislature of the United States shall have the power to borrow money and emit bills of credit."

This is the process by which fiat money begins, i.e.: *emitting bills of credit.* However, the framers of the Constitution were collectively so appalled by the inflation and inherent corruption this process bred, that an overwhelming majority of the Constitutional Convention — amounting to a four to one vote — removed the words "emit bills of credit," from the Constitutional language. Alexander Hamilton spoke for this majority when he said:

> *"To emit an unfunded paper as the sign of value ought not to continue a formal part of the Constitution, nor ever hereafter to be employed; being, in its nature, repugnant with abuses and liable to be made the engine of imposition and fraud."*

The fathers of the Constitution had experienced first hand, the results of fiat currency. Fiat bills were then widely referred to as simply paper money, meaning it was paper only with no guarantees of redemption of anything of underlying value. Paper money, or fiat currency, is not to be confused with the paper bills which are actually receipts or claim checks, which may be redeemed for whatever backs it, normally gold or silver. For example, U.S. dollars up until the 1960's were actually "silver certificates," meaning they could be redeemed at any government mint for their value in silver.

Our early American patriots saw clearly that the government should NEVER again be granted the right to issue paper money without legitimate backing and without a complete check and balance system. Thomas Paine summed up these feelings when he said:

> "The punishment of a member (of Congress) who should move for such a law ought to be death."

Even a corrupt government bureaucracy cannot inflate a fully backed commodity currency; provided, of course, someone is minding the vault. London Times editor William Rees-Moog had this to say:

> "Neither a state nor a bank ever have had the unrestricted power of issuing paper money without abusing that power."

He went on to point out that:

> "There never will be a shortage of politicians willing to spend where they have not taxed, nor is there any shortage of economists wishing to advise them of the wisdom of supporting trade and employment by issuing more money. No money whose issue is controlled by a politician is ever better than the needs the next election will allow."

Article 1, Sections 8 & 10 of the Constitution of the United States say that "Congress shall have the power..."

> "To borrow money ... to coin money, regulate the value thereof, ... and fix the standard of weights and measures ... to provide for the punishment of counterfeiting..."

> "No state shall ... coin money; emit bills of credit, ... (or) make any-
> thing but gold and silver coin a tender in payment of debts."

There is no question that those responsible for drafting the Constitution were careful and precise with their words. The American colonies had previously been flooded with paper fiat money to the incredible
detriment of its citizens. Inflation always follows the circulation of fiat
money and to the best of my knowledge there has never been an exception in the history of the world. Some of the original colonies had
experienced inflation of over 1000%, the results of which wiped out the
lifetime savings of the majority of the colonists. Those that framed the
Constitution understood plainly the danger that lurks where government
is allowed to grant to either itself, or anyone else, a monopoly to create
paper fiat money.

BANKING

Throughout much of history goldsmiths handled the business of
banking. Merchants and citizens brought their gold and silver, usually
in the form of coins, to a goldsmith. The goldsmith's job was to store
and protect these valuables in their vault. For this they charged a fee.
The goldsmith-banker issued paper receipts, which represented claim
checks for the coins deposited with them. These paper bills were generally in a standard and recognized form and were therefore widely accepted as money based on the reputation of the goldsmith, his family
and fortune.

Banking was the act of storing coins and bullion and making loans.
Loans were made from the assets of the banker's themselves, not the
stored assets of others. If a person storing their coins with a banker
wished to earn interest by allowing their gold to be loaned to third parties, they understood clearly that the money was not readily available
for use until the borrowing party had paid back the loan and interest.
Most borrowers wanted paper money, not bulky coins, so when they
received their loans of coin they typically would leave them in the vault
and instead take paper bills representing the gold or silver coin actually
on deposit.

All legitimate paper money was historically 100% backed by gold,
silver, or whatever commodity was identified on the face of the bill.
Paper bills were "receipt money," because they were simply receipts for
an equal amount of gold or silver held on deposit at the bank which had

issued them. Any banker that created paper bills, for which they did not have gold or silver in the vault, was guilty of fraud. Paper money without backing, where people have been forced to accept it by government, is called "fiat money."

A CENTRAL BANK

The Federal Reserve is the central bank of the United States. It was established in 1913. The U.S. had tried such a system in the past and it was abused. Because of this, Americans have viewed with suspicion the centralization of power and authority in banking — especially when it is an imported system, one concocted by the banking families of Germany, England, and France.

The central system gained a foothold after a financial panic in 1907 — one it would appear that was prompted by certain monopolistically inclined eastern and foreign banks. The pressure was on Congress to do something. The answer was a national bank — the Federal Reserve — one that was supposed to become a lender of last resort to the private banking system. The theory was that private banks could turn to the Federal Reserve for loans when other banks were unable to provide them. The Federal Reserve was to pool the resources of participating banks to create an "as-needed" fund for these last-resort loans to provide liquidity in times of uncertainty. Banks were then making money by lending out the large majority of their customer's deposits, rather than simply their own holdings. So, if a number of depositors became insecure about the health of their bank and all tried to withdraw deposits at the same time, there was rarely suffacent liquidity to accommodate such a "run on the bank." When this sort of thing began it typically caused financial panic.

The initial argument for the FRS was convincing, but it has evolved into something far more powerful than simply a lender of last resort and something a good deal more sinister. The Federal Reserve became the entity that controls all banking activities, which in turn controls most business activities and deeply influences the business cycle itself. The Federal Reserve is also the creator of new money out of nothing.

The seven-member Board of Governors of the Federal Reserve Bank, including the Chairman and Directors, have become the most potent force in existence controlling our financial lives. And yet they are unelected and unaccountable to the lives of the very people they control. Though they are more influential than even the highest elected officials, they are appointed by the sitting President and confirmed by the U.S. Senate to serve 14-year terms, with no direct accountability to the voters.

The Federal Reserve is not an agency of the U.S. government, although it is a government creation. It is a corporation owned by banks that are members and that hold stock in it. Every bank that has a Federal charter is required to buy stock in the Federal Reserve and to be members of the system. Banks with state charters have the option of whether or not they wish to become members, but all banks — no matter what their membership status is — are under the control and influence of the Fed.

The Chairman of the Board of Directors testifies before Congress twice per year about how the Fed is handling the nation's money supply and what can be expected in the economy. The media, with great interest, covers these appearances, but most people are simply unaware of their import.

CROSS PURPOSES

The Federal Reserve operates under what has been called the "dual mandate" – two directives from the federal government that many say are contradictory. Congress passed the Employment Act of 1946 and the Humphrey-Hawkins Act of 1978, which is the Full Employment and Balanced Growth Act. These acts call on the Fed to "promote effectively the goals of maximum employment, stable prices and moderate long-term interest rates."

What this means is the Fed has been directed to create economic growth with low inflation. Inflation yes, but hopefully low inflation. Rapid business growth has historically come when the Fed creates more money — lowering interest rates to banks and lending money that had not existed previously. Yet this new money — with nothing backing it — always creates inflation. Inflation, of course, is the "hidden" tax, it is the result of government's over issue of money and it robs the poor and middle class of their hard-earned equity. Only if the economy has grown in terms of productivity and where a substance of widely perceived value backs the new money, can new money be issued without causing inflation.

How much money is created is a decision made by the seven members of the Fed who form the majority of the 12-member Federal Open Market Committee (FOMC). This group has the final say on the cost and availability of money and credit in the economy.

When you send in your taxes, the money eventually winds up passing through the Federal Reserve System, which operates for the government the way your bank operates for you. Checks are issued from the Fed for everything from submarines to Social Security checks.

Those checks, by the way, are due to be phased out by January 1, 1999. That's the date all government payment checks must be issued electronically. Currently the computer system at the Federal Reserve in Richmond, Virginia can handle an average of $988 billion in Federal wire transfers per day. Richmond was selected in 1992 out of banks in the 12 Federal Reserve Districts to be the location of the FRS data processing center. However, personnel at the Federal Reserve Banks in New York, Chicago and Dallas handle automated services. Other FRS centers are in Boston, Philadelphia, Cleveland, Atlanta, St, Louis, Minneapolis, Kansas City, and San Francisco.

WHERE'S THE BEEF?

"Where is most of the money in the banking system today?" asks Bruce J. Summers, the Fed's system-wide director for automated services. "Not in the vault. It's on computer records. We protect the value of the information." They also protect the currency by gleaning out counterfeit and worn bills, which add up to several million dollars each day.

One of the more intriguing things about the Federal Reserve is how it creates money. The picture that comes to mind is of a printing press, churning out sheet after sheet of dollar bills. And, while that indeed happens, the real creation of money is silent and invisible. The Federal government issues securities — debt obligation instruments such as bonds – which the Federal Reserve buys on the open market. It buys these securities in a kind of shell game by issuing credit to the government, which then writes checks against it, and presto — new money is put into circulation.

Let's say you held a U.S. Treasury bond and decided to sell it. The Federal Reserve, using power granted to it by the Congress, would pay you money that did not exist before — whatever the face amount of the security. (It's not the same as when you or I write a check on our bank accounts and the money is then withdrawn. When the Fed does it the banking reserves are added to, not subtracted from.)

Once you've received payment for your security you make the deposit to your bank account. Through the "fractional reserve system," your commercial bank must keep a certain amount of your deposit on reserve – perhaps 10 percent. But it can lend out the rest – what they call the "excess reserves." The person who borrows that money spends it and the business where he or she has spent it can now deposit it in their bank. That bank can now has new money it can lend out. And, so it goes, until the original purchase of the Treasury security could now have multiplied the amount of money in circulation up to nine times the sum of the new money government created out of nothing to begin with. When you add the original government debt to the bank created fiat money the total is approximately ten times more currency put into circulation than the amount of the underlying government debt. The banking system, underwritten by the FDIC, has therefore expanded the amount of money multiple times for every dollar the Federal Reserve has created out of nothing to begin with.

To the degree that this newly created money floods into the economy in surplus of goods and services, it causes the purchasing power of all money, both new and old, to decline. Prices go up because the relative value of the money has gone down. The result is the same as if that purchasing power had been taken from us in taxes. The reality of this process is a hidden tax of up to 10 times the national debt. Americans have paid over the years, in addition to their federal, state, and excise taxes, a completely hidden tax equal to many times the national debt.

Of course, the Federal Reserve can also shrink the money supply by selling securities in its portfolio. The money paid for these securities is absorbed, like a sponge, and taken out of the economy — not actually put into any bank account.

SHELL GAME

If this all seems like a shell game, it's small wonder. A currency with nothing behind it is not only fictitious and dangerous it is simply illegal. Or at least it would be, if you or I or anyone else were to embark upon such an unscrupulous scheme.

It's often said that those who do not know history are doomed to repeat it. We are neither the first generation nor the first nation to try to do business with an artificial currency. But the ultimate consequences in terms of inflation and subsequent creditability have been so disastrous in the past that our founding fathers strove to prevent this kind of corruption in the United States for all future generations.

The U.S. Constitution (Article 1, Sections 8 and 10) already quoted earlier bears repeating, as it stipulated that:

> "Congress shall have the power ... to borrow money ... to coin money, regulate the value thereof, and of foreign coin, and fix the standard of weights and measures; ... No state shall ... coin money; emit bills of credit; [or] make anything but gold and silver a tender in payment of debts."

The drafters of the Constitution were clear in their intent: "coin" money means to stamp pieces of metal. The young country already had its belly full of paper currency. Many states issued their own paper money from 1690 to 1764. It was so much easier to simply print money than risk the ire of citizens by exacting taxes. The result was run-away inflation — as high as 2300 percent in Rhode Island before the Revolution.

This is why the Constitution clearly prohibits states from issuing "bills of credit" or paper money. The flaw, however, is that the drafters did not also directly prohibit the federal government from doing so. In the course of fighting off the British, the Revolutionaries resorted to paper money in order to pay for the staggering cost of providing for men and supplies. At the beginning of the war in 1775, the federated colonies had a total money supply of $12 million. But the Continental Congress issued another $2 million by June, and authorized another $4 million soon thereafter. The presses churned out the money year after year as the war dragged on, until the original $12 million had another $227 million added to it —plus $200 million in money-like certificates issued by the Continental Army — in addition to the money issued by the states. It amounted to an increase of 5000 percent in five years.

The result of all that money chasing goods was runaway inflation. Thomas Jefferson saw what happened and called it by its right name — taxation — which he called "the most oppressive of all because [it is] the most unequal of all."

When the country returned to money backed by precious metals, the country also returned to a stable currency and to prosperity. But this is a lesson apparently every generation must learn anew.

ORIGINS OF THE FEDERAL RESERVE

It was ironic that the very country from which the Revolutionaries sought to free themselves — England — gave them their example of a financial institution that again controls them. Yet that is exactly what happened. Following the example of the Bank of England, the Continentals organized the Bank of North America in 1781. The ambitious name was because they hoped Canada would join them in a continent-wide nation free of British rule. That was not to be their only disappointment.

The Bank of North America – a private bank that functioned as a central bank — was not given the power to directly issue the nation's money, but it could produce bank notes the government would accept. The bank was the depository for Federal funds, and immediately created out of nothing more than a million dollars which it loaned to the government. Other sleights of hand with gold loaned from France, money created out of nothing and loaned to bank officers, brought the bank to low esteem. It was yet another casualty of the Revolutionary War and the bank's charter was not renewed.

The entire concept of a central bank had been discredited. Yet the prospect of the power to create money from nothing is so appealing that the U.S. Congress again succumbed. Congress may have been empowered only to "coin" money, but it desperately wanted to "print" it. And so, Congress pulled a fast one by delegating the right to print money to a separate entity, and then "borrowed" this printed money and spent it. The kicker is that the entity that "lends" this money is actually creating it out of thin air.

Today the IOU's the government creates are the bonds and T-bills you and I buy — with the money the bank has created. Congress has gotten around the Constitutional proscription against creating bills of credit by having the Federal Reserve Bank perform this job.

Thus was born America's second central bank in 1791 — the Bank of the United States. Like the previous bank, the new one was made the official depository of federal funds and was given the monopoly of issuing bank notes. These notes were not forced on the public for private debts, but the government would take them for taxes and duties. The bank was required to redeem its notes in gold or silver. The purpose of the bank was to create money for the federal government, and like its predecessor, issued so much that the result was inflation. In five years wholesale prices rose by 72 percent, which was tantamount to a hidden tax on the citizens. And, as always, it was the fundamental backbone of society that was hurt the worst. Those that faithfully saved money for investment and their retirement saw those savings evaporate through government fraud. The Bank of the United States became a hot political issue in its day, and its charter was not renewed. By 1811, it went the way of its predecessor and was out of business.

The War of 1812 again put Washington in the position of wanting more money than it had. The war was so unpopular that Congress feared levying taxes to pay for it. Yet the past method of conjuring up money out of a central bank was denied to them. Instead, the U.S. government encouraged the proliferation of private banks, from which it borrowed, and then relieved them of the obligation to redeem their notes with gold or silver. The banks loaned out in paper money much more than they actually had on deposit in hard currency. By 1814, when people wanted their silver and gold and the banks were unable to deliver, many of these banks failed, leaving note holders ready to riot.

The chaos in banking gave support to arguments for yet another national bank. In 1816, Congress gave a 20 year charter to the Second Bank of the United States — it was actually the third central bank by that time. In a great irony, this bank refused to accept any notes from other banks unless the notes were redeemable by gold or silver on demand. But when the other banks made the same demand back, the Second Bank of the United States recanted on the issue of hard money.

This bank was more efficient in extending its reach across the young and growing country, so its acts of expanding and contracting the money supply had dramatic impact in the national economy. Once again, the American public wanted a sounder currency. So strong was the sentiment that Martin Van Buren and Andrew Jackson worked within the new Democratic Party to abolish the national bank. When Jackson was elected in 1828, that's exactly what he set about doing. The bank's existence became the central issue facing the nation, until it, too, was finally put to rest by 1837.

Jackson was successful in instituting several monetary reforms — such as requiring the use of hard currency or coin for transactions under $5. But times were changing, people began using checks instead of bank notes for their major transactions. This left bankers the opportunity to once again lend out much more than was on deposit — money in circulation almost doubled in four years. When the contraction in the money supply came, as it inevitably did, banks failed and depositors were the losers.

To protect depositors, states such as New York devised a "safety fund," as early as 1829. New York banks were required to contribute from one half of one percent up to a total of three percent of their total capital stock to this fund. When the crash came in 1837 the banks were swamped with depositor demands for their money. The only thing that saved the system was that the State of New York agreed to accept the now worthless bank notes as payment for canal fees. In other words, the taxpayers picked up the burden, as they have ever since. This system is the precursor to the Federal Deposit Insurance Corporation, or FDIC.

The Civil War, like the Revolutionary War, encouraged the government to create more money. During fiscal year 1861, expenses for the Federal Government had been only $67 million. After the first year of war, expenses rose to $475 million. By war's end they were $1,300 millions. Taxes covered only 11 percent of that total. The national deficit swelled to $2.61 billion.

There was no central, national bank at the time and smaller, state banks were not in a position to create enough receipt money to pay for the war. The North issued bonds to be paid at the end of the war in gold, but that was not enough to pay the bill. An income tax was tried, but it was extremely unpopular. The only option was to print money not backed by precious metals. The $432 million of them printed during the war became known as "greenbacks." In effect, the government became its own Federal Reserve Bank by issuing money from nothing as a wartime expedient.

The pressure of war led to other creative efforts. The National Banking Act of 1863 established a system of nationally chartered banks — not one central bank. But control was firmly held in the East. It was a wartime emergency tool to create a market for government bonds which were transformed into money, a process that later became the model for the Federal Reserve Systems' money creation machine.

What happened is that the Federal government issued government bonds, which the bank purchased. The bank immediately turned them back to the Treasury which exchanged them for an equal amount of "United States Bank Notes," with the bank's name engraved on them. These notes were legal tender for taxes and duties, and therefore most people accepted them as cash. Money was created from nothing — government debt was transformed from bonds into cash.

The money so created during the Civil War was not considered legal tender for all debts — just what was owed to the government. The official money was government issued coins and greenbacks. (Ironically, the South never did issue its own coins — U.S. and private coinage remained legal tender throughout the South during the war.)

Money created in this shell game fashion did become the legal tender of the nation with creation of the Federal Reserve Bank half a century later. With the Federal Reserve System, the government creates money by converting debt into legal tender through loaning to a system of its own creation. The original intention of the Founding Fathers, that America's money be backed by precious metals, was completely thwarted. It was sacrificed as an expedient in waging war. Now that the wars are over, there is no incentive to return to safer ground.

PROBLEMS

What would you do if you had the power to create money out of nothing? Would your area of temptation be toward pleasure, sensuality thrills? That's the temptation of young people. The old, gray heads running the show at the Federal Reserve lean toward the weakness of older men — toward power.

With the ability to create money, the Federal Reserve is a player in the game of co-opting and controlling the world. The FRS is so effective in manufacturing money out of nothing that it has become the model for the IMF (International Monetary Fund). In fact, this organization could not exist without the flow of American dollars created by the Federal Reserve. Central Banks of industrialized nations, just like the Federal Reserve — guarantee loans to developing countries. This means that if the borrower defaults, the taxpayers of the lending nations pick up the debt themselves. This money props up cooperative heads of state by giving them access to vast wealth.

The game that is being played now involves co-opting the heads of state of less developed countries. Our largest and most influential banks make loans to these governments. These countries are rarely able to repay the loans. They then offer to pay the interest only or default altogether. To keep these loans out of the default column, our Fed supported major banks make ever-larger loans so the interest payments can stay current on their books. In this way, the largest U.S. banks are assured of not suffering defaults, booking huge interest income, and will have the taxpayers to bail them out when the debts simply become to overwhelming to refinance.

Former enemies now find themselves beholden to the IMF. Russia and her former satellites now grovel for the dollars that only the Federal Reserve-backed world economy can provide. Thus, entire countries are brought into vassalage to the international fund, to the machine that churns out money from nothing. This system is accountable to no one and is beyond almost everyone's control, yet has as its base of power, the ability to saddle you and I with repaying the obligations it makes.

It bears repeating that when our forefathers spoke of paper money, they were actually referring to fiat currency, or a form of paper money which has no backing and is nothing more than a bill of credit representing increased government debt. This is completely different from a paper currency that represents, in effect, a claim check on something considered of universal value, such as gold, silver, grain, or some other commonly sought after commodity.

George Mason, a delegate from Virginia to the Constitutional Convention stated he had a "mortal hatred to paper (fiat) money." He is quoted as saying, "Paper money is founded upon fraud and knavery." Oliver Ellsworth, the third Chief Justice of the Supreme Court, said:

"This is a favorable moment to shut and bar the door against paper money. The mischief of the various experiments which have been made are now fresh in the public mind and have excited the disgust of all the respectable parts of America."

George Reed, a Delaware representative to the Constitutional Convention, declared that a provision in the Constitution granting the new government the right to issue fiat money "would be as alarming as the mark of the beast in Revelations." And, John Langdon from New Hampshire warned that he would rather reject the whole plan of federation that to grant the new government the right to issue fiat money. George Washington was of a similar opinion as were the vast majority of those assembled to produce, as Gladstone put it: "The ....most wonderful work ever struck off ... by the brain and purpose of man."

So what happened? How did this heroic beginning slide into a situation so wanton that it strips us of our liberty and deprives us of our property?

In G. Edward Griffin's wonderful book entitled *The Creature from Jekyll Island*, which I highly recommend, he says:

"The accepted version of history is that the Federal Reserve was created to stabilize our economy. Even the most naïve student must sense a grave contradiction between this cherished view and the System's actual performance. Since its inception, it has presided over the crashes of 1921 and 1929; the Great Depression of '29 to '39; recessions in '53, '57, '69, '75, '81, a stock market "Black Monday" in 1987, and a 1000% inflation which has destroyed 90% of the dollar's purchasing power."

It takes well over $10,000 to buy now what it took only $1,000 to acquire when the Federal Reserve was formed to "stabilize our economy." This incredible loss in value was quietly transferred to the federal government in the form of hidden taxation, and the Federal Reserve System was the mechanism by which it was accomplished. The details of the creation of the FRS have now largely come to light — it was the brainchild of Paul Warburg, working in concert with the authors of the most famous monopolies of all times, the Rothchilds, Morgans, Rockefellers, and other extremely wealthy influential world players. Daddy Warbucks of Little Orphan Annie fame was patterned after the life and character of Warburg.

Anthony Sutton, former Research Fellow at the Hoover Institution for War, Revolution and Peace, and also Professor of Economics at California State University at Los Angles provides this:

"Warburg's revolutionary plan to get American Society to go to work for Wall Street was astonishingly simple. Even today, academic theoreticians cover their blackboards with meaningless equations, and the general public struggles in bewildered confusion with inflation and the coming credit collapse, while the quite simple explanation of the problem goes undiscussed and almost entirely uncomprehended. The Federal Reserve System is a legal private monopoly of the money supply operated for the benefit of the few under the guise of protecting and promoting the public interest."

America has lost its way. Our government has succumbed to the attraction of spending whatever it will, without the bureaucracy actually having the funds to pay for its excesses. Taxes, always an unpopular issue, can now be reduced while government spending goes unchecked, merely by government waiving their magic wand and "emitting bills of credit" to the Federal Reserve who in turn create more fiat money to put in circulation.

History will not be forever robbed of its lessons. Inflation AL-WAYS follows the circulation of fiat money. Inflation is the hidden tax paid by every one of us as we are robbed of real equity. Every year our money buys less and less and we must work harder and harder to stay even. The average American family is in economic crisis, and is simply unaware of the danger. Our government precipitated this crisis. The very government established by the people to protect them from the kind of counterfeit and fraud the effects of which we are now suffering.

I urge you to implement strategies to protect your privacy, to develop real asset protection, and substantially reduce your taxes. And, I recommend you set something aside that has historical value as money, just in case the worst happens in our lifetime, and we see a temporary collapse of our economic system due to our irresponsible Congress and fiat money. You need to take action now!

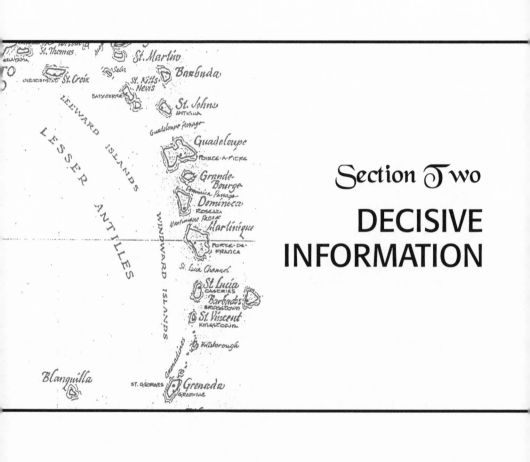

Section Two

DECISIVE INFORMATION

∞ Chapter 7 ∞

OFFSHORE TRENDS

*"Where possible, all business should be domiciled off-
shore in a tax-haven jurisdiction. This is particularly important for Websites and Internet addresses, where there is virtually no advantage in locating in an on-shore, high-tax jurisdiction."*

Lord William Rees-Mogg
Circa AD 1997

THE TAX HAVEN

As long as there has been money, people have wondered how to
keep it. And the more money, the more urgent the question.

The concept of offshore banking is as old as commerce. The Island of Delos off the coast of Greece was one of the places the wealthy
of ancient times stored their treasures. Protected by water, with few natural resources other than a harbor, the leaders of the island learned that
the rich of the mainland would pay handsomely to know their valuables
were safe and protected.

Delos set the pattern for financial havens. For the most part, they
are tiny island nations with limited natural resources located near a major,
thriving economic center. But there is more to it than that today. A tax
haven is often within a country -- such as the state of Nevada within the
USA. Paradoxically, countries that are insensitive to their own citizens'
need for protection and tax shelter sometimes become havens for the
over-taxed and under protected of other countries. The United States is
a prime example of this oddity.

HOW IT BEGINS

A good example of how and why a tax haven nation is developed
is the Bahama Islands. In the early 1960s this string of sandy atolls near
Florida still flew the British Union Jack. Centuries ago, many ships ply-
ing her waters sported the Jolly Roger -- the coves and sheltered beaches

were a paradise for pirates, who creamed the flow of wealth from the galleons of the Spanish Main.

For centuries the islands have been a sleepy backwater -- beautiful to be sure, but primitive and undeveloped. Despite its beauty and comfort, the islands repelled would-be investors with its high-tax philosophy. The result was a net outflow of capital from the islands.

Was it the ancients spirit of the bold and daring pirates or was the fledgling country merely trying to survive? In either event, the leaders realized the Bahamas would never reach their potential unless they reversed the flow of wealth out of the islands. They looked at their options and decided that if their own laws drove money from their country, could they tap into the out-flow of wealth from other, more prosperous nations?

They instituted a two-tier tax system. The leaders decided there would be one set of laws for the citizens of their country, and another for foreigners. At the same time, the Bahamas clamped the lid on any information leaking out about the financial dealings of those with money in the country. They introduced banking privacy laws.

The response was almost immediate. Americans and Canadians seized the opportunity to shield their assets from prying eyes -- and groping hands. The fact that the islands are a beautiful vacation getaway made investing there all the more attractive. Progressive banking laws coupled with a penchant for confidentiality has earned the Bahamas an excellent reputation as an offshore financial center. Total Eurodollars handled by Bahamian banks in 1996 exceeded 250 billions. The second largest source of income for this island nation has become bank service fees!

A GROWTH BUSINESS

Jealousy is a powerful motivator. Other nations, more than 50 of them altogether, saw the prosperity the Bahamas had earned as an offshore banking center and wanted their share.

Like the ancient island-banking center of Delos, these havens tend to be near large economies where citizens' rights are on the decrease and government spending is on the increase. Near the U.S. and Canada, for example, are Antigua, the Bahamas, Belize, Bermuda, British Virgin Islands, the Cayman Islands, St. Kitts & Nevis, the Turks and Caicos, and others. All of these so-called "tax havens" are of rather recent date.

Typically, bank accounts are held in the name of a trust or an International Business Corporation, ("IBC") that has been formed in a tax haven nation. The IBC designation in a tax haven jurisdiction indicates that the ownership of the corporation is foreign to that country and generally speaking has been granted government guarantees that it may operate tax free so long as it's business revenue does not come from within that country. More about this later. U.S. government estimates indicate the formation of 130,000 new IBC's during 1996 in the Caribbean alone. During 1997 and 1998 these numbers continued to rise.

Near Great Britain are the Channel Islands -- Jersey, Guernsey and Sark along with the Isle of Man. Some of the largest financial institutions in the world are located in these smallish, out-of-the-way islands.

Within Europe are the long-time havens of Austria, Switzerland, Liechtenstein, and Luxembourg. And in more recent years Europe has gained Bulgaria, Ireland, and Hungary as new havens for wealth. In the Mediterranean are Gibraltar, (also part of Europe), and Malta. Not to be outdone, the Middle East now have a collection of tax haven jurisdictions of their own.

The island nation of Mauritius in the Indian Ocean, along with the Seychelles, serve as havens for Africa and the Indian subcontinent.

In the Far East, Hong Kong built itself into a financial center with its liberal corporate and banking laws. In 1996, over 15,000 new IBC's were formed in Hong Kong alone. With the change of sovereignty in 1997, the future of this haven is unclear but business is usual at the time of this writing in late 1998. The Philippines and Singapore have passed new laws to attract offshore money. These centers serve the citizens of such countries as Japan and Korea.

Australia and New Zealand citizens use the Cook Islands, Marshall Islands, Vanuatu, Nauru, Western Samoa, and the Marianas, as their havens.

And, oddly enough, as mentioned above, some of the very countries whose citizens place their wealth offshore are themselves tax havens for citizens of other countries. Both England and the United States draw vast sums of money from foreigners. Why is that? Simply because they offer tax advantages to foreigners that are not available to their own citizens.

GO O.J.

Ever heard of O.J. Simpson? He's probably become one of the more famous, and/or infamous, individuals of all time. Simpson was reported in England's The Sunday Express tabloid as having paid that country a visit. But according to the newspaper, his visit was not a vacation. O.J., then the defendant in a civil lawsuit over the murders of his late wife and her friend, was in danger of being stripped of all his money if he lost the suit. Seeking protection for liquid assets, he allegedly stashed $5 million in an offshore bank account on his trip. He supposedly did it by moving money from accounts in the West Indies to Dublin and then to Britain's Channel Islands.

Is it true? We're not likely to know.

VODKA TONIC

Sometimes becoming a tax haven is a tool of manipulation and control. Take the Russian republic of Ingushetia, for example. This tiny area is adjacent to the breakaway republic of Chechnya, which for years has been the scene of a bloody war of independence. Fearful that rebellion could spread to other Muslim-populated areas such as Ingushetia, Moscow took a bold step.

In 1994, Russia granted the tiny republic "offshore" status within the Russian Federation. And according to *The Economist* (March 1996), it is to become a tax haven to the rest of the world as well. The benefits are obvious. The new Hotel Assa, in the capital Nazran, is sumptuous, looking over an artificial lake.

Germans are building an airport. And a new capital -- named "Sun City" and costing $250 million -- is under construction. It's the old concept of the carrot and the stick. The Russians have battered their Chechian minority into staying within the fold. But more effective in pacifying the natives has been the wealth that has come to Ingushetia as a tax haven.

Russia isn't the only country with an internal tax haven. The United States boasts some of the most intriguing tax differentials in the country, as you will see in the chapter about Nevada.

WHY ENGLAND

England has become the mother country to a host of tax havens, and for very good reasons. Remember the Falklands War? Argentina invaded and occupied a barren and practically worthless string of British islands off its own coast in 1982.

Many other countries might have decided it was not worth fighting over and negotiated some face-saving way to exit the scene. But not the Brits. They dispatched an entire fleet -- complete with nuclear weapons -- and were prepared to obliterate Argentina if need be to defend their sovereignty.

Why is that important? Because it demonstrates that any British possession or protectorate is going to remain British until hell freezes over. And that determination breeds a great deal of confidence. That's why many of the countries offering the best asset protection are former British colonies. These Commonwealth countries have enough independence to form their own business and tax laws, yet retain an aura of security through their affiliation with Great Britain.

COMPETITION

The offshore business is so lucrative that countries compete with each other for it. Like any other competition, newcomers must offer advantages the old guard does not. New IBC, privacy, trust, and banking laws are being passed in nation states all around the globe, as jurisdictions line up to serve the citizenry of those disgusted with the bloat of bureaucracy evidenced particularly in the U.S., Canada, Italy, and other European countries.

Some twenty years ago there were few offshore financial centers and their use was surrounded by myths of drug money and other illicit activities. There were few professionals specialized in offshore practice and these were generally focused on only one or two jurisdictions. Today the offshore industry has developed into a major global business, spanning all quarters of the world, involving, in one way or another, approximately half of the world's financial transactions by value. Yes, that's right, HALF THE WORLD'S FINANCIAL TRANSACTIONS BY VALUE!

The International Financial Center, (the new professional name increasingly used to identify a tax haven), is considered a safe and reasonable way to conduct business. IFC's frequently operate 24 hours a day, and have become an integral and important part of the world's financial system.

ELECTRONIC CURRENCY

Smart Cards employ sophisticated electronic technology, but they are still tangible objects. The big leap in the evolution of money is purely electronic currency -- when things are bought and sold and nothing physical changes hands.

"The Cashless Society" spoken of for so long has arrived in stages. First came credit cards -- invented in 1956 by Bank of America employee Joseph Williams. Credit cards became widely popular in the mid 1970s and consumers got used to buying things without cash.

Next came debit cards to directly access bank accounts, and automatic teller machines (ATMs). Direct banking came next, when proprietary software like Quicken gave computer-literate people access to their accounts to pay bills at home.

But it is the Internet, and the ability to access this system from virtually anywhere in the world and do business anywhere else in the world that holds the potential of the next true breakthrough in going offshore. An U.S. Commerce Department and Killen & Associates' study shows a significant growth of electronic purchases in the early years of the twenty-first century.

In 1994, electronic commerce accounted for 4.5 percent of all purchases -- which amounted to $245 billion compared to $5.15 trillion of traditional purchases, which included retail, wholesale, service and mail-order purchases.

They estimated that by the year 2000 electronic purchases would amount to 16.2 percent of all purchases -- a total of $1.65 trillion compared to $8.5 trillion purchased traditionally. And by 2005, they estimate electronic purchases would amount to 19.7 percent of the total. In dollars, that would be $2.95 trillion compared to $12 trillion purchased traditionally.

Of that growth in electronic spending, far and away the fastest growth will be via the Internet, the study concludes. From a standing start in 1994, Internet purchases are expected to reach $600 billion by 2000, and $1.25 trillion by 2005 -- which would be 10 percent of all purchases. Small wonder the Internet has captured the imagination, and why no one wants to be left out.

ARE NEW CURRENCIES REQUIRED?

What will be required to facilitate this expected flow of commerce? New forms of money, perhaps? "There is nothing intrinsic about the Internet that demands new means of exchange," writes Debora Spar, an associate professor at the Harvard Business School in *Harvard Business Review.*

> "There are no technical obstacles to routing and recording even non-traditional transactions through established routes; nor are there demands for new levels of financial oversight or regulation."

In other words, in her opinion, nothing new is required in order for commerce to be conducted on the Internet. The U.S. Dollar and the banking system can handle the business. But is she right?

Apparently, many buyers have agreed with her. Despite warnings about losing control of their credit card number, they have used their plastic to make purchases on the Internet anyway.

The turning point was the security feature in Netscape Navigator, currently the most popular software for finding and manipulating information on the Web. It contains Secure Sockets Layer (SSL) that encrypts data, indicated by a key at the bottom of the screen. This browser enabled on-line banking. Of course it was rapidly followed by Microsoft's Explorer and other similar Web browsers that offer similar security.

In addition to the protection offered by the encryption features of the new browsers, buyers were finally persuaded by their desire to buy the things offered on the Web.

Gateway 2000 Inc., that has become one of the country's leading producers of PCs, sold thousands of computers within months after they put an order form on their Web site. Amazon.Com of Seattle sells several thousand books per day from its Web site. More than 80 percent of its customers complete their transactions on line. The book seller has enough relationships with wholesalers and small publishers that it offers almost 3 million titles, which is more than twelve times the number found in book superstores.

> "We are seeing an almost complete turnaround," according to Michael Wolff, who publishes the NetGuide book series. "There is a perception that technology has improved and the security is there. And it's

also the fact there is so much out there for sale and so the compulsion
to buy is growing."

Besides, consumers think, security on the Internet is no worse than
anywhere else. How, after all, is a hacker supposed to find their credit
card number and their name out of all the data on the Net? And what's
the difference between exposing your numbers on-line and giving it
over the phone to a telemarketer or a waiter? And if a crook *did* get
someone's credit card number, federal law limits an individual liability
in credit card theft to $50.

"The fears about credit card numbers on the Net haven't moved
me that much since I give my credit card to people in restaurants all the
time and they take it out of my sight where I can't see what they're
doing with it," observed Dave Hatunen of Daly City, Calif., as quoted
by Evan Ramstad of the Associated Press.

People have shown they can be weaned away from cash. Electronic transfers and credit card transactions accounted for 18 percent of
the $55 trillion that consumers, corporations and governments spent in
1993, according to Thomas McCarroll (*Time* 1994). The number of electronic transfers increased 200 percent from 1986 to 1993

Checks and cash transactions in the same seven year period rose
only 17 percent. More than 37 percent of consumer payments are by
check. Including consumers, business and government, there are about
55 billion checks written every year. And they are expensive to process
-- financial institutions pay about $1.30 each. Banks end up losing money
on about half of all checking accounts, because the handling costs often
exceed the interest they earn from the money in them.

Electronic transfers, on the other hand, cost about 15 cents each. Is
it any wonder banks want to move us in that direction? Not only banks,
but big check writers also see savings. The U.S. government, for example, recently saved $133 million by paying close to half its hundreds
of millions of bills by computer rather than mail.

Confidence was what was missing. Buying things on the Internet
was simply too unfamiliar. But once the comfort level rose high enough,
the money began to flow. It took a familiar vehicle for the transfer of
money for that to happen, and that was credit cards.

Other means of transferring value on the Internet have evolved, and may or may not survive, depending on their appeal, and on how well the U.S. Dollar/ banking combination serves the needs of Internet commerce.

DIGICASH

The next stage in the evolution of electronic currency is not based on credit cards, but on real money. And the developers invented a completely fictitious money to prove it would work — the Cyberbuck.

If you could just get your hands on a Cyberbuck, you might have a real collector's item. But, alas! It was an electronic currency, with no physical manifestation and not redeemable for any real money.

But the Cyberbuck did prove a very important point: that people are willing to trade goods and services in exchange for what amounts to nothing that is backed by nothing.

The Cyberbuck was the unit of electronic currency issued by DigiCash and its founder, David Chaum of Amsterdam, the Netherlands. Chaum, who received his Ph.D. in computer science from the University of California at Berkeley, and his colleagues at the Center for Mathematics and Computer Science, a government funded institution in Amsterdam, came up with a "blinding" technique that allows numbers to serve as electronic cash.

To demonstrate its viability, he launched an experiment in October 1994 that eventually led to the Mark Twain Bank, through which real money was flowing.

Chaum issued 100 Cyberbucks free to the 30,000 people who participated in his experiment. The Cyberbucks went into participants' DigiCash bank account. Although these Cyberbucks could not be exchanged for real money, their relative scarcity and the goods and services behind them gave them value.

People set up shops at the DigiCash Website and sold things like books and pictures and software -- mostly things that could be transmitted on line -- things most people could live without. But a true small economy evolved, and Chaum eventually cut off enrollment in his experiment a year after it was launched. If anyone wanted in on it, they had to buy someone's Cyberbucks, and it cost a real dollar to get the e-mail address of the person advertising them for sale.

The experiment became a real business, and E-cash (tm) came into being. E-cash is not fictitious money but is the electronic representation of real cash -- primarily the U.S. dollar (USD) and a number of other currencies, as well.

But those anxious to jump on the DigiCash bandwagon face the same risks of collecting arrows in the back that any pioneers do. When you cut through the hype, you find an ingenious set up through which DigiCash has put itself in a no-lose situation, but one in which it warns is customers: "Caveat emptor" -- buyer beware.

When an E-cash withdrawal is made, the PC of the E-cash user calculates how many digital coins of what denomination are needed to withdraw the requested amount. Next, random serial numbers for those coins will be generated and the "blinding factor" will be included. "Blinding" is the bank's way of issuing an electronic note without tracing whom it was issued to. This makes the E-cash as anonymous as paper currency.

The result of these calculations will be sent to the digital bank. The bank will encode the blinded numbers with its secret key (digital signature) and at the same time debit the account of the client for the same amount. The authenticated coins are sent back to the user and finally the user will take out the blinding factor that he introduced earlier. The serial numbers plus their signatures are now digital coins, their value is guaranteed by the bank.

When the user makes a purchase, the coins go to the receiver, who in turn sends them to the digital bank. The bank verifies the validity of these coins and that they have not been spent before (every coin is used only once). The account of the receiver is credited. Another withdrawal is needed if the receiver wishes to have new coins to spend.

DigiCash says that because "E-cash offers full payor anonymity, it is perfect for controversial applications." They explain that the identity of the payor is not revealed automatically, so the payor stays in control of information about himself. But the person who is paid is identified to the bank. At first blush, I'd say this has huge applications for the offshore industry.

But E-cash is not good for money laundering, tax evasion, black market, extortion, or bribes, according to DigiCash. The reason is that all money the payee receives must eventually be given to the bank. "It's not possible to hide from the bank the fact that you received money from the bank (and thereby hide it from the authorities). So tax evasion is definitely out." On the other hand, if the platform operating a DigiCash look alike and the bank charter were both based in a British Commonwealth country that ensures privacy and confidentiality to financial transactions, everyday people could be easily shielded from undue scrutiny.

No wonder DigiCash believes other banks will want to license their software and build a system. The technology behind DigiCash is at the heart of CAFE, a project sponsored by the European Community to develop a pan-European currency system.

BANKS ENTER THE FRAY

CyberCash Inc. of Reston, Virginia and giant banking company Wells Fargo are also experimenting with their own electronic currency. It works much like a checking account. Clients put real money into their electronic money accounts using proprietary software provided free by CyberCash. They spend their money on the Net and at the end of the day, CyberCash clears all transactions and converts the electronic currency back to money.

CyberCash was founded in 1994 by William Melton and Daniel Lynch. Melton had also founded Verifone, which makes equipment to authorize credit card transactions. They managed to convince the U.S. government that their encryption software could not be used to transmit secrets, so it is exportable.

Banks' interest in the Internet stems from a fateful discovery they made when they introduced Automatic Teller Machines (ATMs) as a convenience for customers. Banks learned that the cost of handling an ATM transaction is a fraction of the cost of a traditional one. It made financial sense to move away from bank branches and tellers and in the direction of automating as many transactions as possible at ATMs.

HOME BANKING AND THE INTERNET

Electronic technology also helps banks close branches. The Federal Reserve predicts that American Banks will close as many as half their branches by the year 2000 -- a reduction of 30,000 branches.

Banking from home is so far a tiny portion of the potential market -- accounting for about 2 percent of all transactions. However, recent information indicates this number is growing exponentially. Those who do bank this way enjoy the luxury of avoiding dealing with cash, and its risks of theft and loss. They use Intuit's Quicken or other software and their PC's communications program to work with their banks.

Banks want people to move in that direction, and are doing what they can to "encourage" people. Some bank customers are charged $3 every time they deal with a teller. One bank offers inexpensive checking to customers if they are willing to pay $1 to use a teller.

Banks feel they can charge the customer for the "service" of banking at home or using an ATM, even though these transactions cost the bank a fraction of those done with a real teller. "The banks need that technology to drive their processing costs down," according to Joseph Cady, a consultant with CB Consulting in San Diego.

With the protection of the encryption offered by secured browsers a number of banks have taken the final step -- Internet banking. A new breed of branchless banks is attracting customers with high-yielding certificates of deposit. Since Atlanta Internet Bank opened its virtual doors in August of 1997 it has taken in almost $200 million in deposits. The first half of 1998 saw deposits jump by almost 200%. And, although the bank didn't report its first profitable month until March of 1998, investors have taken notice. The banks stock price has more than doubled in the last few months alone.

Internet banks are popping up all over. This bodes well for anyone interested in moving liquid assets a step away from themselves and into an offshore corporation. You could be a consultant to an offshore company and control the company's cash from anywhere in the world via a portable computer and Internet access.

BARTER CURRENCY

Banks, in their rush to downsize, could find they have lost their hold on customers. "E-cash will be offered by both banks and nonbanks," remarked DigiCash's Chaum.

If Internet commerce swings in the direction of an electronic currency, DigiCash or other look-alike models could just as well work with Microsoft and its 70 million Windows users as it could with banks. And that is a prospect that may well fit with Bill Gates' long-range objectives.

Banks could find themselves "buttons on a network operated by other entities," according to William M. Randle, senior vice president at Huntington Bancshares.

If that seems unlikely, look at what happened to credit card processing. In the mid 1970s, banks owned that business. Twenty years later, 80 percent of card transactions were processed by non-banks, such as First Data Resources Inc.

Just as the banks don't have a lock on Internet commerce, neither does the U.S. Dollar. Chaum's DigiCash hopes to base its E-cash some day on a blend of currencies and precious metals. Today, there is nothing preventing anyone from issuing their own private money. The only question is whether people believe in the integrity of the one issuing it.

Chaum showed in his initial experiment that thousands of people are willing to buy and sell over the Internet using a fictitious currency based on absolutely nothing. It may seem surprising that people are willing to do that, until you think about the world economy. The U.S. dollar is the preferred medium of exchange, but it can't be exchanged for anything, either.

But what if there were an electronic currency backed by goods and services produced by thousands of businesses?   I refer to trade dollars, which are the accounting unit of the commercial barter industry's Trade Exchange segment. Trade dollars don't expire. Trade dollars are impossible to counterfeit.

The trade exchange is a clearinghouse, or marketplace, governed by trading rules which all the members of that particular marketplace have agreed to honor. Trade dollars are -- in effect -- a private money, the only genuine electronic currency.

Professor F.A. Hayek, in *Choice in Currency: A Way to Stop Inflation*, explains why private money such as trade dollars make sense for electronic commerce.

> "There is no reason whatever why people should not be free to make contracts, including ordinary purchases and sales, in any kind of money they choose, or why they should be obligated to sell against any particular kind of money. There should be no more effective check against the abuse of money by government than if people were free to refuse any money they distrusted and to prefer money in which they had confidence."

Paul Suplizio, former CEO of the International Reciprocal Trade Association (IRTA), in his paper entitled, "Commercial Barter Exchanges in Society," wrote:

"Modern commercial barter is a system of trade and payments that is emerging alongside the monetary system of trade and payments. Its instrument of payment -- the trade dollar or trade credit -- is the best illustration today of the privatization of money that Professor Hayek has called for and which Professor Milton Friedman approves."

The trade dollar has all the basic elements of money, as well as some unique characteristics that could make it an excellent choice as a supplemental or alternative electronic currency.

Trade dollars fulfill the essential definition of a currency because they can serve widely as a medium of exchange, as a standard of exchange value, as well as a store of exchange value. They have greater potential as an electronic currency than the U.S. dollar because at least trade dollars can be redeemed for goods and services. For every trade dollar in circulation in a trade exchange there must be an offsetting debit in another participating business owner's trade account. Trade dollars are, in effect, credit lines.

For example, if there were 100 trading business owners in a trade exchange network and each were granted a $10,000 credit line, there could never be more than $990,000 in circulation at any time. Suppose that 99 trade members all drew against their credit line and spent their entire $10,000 at one company.

That would mean the creation of $990,000 in new trade dollars. Each exchange member is bound by trading rules to make immediately available their respective goods and services for 100 percent trade dollars to repay their debt to the system. This means that the trade dollars in circulation are backed by the goods and services of the exchange's indebted membership.

Is this a backed currency? Absolutely! In fact, I cannot think of a better form of currency backing. If all 99 debtors were to repay their obligation through the sale of their goods on trade, the trade dollars in circulation would fall to zero until another credit-worthy exchange member once again accesses the credit line for buying and thereby expands the money supply.

Trade dollars may become one of the most credible electronic currencies for doing business on the Internet because the supply of trade dollars expands with legitimate business demands and contracts as demand diminishes.

No doubt about it — money is changing with the times, and this has major implications for a person with a worldview. The question for all of us is, can we change fast enough with it. Not just money is changing, but everything — and fast.

THE SOVEREIGN INDIVIDUAL

In January 1997 a new book entitled *The Sovereign Individual* was released. Written by Lord William Rees-Mogg and James Dale Davidson, it forecasts the pending collapse of the dominant systems in our society. They are dead serious in their conclusions and amazingly lucid with their arguments. Lord William Rees-Mogg is a financial adviser to some of the world's wealthiest investors. He is a director of J Rothschild Investments, General Electric PLC, and the M&G Group, the largest unit trust (mutual fund) in the U.K. He was formerly the editor of the *Times London* and vice chairman of the British Broadcasting Corporation. Davidson has equally impressive credentials. It is their quote that opened this chapter, it is theirs with which it closes:

> "Citizenship is obsolete. To optimize your lifetime earnings and become a Sovereign Individual, you will need to become a customer of a government or protection service rather than a citizen. Instead of paying whatever tax burden is imposed upon you by grasping politicians, you must place yourself in a position to negotiate a private tax treaty that obliges you to pay no more for services of government than they are actually worth to you."

> "Of all the nationalities on the globe, U.S. citizenship conveys the greatest liabilities and places the most hindrances in the way of becoming a Sovereign Individual. The American seeking financial independence will therefore obtain other passports as a necessary step toward privatizing or denationalizing himself. If you are not an American, it is economically irrational to become a resident of the United States and thus expose yourself to predatory U.S. taxes, including exit taxes."

∽ Chapter Eight ∽

FREQUENTLY ASKED QUESTIONS

"We are not afraid to entrust the American people with unpleasant facts, foreign ideas, alien philosophies, and competitive values. For a nation that is afraid to let its people judge the truth and falsehood in an open market is a nation that is afraid of its people."

John F. Kennedy

PREAMBLE

To the uninitiated, the whole idea of offshore banking is shrouded in mystery. How do I do it? Is it legal? Will I lose my money?

There is much room for misunderstanding and misinformation on these issues. Compounding the problem is the shortage of places to go for straight answers. There are those with a vested interest in planting seeds of doubt in prospective investors' minds. By that I refer to the taxing authorities, bankers and others who seek control over your life.

The more of your money that is offshore, the less that is within their grasp. In Arnold Goldstein's wonderful little book entitled, *Offshore Havens*, comes this quote:

"You may be one of the millions of Americans who are completely hoodwinked by the IRS...our bankers...and countless others who, for their own self-serving reasons, perpetuate the myth and lies about offshore banking. Doesn't everyone believe that offshore havens are evil, dangerous or illegal?

"The fact is that most of America has been duped and deceived by this deliberate avalanche of distortions — even outright lies — about offshore havens. Consequently, most Americans have absolutely no idea what offshore banking is all about. Instead, they believe what they read or hear from a controlled media that paints offshore havens as a hangout for tax evaders, money launders and assorted crooks, and scofflaws. Uninformed lawyers, accountants and financial planners still advise their clients that offshore havens are illegal, too risky, or otherwise unworthy of consideration. They should know better — but don't!"

As with anything else new, there is a learning curve and there are Frequently Asked Questions -- FAQ's. The questions I am most often asked have to do with the legality and appropriateness of investing offshore. Direct answers to specific questions should aid in clearing up misconceptions right up front. You will find additional information about these topics in later pages.

What is an "offshore haven?"

An offshore haven is a country, or jurisdiction, that generally has more lenient financial and banking laws coupled with higher standards of personal privacy, than your home country. Offshore, in the financial world, means a tax jurisdiction other than where the investor lives.

Why use an offshore bank?

Privacy and Asset Protection. One of the most important aspects of offshore banking is personal or corporate privacy and banking confidentiality. Funds and other assets are significantly better protected from creditors, and/or any other form of lien or confiscation action, in an offshore jurisdiction that in your country of residence. Keeping assets offshore considerably reduces the likelihood of litigation from lawyers working on a contingency basis. Legal predators look for deep pockets and will generally not pursue someone who has taken the time to protect themselves from frivolous claims.

Is it legal to have an offshore bank account?

Absolutely! In most Western countries it is perfectly legal to have offshore banking relationships. Questions surrounding offshore banking legalities usually are related to when an investor fails to report offshore income to his or her country of domicile at tax time. In other words, income earned from certificates of deposit or other forms of investment in conjunction with an offshore bank may be tax-free in the country where the bank is located but your country of residence may require that you report it. It has never been illegal for Americans to invest offshore, maintain bank accounts, investment accounts, etc., and it likely never will be.

Is it easier to circumvent taxation offshore?

Yes, it is. Offshore banks do not report earned income to any taxing authorities, or anyone else, even though these earnings may be taxable under U.S. law. Offshore investors are essentially on the "honor system." The IRS estimates that about one third of all the earned income in America goes unreported. What percentage of offshore earnings go unreported is anyone's guess. Notwithstanding, there are stiff penalties for failure to report these earnings. However, it should be clearly understood that ownership of an offshore bank account does not constitute a presumption of tax evasion.

Do I have to pay taxes on money earned abroad?

Yes, you do. If you're an U.S. citizen the money you earn anywhere must be reported. However, if you're living abroad and working for a non-U.S. company you may be entitled to a $72,000 tax fee exemption. And if you're married and you're both working that number is $144,000 a year that could be tax free!

The U.S. Government, as of 1984, required that all U.S. banks transfer to them your Social Security number if you have a checking or savings account, stock brokerage account, mutual fund, money market, or barter account. In any year you earn $10 or more in interest, the IRS receives a report directly from your financial service institution. The IRS matches these reports with what you report on your annual tax return. Foreign banks are not required to comply with these rules unless they advertise in the U.S. That means there is no record of your offshore earnings sent to the IRS.

Properly organized offshore corporations may provide certain tax timing benefits, and in some cases even tax reduction mechanisms, particularly if the offshore corporation is properly "de-controlled." However, just because you open a bank account in a country that has passed bank secrecy laws does not excuse you from the responsibility to report income earned to the taxing authorities in your home country.

What are the primary reasons for having wealth placed offshore?

1. *Privacy* Your rights to privacy are all but gone in several nations, particularly if you reside in or are a citizen of the United States.

2. *Asset Protection* To secure yourself against future predatory litigation. If you earn $50,000 a year or more, you will be sued an average of seven times in your life. And this number is growing.

3. *Tax Planning* Advantageous use of foreign jurisdictions and their tax rules for reduction of tax liability

4. *Estate Planning* Family and Protective Trusts, possibly as an alternative to a Will, for accumulation of investment income and long-term benefits for beneficiaries on a favorable tax basis

What constitutes a favorable jurisdiction?

A desirable jurisdiction should be politically neutral, follow a policy of free trade, not interfere with the commercial activities of corporations established there, and provide reasonable assurances of personal and corporate privacy.

Language, the quality of telecommunications, time zones, availability of professional infrastructure, and other issues are also important.

Most popular jurisdictions have a legal system derived from a western country and greatly favor corporations that are non-resident in nature. There must be a solid commitment to the protection of private property and the promotion of international trade.

Will my money be safe offshore?

As safe as you want it to be. In an age when U.S. banks have failed right and left, you may wonder if your money is safe in the U.S. After all, the number of banks defined as "problem banks" by the Federal Deposit Insurance Corporation increased 750 percent from 1980 to 1988. The FDIC is currently reporting that approximately 1,500 banks in the U.S. are unstable. Even on a per-capita basis there is no such dismal record anywhere else in the world.

While it is true that the Federal Deposit Insurance Corporation insures participant banks' accounts up to $100,000, it is also true that the system would be hard-pressed to make good on its promises in the event of wide-spread bank failures.

To be insured by the FDIC is to live within this bureaucracy's regulatory constraints, which some offshore banks choose to do. Offshore banks typically stay aloof from these constraints because they then have a much wider horizon of opportunities in which to invest than do U.S. banks.

Do offshore banks make riskier investments than U.S. banks?

Not if you look at the relative track records. The Savings and Loan debacle and the hoard of failed U.S. banks -- that together have run up a tab of over $500 billion, an amount we all will pay -- hardly seems like a record to brag about. Add to this the procession of bank executives marching off to prison or being fined. No other industrial country can top this miserable record of mismanagement, ineptitude and corruption.

By contrast, banks in countries that do not have an FDIC to bail them out are very careful how they do business. They realize that their greatest asset is their own success. There are many countries that have their own deposit insurance program. But most often the insurance is through private industry rather than the government. Often enough this insurance can be for the entire balance of an account, rather than only for $100,000.

FDIC does not cover most people with surplus funds in the U.S. anyway. Why, you ask? Simply because most of us want earnings higher than the minute amount paid in passbook savings and therefore we opt for short-term money market accounts, or similar higher interest products. And virtually none of these, whether the funds are on deposit with your local bank or not, are covered by FDIC.

Will I earn more or less interest offshore?

Chances are excellent that you will earn more offshore than in the U.S. Typically, international banks pay higher interest because the interest rates may not be regulated by law -- as they are in the U.S. International banks often operate with lower overhead than do U.S. banks. It is the recognition of this fact that has led to so many American bank mergers and subsequent reduction of overhead -- largely through lay-offs and closing of redundant branches.

Isn't it extremely difficult to do banking offshore?

It doesn't have to be. Banking offshore -- especially in the age of the Internet -- can be practically as easy as banking around the corner. New accounts are opened in offshore centers on a daily basis and millions of legitimate dollars flow through them annually, all without the slightest problem. After all, international finance is the lifeblood of these centers. They frequently have no other source of income, and they need the business. It is true, that to open a bank account internationally usually takes more time and requires more effort than opening an account at the corner branch of your local bank.

Many international banks will allow you to have your money held in the currency of your choice -- such as Pound Sterling, Swiss Francs, Deutsche Marks, or U.S. Dollars.

Secured credit cards are the norm with international banks because they do not ask for your social security information nor complete a credit check on your finances. However, once you've received your offshore card you can charge on it the same way you would a domestic credit card. Conversions are made at your offshore bank if you hold your balances in other than U.S. dollars. The added benefit to you is that the records of these transactions are now overseas, protected from prying eyes.

What do I look for in an offshore bank?

Is the bank well established and reputable?
Do the bank employees speak English easily and
    understand Americanese?
Does the bank have experience in handling customers
    in countries other than those in which they are located?
Can you manage your accounts by phone and fax?
Will you have a personal account manager and will he
    or she complete wire transfers the same day requested?
Are the fees for personal attention reasonable?
Does the bank offer benefits to nonresident customers?
Does the bank routinely handle multi-currency transactions?

Daily administration of an offshore company, if provided by professional corporate managers or a fiduciary such as a licensed Trust Company, will resolve most of your concerns. A good administrator will know the precise requirements of each bank and the most efficient way to fulfill them. In turn, the banks will know from past experience that all accounts opened and operated by that administrator are well managed, monitored and maintained. The benefits of this good relationship are passed on to the client.

How do offshore havens get started?

Certain countries, or legal jurisdictions within countries, seek to make it attractive for you to incorporate and carry on financial activities within their jurisdiction. There are so many tax efficient jurisdictions competing on the world market for your business that it can be somewhat overwhelming just trying to sort through all the positive options.

What's an IBC?

IBC stands for International Business Corporation. IBC is the term most often used when referring to a corporation formed in an offshore jurisdiction where the purpose of the business is to do business in a place or places other than the jurisdiction itself. For example, a person in the U.S. causes an IBC to be formed in Bermuda in order to handle business for anywhere in the world EXCEPT Bermuda.

What maintenance requirements are there for an IBC?

All jurisdictions have at least two requirements:
   1. Maintaining a registered agent or office; and
   2. Paying an annual registration or franchise fee, or flat tax.

Do I have to travel abroad to invest offshore?

No. Offshore investing does not mean that you have to live abroad, or even travel abroad. Offshore investing can be done from your own home through qualified professionals who will function on your behalf with reputable offshore banks and professional firms. Investments within your country of residence can be purchased on your behalf from an offshore location.

Don't you have to be a millionaire to invest offshore?

Definitely not! You can start a bank account offshore with as little as a hundred dollars or so. If you're going to explore overseas investment, you may want to start with $5,000. The more the better, of course, with $50,000 a good level to begin serious offshore investing.

One reason you know so little about offshore banks is that they are prohibited from advertising in the U.S. -- unless they are willing to come under the same regulation as U.S. banks. Which, of course, would destroy the whole point of investing offshore.

≪ Chapter Nine ≫

Fraudulent Transfers

"Currently half the government revenues in the British Virgin Islands, Cayman Islands, and Jersey are derived from offshore financial services. The world's leading financial institutions have all increased their offshore financial services, including Chase Manhattan, Citibank, Goldman Sachs, Fidelity Funds, Charles Schwab, Rothschilds, Royal Bank of Canada, Deutsche Morgan Grenfell, Credit Suisse, Lloyds Bank, Barclays Bank and Bank of America."

Offshore Outlook

FRAUDULENT TRANSFER CONCEPTS

This subject may determine just how quickly or how completely you may transfer assets into structures protecting your estate from future creditors. The laws of the United States provide protection for those who are forward thinking and avail themselves to the structures that legally protect their estate for their heirs. U.S. laws also have serious consequences for those who are merely trying to defraud creditors.

Fraudulent conveyance laws are generally created to protect creditors from debtors who attempt to hide assets to which a creditor might turn for satisfaction of an outstanding but unpaid obligation. Typically a creditor pursuing a legal claim must initiate and win a lawsuit against the debtor. After receipt of an enforceable judgement, the creditor may find that the debtor has previously transferred assets. In theory, this transfer may now hinder, delay, or preclude the creditor from satisfying their judgement. The creditor's remedy would be to go back to court in an attempt to take advantage of various remedies under the fraudulent conveyance statutes.

If the judgement creditor is able to prove to the Court the debtor's transfer was fraudulent, the creditor may attach or levy directly upon the property or asset in the hands of the grantee of the debtor. As an alternative, the creditor may have the Court void the transfer, rather than the creditor proceed against the debtor. The latter is the way most attorneys proceed against debtor's assets on behalf of their clients.

Fraudulent conveyance statutes provide for provisional remedies to protect creditors' rights, who have not reduced their claim to a civil judgement. Likewise, a potential claimant who does not know the extent of their damages or who merely has a potential conditional claim may legally benefit from these provisions.

When a creditor or claimant discovers or believes that you have transferred assets in a way that will hinder, delay, or frustrate the collection in satisfaction of their judgement, that creditor may among other remedies, ask the court for provisional relief such as injunctive relief, restraining orders, attachment, and third party receiverships for the assets.

Any transfer of assets a debtor makes with the actual or constructive intent to hinder, delay, or defraud a creditor is fraudulent. Likewise, transfers by a debtor for less than a fair and reasonable consideration, where the debtor thereby becomes insolvent and incurs debts beyond a reasonable ability to pay, is fraudulent under the law. In these situations, a creditor should have protection afforded by the fraudulent conveyance statutes and gain the relief of the Court, avoiding the transfer to satisfy judgement.

INTENT TO DEFRAUD MAY NOT BE NECESSARY

There are many circumstances where the unlawful actual intent to defraud is not apparent, may not be easily provable, or is in fact not present. There are instances where a debtor may simply gift an asset to a relative, a friend or a person in need for purely charitable purposes. Under the most recent economic times, situations have arisen where a debtor might transfer assets for an amount below fair market value to relieve his or her immediate needs for cash. These examples may be challenged in court as fraudulent transfers without regard to the debtor's subjective or actual intent.

The Statute of Elizabeth was meant to make the described transfer voidable. The creditor may ask the Court to void the transfer and put the parties back in the position they were in prior to the transfer.

"STATUTE OF ELIZABETH" JURISDICTIONS

The law regarding fraudulent conveyances is considered to have begun in England in the year 1570, with the Statute 13 Elizabeth, c.5, referred to as the "Statute of Elizabeth." This statute provided:

I. For the avoiding and abolishing of feigned, conveyor and fraudulent gifts, grants, alienations (and) conveyances ... which ... are devised and contrived of malice, fraud, collusion, or guile to the end purpose and intent, to delay, hinder or defraud creditors...

II. Provided that this Act ... shall not extend to any interest ... conveyance ... upon good consideration and bona fide law fully conveyed or assured to any person...not having at the time of such conveyance or assurances to them made, any manner of notice or knowledge of such, fraud, or collision...

However, early on, the Courts allowed the creditor to proceed directly against the transferred property.

In jurisdictions that have not adopted the Uniform Fraudulent Conveyances Act, the Statute of Elizabeth, or its derivative, is still in place. This statute states clearly that any conveyance made with the intent to "hinder, delay, or defraud creditors" is prohibited.

The language of these statutes suggests a debtor's actual intent must be affirmatively proven. Despite the actual language of the statute, Courts have developed case law supporting areas of constructive fraud, which have been labeled Badges of Fraud. The creditor uses these in proving the debtor's actual intent to defraud.

The courts have recognized that fraud may be established without actual intent to defraud. For example, a debtor who gifts out-right or sells at below market price to a relative and by doing so does not have enough assets to satisfy debt, that conveyance would be presumed to be with the intent to defraud. In some jurisdictions if the debtor retains use or control of the transferred property, the transfer is presumed fraudulent.

Many jurisdictions require proof of actual fraudulent intent, even if under case law the "Badges of Fraud" may be used to prove that intent to defraud. (Badges of Fraud are reviewed later in this section.)

Under these traditional statutes, the creditor may ignore the transfer and go directly after the transferred asset in the hands of the transferee. In order to do this, the creditor must be absolutely sure the transfer was a fraudulent conveyance. If the creditor is incorrect, he may face a lawsuit from the transferee. More typically, the creditor will have the Court avoid the transfer and then levy upon the asset.

UNIFORM FRAUDULENT CONVEYANCE

In the late 1920's, the Uniform Fraudulent Conveyances Act (UFCA) was drafted and circulated among the states for adoption. Approximately one half of the jurisdictions in the United States have adopted the Uniform Fraudulent Conveyances Act. These include: Arizona, California, Delaware, Idaho, Maryland, Massachusetts, Michigan, Minnesota, Montana, Nevada, New hampshire, New Mexico, New York, North Dakota, Ohio, Oklahoma, Pennsylvania, South Dakota, Tennessee, Utah, the United States Virgin Islands, Washington, Wisconsin, and Wyoming.

In these states the Uniform Fraudulent Conveyances Act is the primary statutory law on fraudulent conveyances.

In 1984, there was a new draft promulgated called the Uniform Fraudulent Transfer Act (UFTA). It was intended to repeal and replace the Uniform Fraudulent Conveyances Act.

However, only a few states have adopted this new draft, namely Hawaii, North Dakota and Oregon. Due to the prevailing use of the Uniform Fraudulent Conveyances Act over the UFTA, the discussion in this section will be using the Uniform Fraudulent Conveyances Act, rather than the UFTA. In most cases the outcome will be the same under both statutes.

There are two principal sections of the Uniform Fraudulent Conveyances Act that enable creditors to avoid fraudulent conveyances; (1) avoiding transfers due to actual fraud, and (2) avoiding transfers based on what is called "constructive fraud."

ACTUAL INTENT FRAUDULENT CONVEYANCES

Actual intent fraudulent conveyances are instances in which a creditor has clear proof demonstrating the debtor consciously intended to hinder, delay, or defraud their creditor. Section 7 of the Uniform Fraudulent Conveyance Act addresses actual or intentional fraud in pertinent part as follows:

> "Every conveyance made and every obligation incurred with the actual intent, as distinguished from intent presumed in law to hinder, delay or defraud either present or future creditors, is fraudulent as to both present and future creditors."

The Uniform Fraudulent Conveyances Act uses language already set forth under the Statute of Elizabeth. Both require actual intent. It is pertinent that present and future creditors may avoid a transfer as fraudulent under Section 7.

Therefore, if a transfer is made with the intent to defraud someone who is not yet a true creditor, that transfer is still deemed fraudulent. This has been taken further under case law, Masomi Sasaki v. Yana Kai, 56 C.C. 2nd 406, and its progeny, wherein there seems to be precedent for those who become creditors after a transfer, not needing to demonstrate the debtor specifically intended to subsequent creditors or to defraud a particular subsequent creditor, i.e. An actual intent to defraud either a present or future creditor, will give rights under this statute to both.

Evidence of actual intent is rarely readily available to creditors. Difficult or nearly impossible to produce, creditors must rely instead on the "circumstantial evidence" of fraud that developed under the Statute of Elizabeth and frequently referred to as the Badges of Fraud. These are incidental or collateral circumstances that usually accompany a fraudulent transfer, such as an uncharacteristic transfer of assets, transfers to relatives for less than fair market value, unreasonable or insufficient transfer consideration, or transfers still leaving the transferor in possession or control, etc.

Badges of Fraud are not conclusive evidence, but are often considered by the courts to be "circumstantial evidence" of fraud.

BADGES OF FRAUD

1. Insolvency by the transfer.
2. Lack or inadequacy of consideration.
3. Family, friendship, or other close "insider" relationship among the parties.
4. The retention of possession, benefit, or use of the property in question.
5. The existence or threat of litigation.
6. The financial condition of the debtor both before and after the transfer in question.
7. The existence or cumulative effect of a pattern of transactions or a course of conduct after the onset of financial difficulties.
8. The general chronology of events.
9. The secrecy of the transaction in question.

10. Deviation from the usual method or course of business.

CONSTRUCTIVE FRAUD

A transfer of most or all of a debtor's assets, leaving the transferor with nothing to their name, has been held as a sign of fraudulent intent.

Transfers where the transferor has retained possession in the absence of any commercial or business purpose.

Transfers for unreasonably low consideration or purport to be more than what the asset is worth.

Some courts have held transfer documents that contain the very language "this is a legitimate transaction" would only do so if it were done in contemplation of fraud.

The Uniform Fraudulent Conveyances Act has set forth factors under Section 4(b) which should be given consideration in determining whether actual fraud exists. Under current law the factors in Uniform Fraudulent Conveyances Act Section 4(b) are the types of acts considered to be Badges of Fraud.

Section 4(b) of the Uniform Fraudulent Conveyances Act reads in pertinent part as follows:

"In determining the actual intent under subsection (a)(1), consideration may be given, among other factors, to the fact that:

1. the relationship between the transferor and the transferee was a close one;

2. the transferor retained possession or dominion after the transfer;

3. the transfer was concealed;

4. prior to the transfer a creditor had sued, or was threatening to sue the transferor;

5. the transfer was of substantially all the debtor's assets;

6. the debtor has absconded or has removed or has changed the form of the assets remaining in his possession so as to make the assets less subject to creditor process;

7. the value of the consideration received by the debtor was not reasonably the equivalent to the value of the assets transferred or the amount of the obligation incurred;

8. the debtor was insolvent or heavily in debt or reasonably should have expected to become so indebted;

9. the transfer occurred shortly before or after a substantial debt was incurred.

Proof of the existence of any one of the factors listed in this subsection does not in itself constitute prima facie proof that the debtor has made a fraudulent transfer or incurred a fraudulent obligation."

As can be easily seen, these represent "circumstantial evidence," or "badges" of a fraudulent intent.

They are not conclusive, nor does any one or combination mean there is actual fraud. It does however, give the Court, and the creditor's attorney, a rational to attempt to convince the Court that the transfers were fraudulent, rather than a family, commercial, or business transaction.

It is generally difficult to prove actual fraud. There is rarely a "smoking gun" type of evidence, and the Badges of Fraud require an extreme amount of research on the part of the creditor. Due to this difficulty, the law has allowed several methods of establishing fraud without any actual intent to defraud. Therefore, the law can determine a transfer was fraudulent irrespective of the actual intent of the transferor.

The Uniform Fraudulent Conveyances Act at Section 4 also contains the principal provisions regarding "constructive fraud."

Section 4 reads in pertinent part as follows:

"Every conveyance made and every obligation incurred by a person who is or will be thereby rendered insolvent is fraudulent as to creditors without regard to his actual intent, if the conveyance is made or the obligation is incurred without a fair consideration."

The legal theory behind the idea of "constructive fraud," or allowing a transfer to be deemed fraudulent irrespective the proven intent of the transferor, is someone who knows they have no money, has or will be incurring new debt, yet transfers assets out of their ownership, "should" know the transferred asset is the only thing of value the creditor would be able to attach if the debt, was not paid. Since the transferor "should" have known that result of their action, the law therefore will deem the transfer was a constructive fraud.

AN EXAMPLE

The law would probably deem as fraudulent, the gifts or transfers of property of an insolvent person to their child, while not receiving any or adequate consideration in exchange. Therefore, if a debtor transfers away property without receiving a reasonably adequate commercial exchange in return, it would be determined that it is so prejudicial to the creditor, who under equitable law owns the property. The law will avoid the transfer in order to give the creditor a remedy, irrespective of the actual intent or thoughtfulness of the debtor.

The Uniform Fraudulent Conveyances Act presents three "presumed-in-law or "constructive fraud" transfers. All three address a person who is insolvent, will soon become insolvent due to the transfer of the extent of the transfer, or is near insolvent, while not receiving reasonable or adequate consideration for the asset transferred.

The three categories of constructive fraudulent transfers under the Uniform Fraudulent Conveyances Act are:

1. Transfers by an insolvent for less than fair consideration, or for less than a reasonably equivalent exchange.

2. Transfers for less than fair consideration by a businessperson without retaining sufficient capital to meet the likely future needs of that business.

3. Transfers for less than fair consideration by anyone, businessperson or consumer, without retaining enough property to meet his likely future debts as they become due.

The majority of litigation by creditors or by a bankruptcy trustee regarding fraudulent transfer involve one of these three "presumed-in-law" or "constructive fraud" premises for the transfers.

FAIR CONSIDERATION

The law regarding Constructive Fraudulent transfers determines the standard of fair consideration or reasonably equivalent exchange. Under this standard however, the transferor need not receive the exact market value of the property. The law usually allows for something less than fair market value.

The law has allowed a certain amount of flexibility due to actual market conditions. People often sell property for less than fair market value, due to the necessity of quick cash, or because they have incor-

rectly valued the property, or have sold to a buyer who has out negotiated them. Due to these realities of our free-market society, the standard is still a debatable point.

Under several notable Court cases, the bench mark for "fair consideration or reasonably equivalent exchange" has been determined to
be at least 70% or more of the fair market value, the Court is likely to
determine that fair consideration was not had and would rule a constructive fraud had taken place.

This 70% rule is merely a guideline. There are instances that may
make it "reasonable," under specific circumstances, to sell a property
for less than the 70%, and the Courts have so held.

AFFIRMATIVE DEFENSES

Both the Uniform Fraudulent Conveyances Act and the Federal
Bankruptcy Code provide a defense for good faith transferees who give
value.

The Bankruptcy Code at Section 548 (c) provides as follows:

"Except to the extent that a transfer or obligation voidable under
this section is voidable under Sections 544, 545, or 547 of this title, a
transferee or obligee of such a transfer or obligation that takes place for
value and in good faith has a lien on or may retain any interest transferred or may enforce any obligation incurred, as the case may be, to the
extent that such transferee or obligee gave value to the debtor in exchange for such transfer or obligation."

The Uniform Fraudulent Conveyances Act considers a conveyance made for "fair consideration" when either (1) in exchange for the
debtor's conveyance, "as a fair equivalent therefore, and in good faith,
property is conveyed or an antecedent debt is satisfied" or (2) the debtor's
conveyance is received in good faith to secure a present advance or
antecedent debt in amount not disproportionately small as compared
with the value of the property, or obligations obtained.

GOOD FAITH BUYER

To successfully avoid a transfer as fraudulent and obtain the transferred asset to satisfy their judgement, a creditor must prove the debtor's
fraudulent intent (whether actual or constructive), and the transferees,

the person acquiring the asset purchased in "bad faith," attempt to avoid their obligations to their creditor.

Under the Uniform Fraudulent Conveyances Act at Section 9, a person acquiring an asset, has total protection under the law if they acted in good faith and pay reasonable or equivalent value. If the debtor had actual fraud as the bases for the transfer and it was easily proven, the creditor or the bankruptcy trustee will not be able to avoid or take the transferred asset from the person who has purchased in "good faith." They would be protected from attack.

The Uniform Fraudulent Conveyances Act at Section 9, requires the "good faith purchaser" to meet the following three requirements:

1. He or she takes the property in good faith.

2. He or she takes the property without knowledge of the fraud that the creditor is seeking to perpetrate.

3. He or she is given fair consideration - that is, a reasonable equivalent exchange for the property received.

If any of the above three elements in the test of the bona fide purchaser is not met, they will not have the protection of the Uniform Fraudulent Conveyances Act. Under this rule a person purchasing for fair market value, having knowledge the transfer of the asset would delay, hinder, frustrate or preclude a creditor of the transferor, then the transferee will not be deemed a good faith or "bona fide" purchaser. The transferred asset would be attachable by the creditor or bankruptcy trustee.

INADEQUATE CONSIDERATION

What if the opposite of the above situation exists, where the person acquiring the asset does so in total good faith and with no knowledge of any creditors, they negotiate paying significantly less that the fair market value, even below the 70% test mark? The principal cases in this area show the law requires the asset to be delivered to the creditor. It is only delivered pursuant to a lien in the purchaser's favor in the amount of the actual consideration the purchaser gave for the asset. This is not fair market value or its replacement value.

In essence, the law will protect the purchaser's out of pocket expense of the purchase. The Courts consider total protection of one who negotiates to the exclusion of a creditor's rights would be too unfair. Therefore, at the sale of the property for fair market value, the Courts would deliver the purchase amount to the transferee. The remainder would go toward satisfying the creditor's judgement.

ISSUES CHECKLIST

1. Act when your "legal seas are calm." Whether or not a transfer was in contemplation of a creditor's claim against you is the main focus of a fraudulent transfer claim. It is therefore paramount to "judgment proof" your assets in advance of legal or financial difficulties.

2. If possible, avoid dealing with close family members, as such transactions are naturally vulnerable to attack. Transfers to trusted advisors or business associates are less likely to be challenged.

3. Maintain paper trails to support your transaction. As you know with corporations, to keep that entity legally formed the "formalities" must be maintained. This habit should be kept up in all your asset structures. In areas subject to an inquiry it is wise to have supporting documentation, showing capitalization or consideration exchanges.

If you owe monies to a friend or relative, have the debt formalized in writing or a promissory note. No matters how bonafide the transaction, reconstruction is difficult, time consuming with pertinent facts being forgotten.

4. To gain maximum protection in forming asset protect structures, have reasons other than asset protection for the transaction. If the asset protection structure is being set up at the same time as the rest of your estate plan, it is estate planning. If it is being set up when you start to do investing overseas, it is global positioning for better access to your investments. If gifts are made to relatives at special occasions the gift is for other reasons than merely sheltering assets. Timing is important.

5. Seek advice from professional counselors. Advice from your attorney to transfer your assets to your spouse for estate planning purposes or for tax purposes can help negate the inference of fraudulent intent on your part.

6. Numerous transfers are less likely to be challenged. The Courts are less likely to overturn transfers of different assets, to different persons, that are made at different times, for different reasons. Likewise, regular or consistent transfers will support the most recent transfer as normal and not intended to defraud the recent creditor.

7. Never attempt to conceal assets from known creditors or while in a bankruptcy proceeding. Such activity is dealt with harshly and may "unravel," what you have done prior to such activity, and had done le-

gally. There is a subtle, yet distinct difference between lawful asset protection and privacy, and unlawful asset concealment. Follow your attorney's advice to be able to defend the actions you take.

8. State statutes of limitations for fraudulent conveyances are usually from three to six years. In Federal bankruptcy Court, the Court's trustee is limited under Section 548 of the Bankruptcy Code from setting aside transfers "made or incurred on or within one year" from filing the bankruptcy petition. The trustee does have the option of proceeding under State law to gain the benefit of a longer statute of limitation.

9. Don't wait. Even if your legal circumstances are not as calm as you might like, you can do some planning and asset transfers. And, although a legal structure put in place now may not protect you entirely from a potential creditor you are faced with currently, getting started could protect you against future and yet unknown creditors.

10. Do not rely on the "economic sense" of your creditor. Creditors generally pursue cost-effective means of collecting debts, which is good from an asset protection perspective. However, it would be unwise to believe that a fraudulent transfer will protect your assets simply because it will not make economic sense for your creditor to continue. Whereas it is true that to pursue this type of claim is typically expensive and time consuming, the penalties of fraudulent conveyance are a risk you should not be willing to take.

∾ Chapter 10 ∾

OFFSHORE PRIVATE BANKING

"Offshore banks are jurisdictionally immune to service of process. Under no circumstances can an offshore bank (based in a legitimate tax haven country) divulge financial information about you to a third party ..."

A.S. Goldstein, JD, LLM, Phd

JURISDICTIONS AND LEGAL STRUCTURES

Twenty years ago there were few offshore financial centers and their use was surrounded by myths of drug money, and illicit activities. Today the offshore industry has developed into a major global business, spanning all quarters of the world, involving, in one way or another, half of the world's financial transactions by value.

The "Offshore Financial Centre," sometimes called an "International Financial Center" or "IFC," is the professional name increasingly used to identify a legal tax haven. An IFC is generally a nation or independent jurisdiction that has passed important legislation to protect international clients. ***The use of International Financial Centers is considered by sophisticated money managers worldwide to be a safe and reasonable way to conduct business.*** In fact, about one in four Americans who earn over $100,000 a year now enjoy use of one or more safe haven jurisdictions.

Although the concepts of private banking go back to the dawn of civilization, the Swiss are generally accredited with developing the process into an art form. The strategic location of Switzerland, at the center of Europe, found its citizens in constant contact with their larger neighbors on all sides. Being pragmatic, the intelligent option was for them to stay neutral when their neighbors were in conflict.

While most of Europe's borders were constantly changing Switzerland's remained firm. In Switzerland, government was not allowed to force disclosure of business secrets, or the existence of trust property, nor could private property be expropriated. Due to inalienable personal property rights, the rights to privacy, and the encouragement of free enterprise, the concepts of private banking matured.

Private banking services for the well to do is not new. Most large banks throughout the world have a system for providing the affluent with special service. However, private banking means something quite different in the U.S. and Canada than it may in the Bahamas, Cayman Islands, or Nevis. For starters, American and Canadian banks operate in an environment where personal privacy is no longer regarded as a "right" and therefore the very name "private banking" is a misnomer. The U.S. form of "private" banking is in reality "personal" banking, or traditional commercial banking with added personal service. There is absolutely NO privacy to private banking in the States.

The term private banking is on the increase in North America. Most of the larger financial institutions have someone officially assigned to provide their version of "private banking." True private banking services rarely provide such things as checkbooks, ATM access, and drive-through tellers, what most people think of as a traditional banking service. Instead private bankers control such things as Private Demand Deposit Accounts, Private Savings or Investment Accounts, and Private Treasury and Certificate of Deposit accounts for their customers.

A typical private banker, or trust officer, will wire funds upon request, sign contracts, handle virtually any kind of financial transaction, and generally do whatever their customer needs done, all without ever revealing the person whom they represent.

Banks and trust companies are licensed by government. In the case of a British Commonwealth country, it will typically be the Minister of Finance that endorses approval for a bank formation or trust company appointment. A trust company charter, like a bank charter, is only granted after careful examination of the principals and their individual credentials, their business plan, and a review of the capital resources and other specific financial criterion.

Once appointed, a licensed Trust Company is generally empowered with the rights to form International Business Companies (IBC's), Limited Liability Companies (LLC's), International Exempt Trusts, Asset Protection Trusts, (APT's), etc. They are also empowered to open and operate bank accounts for third parties, act as a registered agent, trustee, nominee shareholder, or director, and generally provide the various services of a private banker.

Normally, and unless a trust company has been granted an international bank charter, a trust company officer is not permitted to hold third-party funds in their own accounts. On the other hand they may function as the officer of an IBC, for example, and be the nominee signer on that company's bank account. The power to handle third-party banking by a trust company is quite similar to the private banking services provided by the Swiss. In the case of Nevis American Trust Company, for example, it administers Exchange Bank & Trust Inc., an international private bank. Customer accounts issued by this institution are extended exclusively to clients of the trust company.

For those unfamiliar with these kinds of services, the entire concept may seem unsafe. Nevertheless, according to the latest information on money handling, it would appear that approximately *one half of all the daily money transactions worldwide are handled through International Financial Centers*. This amounts to about 2 trillion dollars in business that flows through offshore centers daily! The numbers are huge, and precisely because they are so incredibly large, no emerging financial jurisdiction can afford to let a scandal destroy it's reputation and interrupt this growth industry. Once level-headed legislation has been enacted, trust companies, registered agents, and private bankers, become the key ingredients to the success of every offshore financial center.

The world of "offshore" is surrounded in its own mystique and language. And for many, this aura can be disconcerting. It is worth remembering that the real differences between an offshore jurisdiction and an onshore jurisdiction are few. Any person with a reasonable grasp of their domestic business practices is equipped to begin navigating the world of international financial centers.

A recent staff report commissioned by the United States Congress sums up the value in going offshore:

> "The offshore financial market has many advantages for rational economic operations. **The reasonable expectation, when one learns that an entity is engaged offshore, is that it is there for honest economic reasons, buttressed by whatever advantages privacy holds.** The major categories for offshore use are to profit from higher interest rates when lending, to enjoy lower interest rates when borrowing, to escape taxation, to enjoy greater business flexibility by avoiding regulation in an efficient market, to enjoy the protection of confidentiality when engaged in activities..."

U.S. Congress Staff Report

PRIVACY & CONFIDENTIALITY

Keeping financial transactions private in some countries is against the law, in other countries it is a violation of law to reveal anything about anyone's banking or financial activities. Of those countries claiming its citizens are free, the largest and most recent source of personal privacy violation has become the United States. A pertinent example of their rapidly expanding citizen control laws is that financial institutions must now automatically report to government on the banking, bartering, and securities business of its private citizens.

The alarming increase in citizen control laws has been achieved under the cover of fighting the "war on drugs." The assault on personal rights, including privacy, is always justified with convincing arguments about the common good and how the state is "improving" the quality of the protection it provides its citizens. On closer examination one may observe that the "common good" always coincidentally happens to benefit the political concepts of the politicians in power and that the individual's loss of personal power is transferred to the bureaucracy.

In an increasingly hostile environment privacy is essential to risk planning. The clientele of offshore trust companies typically seek confidentiality in their affairs to protect assets from disasters, unwarranted third party interference, and to reduce an ever-growing burden of unnecessary disclosure. It is a trust company's business to provide legal structures and potentially private banking services to protect client assets, insure privacy, and reduce risk, taxes, and costs. A policy statement extract from Nevis American Trust Company Limited pretty much sums up the offshore attitude:

> *We believe firmly in each individual's right to pursue aggressive and unrestrained enterprise and that it may be best developed through a secure, reliable, confidential, and tax friendly jurisdiction.*

MAKING DEPOSITS OFFSHORE

Making deposits in an offshore account is a simple matter and no different from making a deposit in your home country, however there are other things you ought to consider. Depositing checks in an offshore account is not generally a good idea if the checks are drawn on accounts in your country of residence. To begin with the check clearance time to "make good" paper deposits is thirty days or more, so wire transfers are the norm for international banking. If you feel strongly about implementing bank privacy tactics as a part of your overall privacy and asset protection strategy, then you may want to "break the money paper trail."

There are no restrictions on the flow of capital between most countries in the free world. There are some foreign exchange requirements placed on citizens of Barbados, South Africa, and the like, but by and large anyone from North America and Europe is exempted from these worries. Reporting requirements are another issue entirely. For example, anyone who transports $10,000 or more in or out of the U.S. is required to file IRS Form 4790.

If you currently bank in any one of a number of European countries, the U.S. or Canada, your bank may be required to report a transfer from your domestic account to your offshore account. In the case of the U.S. wire transfers of over $10,000 made to an offshore company or bank account require your bank to make a routine report to the U.S. Treasury. Currently there are tens of thousands of these reports filed daily and the IRS is swamped with inbound records and does not yet have the resources to examine them in a timely manner. At last report they were beginning to perform cursory review of Form 4790 reports from a period four years earlier and looked to be falling further behind.

Cash is still a good method for making transfers from your personal onshore account to a private offshore account. If you are from the U.S. you are required to disclose if you have over $10,000 on your person when crossing a border. However, if you are traveling with a companion you may legally cross a border with pennies less than $20,000 and be under no obligation to report it.

Due to x-ray equipment and increasing airport surveillance you should not board an international flight with more than the reportable limit of cash or negotiable financial instruments. In June 1998, the *Oregonian* newspaper carried an article that included the statement that a dog trained to sniff money caught a boarding passenger at an airport terminal with over $300,000 in his carry-on luggage. The money was seized, notwithstanding the passenger was ultimately able to prove he had earned the money legally and was not evading taxes or breaking any criminal law. It seems that the passenger was not a US citizen, and that he had a high distrust of all governments and government sponsored banks. The Fed argued that their right to the money was based on the fact that he forfeited his right to his own money the moment he refused to complete the appropriate government form indicating he was transporting funds of over $10,000.

Within the United States there have been over 200 forfeiture laws implemented in the past few years, and our bureaucracy has developed a nasty and very aggressive habit of seizing money wherever they can find it. Of course these laws were passed "to get the drug dealers," but taking money from average citizens is much easier. Incidentally, U.S. agencies who seize money get to keep it, and chances of getting your money back from a government agency is virtually nil. So, proceed with care if your objective is to move blocks of cash outside the States.

ATM's have become ubiquitous and are a simple way of withdrawing smaller sums of cash to stockpile for eventual offshore transfer. This is not illegal. And it is, after all, your money. Money orders and to some extent Cashier's checks may be purchased for use in cutting the paper trail if acquired for cash. But do not purchase these from your own bank and keep the amounts less than $3,000 if banking privacy is a serious issue with you.

Even if you sign your own name on traveler's checks when purchased, a computer program that has access to traveler's check data bases to scan for a specific name does not yet exist. When sending these instruments through the mail make sure to include instructions that the traveler's check(s), money order(s), or cashier's check(s) be cashed and deposited into whatever account you are seeking to fund.

Federal Express is still a secure way for moving financial instruments, regardless of what you may have heard to the contrary, and it is done everyday all over the world. However many of us feel insecure about shipping untraceable cash. It is also important to remember to not violate your home country laws in this regard. Therefore, if you elect to ship cash or other financial instruments make sure to send less than $10,000 per pouch. There may be other precautions you will want to review with personnel at the receiving end prior to shipment, if you select this approach to moving money offshore.

Some business owners and professionals have purchased educational materials and consulting work from offshore vendors for exploring the expansion of their business into the international marketplace. These expenditures are normally considered legitimate business expenses. Occasionally an offshore vendor has been known to issue a discount, or refund a purchase altogether, and deposit the money directly into an offshore account.

THE OFFSHORE ADVANTAGE

A process known as re-invoicing is a favorite strategy for moving funds offshore. In a typical situation a person might purchase supplies or services for their onshore business, such as a dental office, from an offshore source with which they have some connection. (Perhaps the offshore company is their own international business company "IBC.") The IBC might direct a vendor to drop-ship dental supplies directly to it's owner's onshore dental office and bill the IBC. The price paid by the IBC for the dental supplies would be less than the price the IBC would ultimately invoice to the dentist. Therefore, net reportable income is reduced for the dentist and the spread between the underlying cost paid by the IBC and the price invoiced the dental practice would accumulate offshore. This kind of approach is standard business procedure all over the world in tens of thousands of transactions every day from the very small to the largest companies in the world.

Curiously enough it is perfectly legal for U.S. citizens and those from most other countries, to gamble at offshore casinos. An attempt by the Justice Department to close down Internet gambling is in play and the U.S. Senate voted overwhelmingly on 23 July 1998 to ban gambling on the Internet. However, and although there are approximately 140 on-line casinos currently in operation and numerous sports betting operations, the Internet gaming business is projected to be a 10 Billion industry by the year 2000, according to Senator John Kyl of Arizona. In addition to the Internet there are a considerable number of offshore telephone bookie operations reached by international 800 lines. One can send money to a gambling account offshore for virtually any sum. There are those who routinely claim large losses from offshore gambling when in reality after the deposit is received into a gambling account the money is transferred to another destination. Of course this is not "legal" because one is "falsely" claiming a gambling loss. On the other hand, those who pursue this strategy tend to believe their claim is justified because of the greater evil inflicted by an increasingly dishonest government. The oft quoted phrase, "You can trust me. I'm from the government." is considered by most of the internationally enlighten to be an outrageous lie.

Although there are numerous ways to move money safely into privacy, perhaps the easiest is simply to invest funds offshore, report it, and be done with the entire matter. For example, an individual can purchase shares in an offshore private company and where they own less than 10% of the total shares issued, the transaction is not reportable. Investments in offshore mutual funds, annuities, real estate, etc., generally need be reported, but it does move money safely offshore and without tax consequences until or unless your investment creates reportable earnings on profits of some sort. Money held offshore is immune from almost all forms of judicial proceedings from your home country, particularly if you are careful to select a non-treaty nation with a good history of banking integrity. There are literally millions of Americans who maintain offshore bank accounts in safe harbor jurisdictions and sleep better at night for it.

There are numerous other effective strategies that work well and serve the needs of millions, notwithstanding government's tightening net of worldwide surveillance. Offshore clients tend towards those of higher income and larger net worth and range from the famous of Hollywood and sports figures, to lawyers, medical practitioners, accountants, and other professionals. Independent business owners and international travelers are two other large proponents of the use of offshore services. More recently a growing paranoia, particularly in the U.S. is fueling immense interest by average citizens in the offshore arena. It is absolutely clear that the more aggressive governments become in restricting citizen's rights, the more those citizens look for back-up options to the Big Brother mentality.

OFFSHORE CREDIT CARDS

Offshore customers seeking financial flexibility can secure corporate credit cards in the name of an offshore corporation. The signer's name appears on the face of the card below the name of the corporation, however the signers name may not be included in the magnetic strip information on the reverse side of the card.

A private, secured corporate Gold MasterCard, for example, is available within 72 hours through Exchange Bank and Nevis American Trust. Cash advances may be secured from over 18,000 ATM's around the world, and of course MasterCard is accepted at more locations worldwide than any other card. A deposit equal to 1.5 times the card credit line amount is required to serve as collateral. (Minimum $7,500 to secure $5,000 credit line.) No credit check is made, and there is no request for the signing customer to provide taxpayer identification information. The deposit placed with Exchange Bank, which secures the credit card, is interest-bearing at their passbook savings rate. The charge for securing a private, offshore Corporate Gold MasterCard is

$250, plus card charges.

Credit card clients generally request that their trust company receive monthly card statements and pay the amount due from the appropriate offshore corporate IBC bank account. It is best that you instruct your trust company to not mail bank and credit card statements into the U.S., but rather fax them when appropriate, as various government agencies routinely break the law and read through citizen's personal mail.

On a recent trip to the Bahamas, my wife and I watched a unit of the U.S. Customs office opening air courier packages, copy their contents, and reseal for delivery. Walking boldly to this group of busy bureaucrats in an isolated section of the airport, and speaking with some authority, I asked if they were making certain they did not miss any information no matter how benign it appeared. With some confusion they responded to me confirming that the contents of every envelope was being copied according to their instructions.

This of course is a flagrant violation of our rights as citizens, but no one is likely to do much about it. It is hard to believe that the people of the United States of America now permit this kind of conduct without violent resistance. The bottom line is that citizens have become afraid of their own government and do not want to attract attention to themselves by raising their voice in opposition. Unfortunately this is exactly the course of events that transpired in pre-war Germany and the former Soviet Union. We need to recognize tyranny for what it is, regardless of where we see it.

As I argue elsewhere in this book, we are now in the midst of a revolution, what might almost be called a "stealth" revolution, because the masses are simply unaware of its existence. This revolution is not about blood and bullets; it is all about education, economics, and free choice.

If you wish further information on offshore trust services you may want to call Offshore Corporate Services at 888-684-2622 or Nevis American Trust at 869-469-1614.

∞ Chapter 11 ∞

SHOULD YOU GO OFFSHORE?

"There never will be a shortage of politicians willing to spend where they have not taxed, nor is there any shortage of economists wishing to advise them of the wisdom of supporting trade and employment by issuing more money. No money whose issue is controlled by a politician is ever better than the needs the next election will allow."

Lord William Rees-Moog

IF TAXES ARE YOUR ONLY REASON FOR GOING OFFSHORE

A growing number of moderately successful individuals, business owners, and professionals are considering offshore options. Most appear to be focused on the fundamental issues of: PRIVACY, ASSET PROTECTION, HIGHER INVESTMENT RETURNS, AND TAX SHELTER. More recently a number of inquiries seem to be targeted exclusively on tax issues. This is a mistake.

If the only reason one has for going offshore is tax avoidance I recommend strongly that one seek the assistance of a qualified tax attorney and explore the myriad of opportunities available for domestic tax deferral. Both Revenue Canada and the IRS have taken the position that if the *primary* reason an offshore option is invoked is taxation based, this motivation is sufficient grounds to deny tax benefits. It is important therefore that anyone considering an offshore business opportunity do so for reasons OTHER than tax issues alone. Yes, the tax issue may be <u>a</u> reason for going offshore but it may not be the *only* or principal reason for doing so.

There are a number of very important reasons for one to consider using a Offshore Financial Center such as Nevis, West Indies from which to base critical financial activities. Motivating factors may include:

- An offshore company can invest in global securities including top performing mutual funds not available to U.S. citizens, Canadians, and some Europeans.

131

- Privacy is often integral to risk planning. Offshore clients typically seek confidentiality in their affairs to protect business strategies.
- An offshore jurisdiction such as Nevis offers the best Asset Protection resources available to anyone, anywhere, in the world.
- An International Business Company ("IBC") is TAX-FREE and there is no business activity reports of any kind required in Nevis.
- There are no reports to your home country regarding a corporation's banking, investments, stock trading, or other financial activities, if your company is based in a secure offshore jurisdiction.
- An offshore corporation can be effectively employed in pre-planning for such things as: divorce, business break-up, corporate re-organizations, and the re-structuring of all forms of business and personal financial relationships.
- Premier offshore jurisdictions are less business invasive allowing for aggressive and unrestrained enterprise with lower overhead.
- An offshore corporation may be used to file first position liens against assets and property in your home country thereby closing the "apparent" window of vulnerability to legal predators, and stop frivolous litigation before it commences.
- By titling property into an offshore company, you can transfer real estate, cars, boats, and other titled assets easily and confidentially by simply instructing your offshore trust officer of the new owner, or handing over bearer shares in the offshore company to the buyer instead of re-titling property when sold.
- An offshore company may be used to segregate high-risk investments from other more secure holdings.
- The offshore option may be used as an effective prenuptial agreement.
- Offshore structures can protect retirement funds from possible bankruptcy or other legal conflicts.
- Informed estate planners know that offshore structures can provide the most effective mechanisms for the transfer of assets to the next generation in an efficient and discreet fashion.
- An offshore company used in conjunction with a nominee director/officer allows you to conduct business transactions and remain completely anonymous.
- By transferring assets out of harm's way, different types of insurance costs may be substantially reduced.
- An offshore company may be used as a holding vehicle for troublesome properties.
- When used in conjunction with a domestic company, an offshore corporation can reduce many kinds of taxes by shifting earnings offshore.
- An offshore corporation can secure you debit or credit cards with all

paper and electronic records maintained offshore under Crown Privacy Statutes thereby providing confidentiality in ATM and credit card use.

- An offshore corporation used in conjunction with a carefully structured plan may be able to legally defer, or avoid altogether, domestic federal income taxes.

Several high tax countries have enacted anti-avoidance legislation designed to reduce the use of tax haven countries for strictly tax avoidance reasons. Tax haven countries are now generally referred to as Offshore Financial Centers, or International Financial Centers (OFCs or IFCs). It is interesting to note that their very existence substantially began as an effect of U.K. and American efforts to reduce aid to specific developing nations. Instead of providing foreign aid, legislation was passed to grant tax incentives for multinational corporations to invest in target offshore jurisdictions.

Corporations based in an IFC may derive substantial tax benefits from their activities provided they know the rules and follow them carefully. It is important to remember however, that as long as a person remains resident in another legal jurisdiction they are subject to the tax laws of their respective country.

The simple act of setting up an offshore corporation does not automatically reduce tax liability for the individual. For example, if you are a U.S. person the implications of your offshore company being designated a *"Controlled Foreign Corporation,"* a *"Foreign Personal Holding Company"* or a *"Passive Foreign Investment Company"* are matters that should be addressed by an informed accountant or tax attorney. (See the Offshore Tax Guide included in the Appendices for more information on this subject.) To avoid being considered one of the above, an effective plan to "de-control" an offshore company is a critical part of the offshore strategy.

Notwithstanding efforts by some governments to reduce the use of IFC's, they have become a critical part of the tax planning strategies of individuals and corporations in most first world countries. The offshore industry is a huge growth business with 130,000 new offshore corporations formed in the Caribbean during 1996 alone. People of moderate net worth are increasingly using the resources of offshore trust companies, to take advantage of privacy, asset protection, and investment opportunities unavailable to them in their home country.

Why do offshore mutual funds based in an IFC frequently outperform those in Europe and North America? Because they are generally based in tax-free jurisdictions, AND because the securities regulators in countries like the U.S., for example, require that pooled investments like the typical mutual fund, provide exhaustive and extremely expensive registration filings before an investment may be offered to their residents. Most of the top performing offshore funds find the registration costs unnecessarily demanding and uneconomical in high tax countries. Instead, IFC based funds invest the money saved and improve overall profitability. The result of this choice for greater returns and less legal hassle is that the top performing mutual funds in the world are unavailable to the citizens of some countries. This situation is particularly prevalent in the U.S., where the costs of government oversight and compliance are the highest in the world.

Further complications for U.S. residents is that although it is their right to bank, or invest virtually anywhere in the world, the top performing 5,500 offshore mutual funds will not allow a U.S. person to invest with them. Offshore mutual funds simply want to avoid the harassment they've learned to expect from the U.S. government. Even though many of these funds are fully vested in U.S. stocks, they insist that their investors NOT be domiciled in the U.S.

The Microbial Guide to Offshore Investment Funds, a publication of the *Financial Times* of London, lists the 5,500 funds unavailable to U.S. citizens. Standard & Poors purchased this publication in December of 1997. Their 1997/98 book includes an in depth survey of the top 350 performing funds. Some of these funds have achieved five-year returns of several hundred percent. It's interesting to note that all these funds are based in traditional tax haven countries. For example: 54% are in Luxembourg, 13% in Guernsey & Jersey, 9% in the Isle of Man, 5% are in the Cayman Islands, 4% in Bermuda, 2% in the British Virgin Islands, and the rest are scattered throughout the globe. Only Luxembourg is a land locked nation, the rest are British Commonwealth Island jurisdictions. It is also interesting to note that a number of the successful tax-free offshore funds have U.S. Fund Managers who are also administering "mirror" domestic "taxed" funds.

An offshore company can easily invest in almost any fund, worldwide, and the earnings are tax-free. However, the owner(s) of the offshore company, if resident in the U.S. for example, are required by government edict to voluntarily report the gains their offshore company has earned on these passive investments and pay the appropriate tax.

The decision to utilize an offshore trust company to form and operate an offshore corporation is extremely easy to implement. However, remember that if tax avoidance is the only, or even the primary, motivation for going offshore one should expect obstacles that must be dealt with prior to taking action. On the other hand, if your goal is to access new markets, take advantage of business and investment opportunities unavailable at home, regain your privacy, and protect assets from frivolous and predatory litigation, use of an offshore corporation can reap extraordinary benefits.

THE CHAIN REACTION

A family living at the poverty level in the United States has a higher income than the median family income in 150 other countries.

The average senior citizen today will receive $250,000 more in lifetime Social Security and Medicare benefits than they and their employers paid into the system, including the interest earned on those payments.

The richest 1% of Americans earn 15% of total national income but pay 28% of the federal income taxes.

The estate tax paid by wealthier Americans at their death is equivalent to 55 percent of everything they have, this added to the tax already paid on the income which purchased these assets brings the total tax on the assets of the wealthy to about 94%!

The World War II generation are passing their assets on to their heirs, an amount which totals about $10 trillion.

If the federal government confiscated every penny earned each year by every millionaire in the United States, they would only raise enough to run the federal government for six weeks.

Taxes continue to rise, bureaucracy continues to expand, the National Debt continues to grow, government refuses to operate within a balanced budget.

The richest countries in the world are tax shelter nations.

In the publication entitled, *Free to Choose* by Milton Freedman (the Nobel Prize-winning economist), he had this to say:

"Social Security has been promoted through misleading labeling and deceptive advertising. Consider a paragraph that appeared until 1977 in a Department of Health, Education and Welfare booklet entitled "Your Social Security": The basic idea of social security is a simple one: During working years employees, their employers, and self-employed people pay social security contributions which are pooled into special trust funds. When earnings stop or are reduced because the worker retires, becomes disabled, or dies, monthly cash benefits are paid to replace part of the earnings the family has lost.

This is Orwellian doublethink. Payroll taxes are labeled 'contributions' or as the Party might have put it in the book 1984, 'Compulsory is Voluntary'."

Picture a mousetrap, pried open and set to snap. But instead of cheese at the trigger, there is a ping pong ball. If you were to somehow spring that mousetrap, the ball would go flying.

Now envision a vast airplane hangar full of such mousetraps, packed side by side. Now picture yourself in the middle of these mousetraps -- extending far off into the distance in every direction -- holding a single ping pong ball.

You have but to drop that solitary ping pong ball in order to set off a virtual bedlam of mousetraps snapping and balls flying. This is a chain reaction, and is the principal behind nuclear weapons.

There is no moral dimension to this phenomenon. Both the mousetraps and the ping pong balls are acting according to physical laws, behaving according to their natures. They cannot do anything else.

People are the same. There has always been such a thing as "human nature," and try as we might, people cannot help but behave in accordance with it. The argument comes in defining human nature. Are we "creatures of light?" Are we basically "good?" Or is the human heart, as the prophet Jeremiah proclaimed, "desperately wicked and deceitful above all things -- who can know it?"

Human nature is very much at the center of what is to come because of the mousetrap and ping pong ball phenomenon. When there were relatively few people on earth and they were separated from one another by great distances, it didn't much matter how one individual or group of individuals behaved. Whatever action they took -- for good or for ill -- affected a small number of others in the immediate area.

But at the turn of the millennium, we are connected as never before, through international trade and the Internet. Whatever happens in one place has the potential of an immediate impact practically everywhere at once. Which is why each of us must consider human nature in making long range personal decisions.

Will the Internet ease international tensions by bringing people together in a community forum of mutual understanding? Or will it be used by international terrorists to plan nuclear, germ, or chemical attacks? Will it become a system for medical, humanitarian, and philanthropic enterprises to meet ever-greater human needs? Or will it make it easier for swindlers and pornographers to spread their corruption?

The answer, of course, is both. Whatever is in the human heart -- for good or otherwise -- will be fulfilled at an exponential pace in coming years. The seed of human potential, now germinated and flowered, will soon bear fruit.

Those who took a sanguine view of human nature were dealt a devastating blow with the collapse of Communism. This political system was appealing to many because it promised equal distribution of wealth -- from each according to their abilities; to each according to their needs.

Such an idea seems quaint today, but it has its roots in New Testament teachings, about how primitive Christianity was to organize itself as a social structure until Jesus Christ returned to Earth. The hard-nose part of the same teaching -- if you do not work you shall not eat -- is the part that most people under Communism chose to ignore.

Understanding human nature is the only reason to once again beat this dead horse. Many people would receive something for nothing if they could, while there are others who will produce and give to the extent they are able. The Communist system did not take that reality into account. It failed because there were too many people hoping for a free ride on those willing to produce.

Of course, Communism did serve a purpose. As long as there was a viable alternative to free enterprise capitalism, the tendency of the strong and productive to accumulate a greater proportion of wealth was held in check. Now that balance is gone.

The result has been that the rich are getting richer -- certainly relative to the poor. The richest 358 people in the world have net worth equal to the annual income of the poorest 45 percent of humanity, or about 2.3 billion people. The trend toward concentration of wealth in fewer hands is accelerating. Former Third-World countries had something to bargain with in the past -- either natural resources or votes in the United Nations.

(Ironically, the vote in the UN is still a saleable commodity despite the end of the Cold War. The governments of some small countries have their entire budget deficits covered by wealthy governments such as Taiwan and South Korea.)

So much wealth concentrated in so few hands hardly seems fair to those individuals and nations who do not have as much. It is especially galling to see it passed along from generation to generation. And that is why laws are enacted to harvest this accumulated wealth from families and spread it around. Defenders of the tax point to the Vanderbilts and Rockefellers at the end of the 19th century, who accumulated vast fortunes while millions were penniless. This is the impulse behind confiscatory inheritance taxes.

In the United States such a death tax can consume as much as 55 percent of an estate. Today's fortunes are mostly made through family businesses or farms and the value is in the equity of these enterprises. But with confiscatory taxes, these generators of wealth are pried out of the hands of families and sold to big corporations in order to satisfy inheritance taxes. Such inequity has spawned the Kill the Death Tax Coalition, and other groups, to oppose inheritance taxes by lobbying for legislative reform.

But until you really can fight City Hall, there are alternatives to losing family-built enterprises to taxation. And these alternatives often involve using offshore investment vehicles for privacy, asset protection, and legal tax avoidance. The offshore financial services industry has grown to such an extent that the amount of money protected in offshore sanctuaries is now equivalent to one year's personal income for the entire United States. This is equivalent to the entire U.S. national debt. So what do you think? Should you go offshore?

CARTE DE L'ISLE DE NIEVES

Echelle d'une Lieue commune.

Section Three

THE SOLUTION

∞ Chapter 12 ∞

OFFSHORE STRATEGIES

"About one in four Americans who earn over $100,000 a year now invests offshore."

Arnold S Goldstein, JD, LLM, Phd

WHO'S WHO OFFSHORE?

Some of the biggest and best names in American industry have gone offshore. Companies like Boeing, Weyerhauser, Sears, Firestone, Exxon, Caterpillar, Monsanto, and most of the Fortune 1,000 companies.

American Express, Citibank, Chase Manhattan, Bank of America, and literally hundreds of mainstream banks know that their earnings depend upon tax-free offshore profits. Take a look at the financial statements of the most substantial banks and financial institutions in America and you'll discover that their largest profit centers may come from offshore activities. Banking and financial service profits in an offshore financial center are virtually tax-free because dividends, interest and capital gains are not considered taxable income to these firms.

Many people mistakenly believe that tax avoidance and asset protection tools that are not well known by the majority of people are somehow less effective or less legal. This is simply not true. Why is it we instantly believe it's perfectly legal for the Rockefeller's to implement an offshore strategy but highly suspect if it's our next door neighbor?

In the opening address of the 6th Annual "Money Laundering, Cyberpayments, Forfeiture, Offshore Investments, & Securities" seminar held at the Marriott Marquis in New York City in mid May of 1996, Walter H. Diamond, Editor and Economist had this to say:

> "Within the past decade, the once eye-catching words "Tax Havens" have given way to the far more acceptable term of "Offshore Financial Centers." Reflecting its increasing importance in the world of international finance, the Offshore Financial Center has vastly improved the global image of the continually popular "Tax Haven."

Today, the offshore financial base with $5 trillion of investment funds is a powerful necessity in the daily operations not only of financial institutions but also multinational corporations, small and medium-size companies, and executives in the legal, accounting and investment counseling professions."

"Of the $5 trillion in offshore financial centers today, approximately 40% or $2 trillion is estimated to represent offshore trusts, principally handled by financial and trust companies acting as trustees. Latest surveys indicate that the rapidly growing asset protection trusts account for about one-half of trust funds, or $1 trillion. The remainder covers the original foreign trust that began to attract funds in the early 1970's. However, because of the tremendous onslaught of attorneys and management service firms to protect their clients from malpractice suits, insolvency claims, and creditors in general, the ratio is expected to rise to 60% of the total trust funds by 1997."

Walter Diamond concludes his 13 page keynote address with the following:

"In conclusion, it is my firm conviction that offshore investment operations are here to stay and will expand rapidly in the future. This is predicted despite threats heard in Europe that government restrictions and additional negative lists currently taxing income of residents of countries whose parent companies have tax haven affiliates will be the downfall of offshore centers. In fact, I believe that the 21st Century will be known as the era of offshore domiciles."

AN ECONOMIC EQUIVALENT TO THE BERLIN WALL

The Berlin Wall will be remembered as an icon that spoke of absolute tyranny. It was build by the communist bureaucracy to keep its citizens from escaping to freedom. The present administration of the United States is, in effect, erecting the equivalent of a economic "Berlin Wall" to keep its citizens from placing their income or other assets outside the U.S. Our freedom and our rights are being dramatically curtailed.

President Clinton signed into law the Small Business Job Protection Act of 1996 on August 16, 1996. Contained within this legislation are significant changes to the formation, reporting, and application of tax rules for foreign trusts with U.S. connections. Evidently all foreign trusts must now be rendered "domestic" by either transfer of jurisdiction or by appointment of a U.S. registered agent.

Under the new law, if you are connected in any way, either as grantor or beneficiary, to an offshore trust, the trust itself shall be considered a U.S. revocable trust. This new law requires that reports be provided and that penalties be assessed such that it makes foreign trust systems, as currently organized, virtually obsolete. Internal Revenue had earlier taken the position that all foreign trusts were considered revocable grantor trusts regardless of the irrevocability of the document itself. By definition this would make all offshore trust earnings taxable to the grantor.

Lest anyone should consider not reporting their affiliation with an offshore trust, you might consider that were IRS to assume you were affiliated, they would likely assert their right to "estimate and assess." It is then up to you to prove they are wrong, which in turn would require both you and the target trust's trustee to provide documentation to demonstrate your innocence. Not fun at all.

The newly passed legislation requires that every offshore trust report their assets held in trust, the earnings of the trust, and the name of the trustee.

> "The IRS has become a symbol of the most intrusive,
> oppressive and nondemocratic institution
> in our Democratic Society."
>
> Fred Goldberg, former
> IRS Commissioner

WINGS FOR COWS

Frequently we hear of taxpayers being likened to "sheep waiting to be shorn," or "cows at pasture waiting to be milked." It has been suggested that those working in the offshore arena be considered "angels of mercy" giving wings to cows. It's sad but true, that government increasingly treats it's citizens as little more than cows, to be milked when, and as, they see fit.

One interesting strategy that gives wings to cows — wings possibly strong enough to clear the new tier the Clinton administration has added to their economic "Berlin wall" is the following. This example, reviewed for the first time, will likely seem complex, but taken step by step, particularly with the aid of professionals, you could be flying in no time. But, before we plod through this particular scenario, it might be wise to remind ourselves of what US Supreme Court Justice, Judge Learned Hand had to say regarding those reorganizing their affairs in such a way as to reduce taxes:

"Over and over again courts have said that there is nothing sinister in so arranging one's affairs as to keep taxes as low as possible. Everybody does so, rich or poor; and all do right, for nobody owes any public duty to pay more than the law demands: taxes are enforced exactions, not voluntary contributions. To demand more in the name of morals is mere cant."

Judge Learned Hand
Supreme Court Justice

The particular strategy set forth below calls for the use of Trusts in conjunction with a Limited Liability Company (LLC) and an offshore International Business Corporation (IBC) to achieve the benefits of privacy, asset protection, and legal tax reduction. This strategy has been prepared in light of the recent changes in the 1996 laws. For this illustration we will assume that you are a self-employed dentist in the U.S., practicing in the State of Oregon.

CALCULATING THE TAX

The maximum personal Federal Income Tax rate is 39.6%, the next level down is 36%, and for our example we'll use the lower of these two rates. Social security is assessed at 6.2% on the first $65,400 in earned income and must be paid by both employee and employer. In that a typical dentist is self-employed he or she will have to pay the combined amount of 12.4%. There is also a 1.45% Medicare tax, again, it is paid by both employee and employer and therefore totals 2.9%. In addition, our dentist friend gets to pay Oregon State Income Tax of up to another 9%.

All of these percentages add up to a whopping 63.9%, assuming we use the lower of the two upper Federal Income tax tiers. In the case of social security the 6.2% tax drops off after the first $65,400 in earned income, at least for calendar year 1997. But, as they say on television, that's not all folks.... there's another .62% tax on total income for TriMet, which is Portland's tax for a rapid transit system. In addition, our over-taxed Oregon dentist friend is privileged to pay just about the highest property taxes in the U.S., coupled with some of the highest gasoline taxes at the pump. Okay, so why would I bother to use such an extreme example? Simply because I have such an inordinate amount of dentist friends who live in my home State of Oregon. (There is one taxation bright spot — Oregon doesn't have a sales tax.)

All the tax tables aside, let's simply assume our dentist friend is paying a maximum tax average of around 56%, and we'll forget the property taxes, the gasoline taxes, and all the taxes already incorporated in the cost of various items purchased in the stores.

A SAMPLE STRATEGY

The following example is provided to aid readers in expanding their grasp on the potential for integrating offshore planning in conjunction with a domestic business, rather than representing an actual strategy recommended by the author. The example that follows has never been actually used, or recommended, by the author. There are perhaps as many as one hundred combinations of core-strategies recommended by asset protection and tax attorneys that involve one or more offshore legal structures.

1. Form LLC in Nevada, with the Dentist as the manager.
2. LLC forms a business venture relationship with an IBC in a tax-free jurisdiction. (Dentist receives appointment as managing consultant to the IBC.)
3. IBC forms offshore trust with itself as beneficiary.
4. Trustee of offshore trust forms U.S. Trust.

Note: Both the offshore and domestic trusts will require that 100% of their annual income be distributed to their respective beneficiaries each year.

HOW AND WHY IT MIGHT WORK

The LLC is formed in Nevada because, as pointed out in a later chapter, there is no state income tax in this jurisdiction, and Nevada provides greater confidentiality than any other U.S. jurisdiction. An LLC, as you may recall, is a rather recent form of corporate-like structure. It can be visualized best by thinking of it as a partnership with corporate protection. The LLC is formed of members as opposed to shareholders; it takes a minimum of two members to form an LLC.

Members of a LLC can be any person or entity anywhere in the world. One of the members becomes the managing member, which is exactly the same function as president for a corporation. The manager has all the needed authority to operate the business, pay bills, hire staff, etc. In this example the domestic LLC owns and operates the dental practice, and the dentist is an employee of the company.

As the company profits grow, the members elect to expand into other business activities, perhaps offshore financial investments. Using the services of an offshore trust company such as Nevis American Trust Company Limited, they locate a suitable International Business Corporation, (IBC) in a tax free jurisdiction to serve as a willing partner in their expansion. The LLC is able to pay the deductible expense for this legitimate business consultation.

Soon thereafter, the manager of the LLC (our dentist friend) receives word of his or her appointment as managing consultant of the IBC. He or she is then given responsibility for the source and application of funds for that company, subject to approval by the IBC's managing director.

The IBC now decides it is in it's best interest to form a simple offshore trust with itself as the beneficiary and to grant the trust sufficient funds to enable it to initiate its business activities. The trustee for the offshore trust to be a qualified, licensed, trust company in the jurisdiction that the trust is formed. The terms of the trust would call for the distribution of all profits to the beneficiary annually.

The trustee of the offshore trust contracts with an independent trustee or lawyer in the U.S. to form a simple domestic trust and act as it's trustee. This trust will also be responsible to send it's profits to it's beneficiary annually.

The settlement of the domestic trust would be so structured that there were sufficient funds on hand to acquire a 90% interest in the domestic LLC.

HOW IT ALL SHAPES UP

The entities are all in place and the practical application follows. Within the U.S. all sales of product or services that will be consumed within the United States will be handled by the Nevada LLC. It will report its revenues and net income on IRS form 1065 annually. Because it is taxed as a partnership it will show 10% distribution to the founding members and 90% distribution to the domestic trust. Distributions would be reported to IRS on form K-1 in concert with partnership tax law. There would be no taxes paid by the LLC, rather the tax burden is borne by the members.

The domestic trustee receives the 90% distribution of profits from the LLC and in turn distributes these funds to its beneficiary, the off-shore trust. Since the trustee is required to report the profit and pay the tax, he or she would cause to be filed IRS form 1041, commonly known as the fiduciary tax form. Because the trustee had already distributed the funds received from the LLC to the offshore trust, (its beneficiary), there will be no taxable profit.

Since the offshore trust receives its funds from within the U.S. and they are therefore considered "source funds" the trustee will be required to report them to the IRS under the new legislation. However, since the offshore trust is also a simple trust with instructions to distribute its effective earnings to the beneficiary annually, when it files IRS form 1040NR it will also show no taxable income.

SAMPLE STRATEGY SUMMARY

The funds received by the LLC's offshore business partner, the IBC, have come to it through an offshore trust. Therefore these funds are considered NON U.S. source funds and are therefore not subject to any tax extension of the U.S. Tax Code. In addition, any business the managing consultant of the IBC, the dentist who is also the manager of the LLC, is able to develop with offshore entities should always be done through the IBC.

If both sides of a given transaction are offshore, they are not sub-ject to U.S. taxes. That is, assuming neither party to the transaction is an entity owned by a U.S. citizen or resident. Of course, if our dentist friend wants payment for consulting services to the IBC, he or she will have to pay taxes on all the funds received for this activity.

What has happened in this example is simply that 90% of the prof-its generated by the dental practice have moved offshore to a tax-free jurisdiction where they may be invested in higher yield securities than are available to citizens of the U.S.

Complicated? Yes it certainly sounds like it the first time you come across a strategy like this. But, once in place the pieces should operate smoothly. There are initial set up costs and ongoing administra-tive costs for operating the IBC, and both trusts. However, the good news is that once in place the annual administrative fees are relatively low.

Setting up an offshore structure can be the most practical and cost effective insurance you will ever acquire to protect your hard-earned estate. It will definitely provide you enhanced privacy and access to greater investment returns, and you may be able to enjoy the added benefit of significant tax deferral or legal tax avoidance.

There is no panacea for offshore asset protection and tax deferral structuring. A mechanism that will give you superior asset protection may not provide privacy or have sufficient tax advantages. There is no one "perfect" structure. An experienced planner will therefore recommend a program or strategy that may incorporate several, or even many, different devices that meet the particular needs, circumstances, and desires of a client.

THE BOTTOM LINE

In the final analysis, is a strategy such as the one set forth above worthwhile? Well, remember that 56% tax rate way back at the beginning of this example? How do you feel about ninety percent of profits beyond the prying eyes of predatory litigators? How do you feel about privacy guarantees? Do you want to take advantage of higher investment returns, even in such basic financial products as CD's? Does it make sense to you to have a piggy bank located offshore? You be the judge.

Is there any guarantee a strategy like the one set forth above will work? In the final analysis, there is none. However, if you have legitimate motivations for wanting to be involved offshore beyond the issue of federal income tax, the chances that a workable program can be developed to suit your needs is quite high. And, it is important to point out that you should avoid any attempt to replicate someone else's "cookie cutter" approach. Going offshore can be exciting, fun, and thoroughly beneficial, but do not implement a plan without seeking the aid of a competent professional.

To be successful, a plan will require that a specialist in this field review carefully all of your relevant circumstances and fully understand your particular goals. He or she must be thoroughly informed as to your potential or actual legal exposures at the time the strategies are to be implemented in order to avoid fraudulent conveyances. The number of structures necessary to accomplish your needs varies according to your particular circumstances.

There are many legal and ethical devices that can and should be used to protect the assets of those in every income bracket. If you have a home, a bank account, investments, corporate securities, valuable family heirlooms, or you feel that you just can not afford to start all over again, then your assets are at risk in today's litigious and predatory environment.

> "Where I live in Alexandria, Virginia, near the Supreme Court building, there is a toll bridge across the Potomac River. When in a rush I pay the toll and get home early. However I usually drive outside the downtown section of the city, and cross the Potomac on a free bridge. If I went over the toll bridge and through the toll without paying I would be guilty of tax evasion. However, if I go the extra mile and drive outside the city of Washington to the free bridge, I am using a legitimate, logical and suitable method of tax avoidance. And, I am providing a useful social service as well."

> Louis D Brandeis
> U.S. Supreme Court Justice
> 1941

Doug Casey, a friend and investor in a business I founded some years ago, has become world renowned for several best selling books he's authored on finance and investing. He has championed the term "international men" to describe those enlightened people who assume greater personal freedom by learning to operate multi-jurisdictionally. All of his books are excellent, but I particularly like *Strategic Investing For the Nineties* and I recommend it as an excellent text for understanding global influences on local economics.

Author Dr. William Hill calls the folks that wake up and move on to become multi-jurisdictional people "PT's," which stands for "Perpetual Travelers," a term that refers to the status afforded them under various legal jurisdictions. (Some refer to PT's as "Prior Taxpayers.")

Lord William Rees-Moog describes the self reliant, internationally-enlightened among us as "Sovereign Individuals." I call them **PRUDENT!**

∞ Chapter 13 ∞

REGAINING YOUR PRIVACY

"In today's information age, personal privacy is virtually extinct.... Just a glimpse into the case files of any federal investigative, local law enforcement, or private investigative agency provides unique insight into the degree to which MILLIONS of people's private lives are being researched, scrutinized, and even exploited."

Surveillance Countermeasures
ACM IV Security Services

PRIVACY STRATEGIES

If you have read this far, you probably have decided that privacy is a commodity you want to have. I have your attention and you have shown interest.

Unfortunately, privacy is not a commodity you can buy off the shelf. It is, however, a quality you acquire through a series of decisions and actions. But to be successful, you must organize a plan of action whose goal is the state of being we call "privacy."

Compare achieving privacy to wellness. It isn't something that happens overnight. To become a well person you must develop habits and behaviors that protect your health — proper exercise, rest and food. The same is true of privacy. If you have lived a life of public displays of wealth and conspicuous consumption, you can't expect to fade quietly into the woodwork.

To achieve privacy, then, you must make a fundamental decision about what is important to you. Is it more important to let the world know you have been successful through fat bank accounts and many properties owned in your name? Or is it more important to protect what you have from marauding suers and government bureaucrats?

Achieving privacy, then, is in reality a spiritual journey. You must consciously decide to put aside the show and splendor that so beguiled you in the past, and live more simply. Prestige kills privacy — humility protects it. Make it your ambition that the press describes you as "a private person" living "a quiet life." This approach to life is not underhanded or unethical. It is wisdom from ancient days.

STANDARD BUSINESS PRACTICE

Learning humility inevitably brings you to the state of mind that you develop an alarm system regarding things that will draw the wrong kind of attention. By that I mean, the kind that will get you audited by the IRS, or investigated by any one of a host of three letter government agencies endeavoring to justify their existence. .

The kinds of things to avoid are those that set off red flags with government. And by that I mean anything that isn't standard business practice. Corporations are about the only asset protection vehicle that will not automatically attract the attention of the authorities. But things like your own private church, a charitable foundation that holds your assets — these things are often suspect. Accepted business practices include such things as leases, consulting fees, loans, and trusts.

Part of the lifestyle of privacy is keeping a low profile politically. Republican, Democrat, Independent — those organizations are mainstream. Charitable groups such as orphanages, colleges, service clubs are all acceptable places to invest your energy. But tax revolt groups, anti-Bureau of Alcohol, Tobacco and Firearms — anything that smells of the fringe — is likely to cost you privacy. If you are committed to a cause or a movement and have a major grievance and want to lash out at the world, get a soap box but forget protecting your assets. Remember — invisibility is the soil privacy grows in best. The more visible you are, the more likely you are to attract government investigation or predatory litigation, or both.

If you have assets to invest overseas, chances are you are engaged in some sort of profitable activity. You probably do not have the time to travel all over the world looking for the right place to sequester your assets. You probably need help in this most important task.

There are those who recommend against using anyone in the U.S. to set things up for you offshore. Your accountant's files are readily available to government inquiry and frequently to civil litigation, and even your attorney can be pressured to reveal confidential information. Recent changes by the new, "friendlier" IRS will allow your accountant some "client privilege." However, if the IRS suggests they are concerned about a possible criminal infraction the privilege is automatically revoked. What you need is someone who has first-hand knowledge of the jurisdiction where your assets are going, is trustworthy, and whose records are not available on shore.

It's always a good idea to get to know the primary individual who will be managing your funds overseas. And yet, going to tax haven countries yourself to meet with a potential agent may delay this kind of positive move indefinitely. Further, if you take a trip to the Channel Islands or some other place known only as a tax haven, chances are good you may become a target of any one of a number of federal agencies looking for tax evaders.

Of course, no matter who you deal with, there are firms or individuals who may not be worthy of your trust. References make good sense, but not the names of U.S. clients. For example, the government where your agent is based will generally advise you with a simple telephone call if there have been any complaints registered against the Trust Company you are considering doing business with. In addition, bank and influential third party reference letters are standard protocol all over the world.

RECLAIM PRIVACY

To reclaim your privacy, I recommend you consider what information about your life you are willing to share with the world, and then take back the rest. To begin with, no one really has the "right" to know your address and telephone number — certainly not your bank. They require an address in order to issue you checks, true. But it doesn't have to be the address of your domicile.

Mail services rent private mail boxes and message telephone numbers. The address will appear as a suite number or an apartment number. With your new address, you can obtain a new driver's license and another piece of identification.

Now that you have a new address, close out the checking and savings accounts you already have. Then, choose a new bank and start over with your new address and telephone number. The bank can send its statements to the new address and your domicile address is once again your own business. One caveat regarding such addresses — we are not the first ones to have thought of using them for secrecy. As a matter of fact, law enforcement often uses them in their own covert or sting operations.

Remember that the checks you deposit to your account are recorded and reported. Therefore, if checks issued to you are written to a bank with a local branch, it makes sense to cash those checks at those banks.

153

This is true of pay checks, checks from clients — anyone whose dealings with you are your business alone. You can then deposit the cash or a money order to your own checking account.

If you do decide on money orders, buy them at banks other than those at which you cashed the check. When checks are cashed and money orders subsequently purchased, a notation is made of what transpired. You can buy money orders at the Post Office, at supermarkets or other banks. Because it is true that you are at risk when you stroll about with large amounts of cash on your person, it is a good idea to change your routine frequently when cashing checks. If you take these steps, however, the payoff is that there is now no record connecting the source of your income with your bank deposits.

As we mention elsewhere in this book, the transactions through your bank account are recorded and reported to the government. When you use checks to buy things in stores, you are often required to produce two pieces of identification, which is written on the check. This information is also often compiled into private databases. It could include everything from your name, address, birthdate, Social Security number, bank account number and driver's license number. If you want to keep to yourself who pays money to you as well as who you pay money to, then it makes very good sense for you to reduce use of a U.S.-based checking account.

There are other, more anonymous, ways to pay bills. For example, money orders and travelers checks are non-revocable forms of payment that are accepted just like cash. Banks and AAA and others who issue these instruments protect the recipient against loss, so they are actually preferred over checks that could bounce. There is sometimes a charge for traveler's checks, but if you shop around sometimes you can get them for free. You can use these to pay rent or mortgage payments, utilities, goods and services — you name it. Meanwhile, you can move to a new neighborhood or even a new community, change your telephone number, and your financial transactions do not give you away.

PRIVACY OFFSHORE

To gain even more privacy, this is the time to move your savings to an offshore bank. Before you do, be aware of the Foreign Account Declaration Form -- form TD F 90-22.1. Penalties for failing to report foreign accounts can be as much as five years imprisonment and $500,000 fine. These penalties can be imposed, however, only when you have failed to report in order to dodge taxes or cover up a criminal activity. You can't be punished for not filling out the form, as long as you report the income under "miscellaneous income" on your form 1040 and pay the appropriate taxes.

As discussed elsewhere, foreign banks are not obliged — as are U.S. banks — to report interest earnings to the IRS. You are required by law to report the interest income yourself, but at least this way you are in control of what is reported.

A further caveat, not all foreign countries are created equal when it comes to protecting your privacy. Uncle Sam is still a big player in the world and carries a lot of clout — especially with some small countries that depend on the U.S. for trade and aid. The U.S. has arrangements with some countries that give IRS easy access to your records --- all part of on-going treaties and agreements between countries. If the country in question doesn't go along — no treaty with the U.S. With no tax treaty, it means people doing business in both countries can be taxed twice on earnings, thus discouraging trade with that country.

The Cayman Islands are an example of capitulation to the U.S. government. In 1989, the Caymans introduced new laws that allowed U.S. investigators more access to bank records of Americans there. The U.S. threatened to make it difficult for tourists to visit the Caymans if the changes were not made. The pressure also came through the government of Great Britain, which controls the Caymans as a Crown Colony.

There may actually be more protection in Switzerland. To access your records there, the U.S. government would have to send an agent to that country to present evidence to a magistrate that you are involved in international drug deals, murder, torture, kidnapping or forgery. The Swiss will consider requests for information – but they do not grant it automatically. The point here is that offshore banking centers vary in the amount of privacy they offer, and here is where someone familiar with the differences can save you a lot of headaches.

Offshore banking varies country by country in the amount of backbone they show the U.S. government. Private lawsuits are another matter. Offshore banks are not subject to American legal jurisdiction, so they cannot be compelled to provide information because of a subpoena in an American lawsuit. The exception is if the bank in question has branches in the U.S. or advertises here -- then the banks may have to submit to U.S. law.

This is important because in the discovery phase of a lawsuit in the U.S., a sharp lawyer will try to get his or her hands not only on your bank account but also on your credit card files and loan applications -- anything that will reveal your assets so they can be seized. With an offshore account, this information is protected. Writs of execution, or attachment orders issued by U.S. courts, generally have little impact on your wealth held offshore.

You get further protection with an offshore account because you are entitled to a credit card issued on that bank. That means you can charge to your heart's content, anywhere you want, and the information stops at your offshore bank. If you charge on a domestic domiciled bank however, the information could become part of a database that is sold to whoever is willing to pay the price.

THEFT CONTROL

There are others who are out for your assets besides the government. Thieves can gain access to information about you by stealing identification, and cause worlds of problems. If your wallet or purse is stolen, for example, it probably contains your driver's license, credit cards, ATM card, Social Security card, perhaps even a copy of your birth certificate or checkbook.

If you are lucky, you have been hit by a low-grade thief who wants and understands only cash and tosses the rest away. But chances are the thief wants to use your ID to make purchases on your credit cards and checking account. It's no problem to buy loads of merchandise on your credit card, then take the stuff back for cash. The thief can even use your identity to open up new accounts, not pay the bills, and damage your credit. To protect yourself, it's best to minimize the amount of information you carry around with you. You really have no need to take your Social Security card, birth certificate or passport with you, unless there is a specific reason.

If you take keys with you, it is naive to assume putting your name and address on them will result in their return. What's more likely to happen is that the thief will go to your home and loot it while you're out looking for the lost keys.

The same is true for funeral notices. If a family member has died, do not print the home address in the funeral notice, or if you do, make sure someone remains in the home during the service. There are thieves whose modus operandi is to read these notices and ransack the house while you're most vulnerable.

Keep a list of your credit cards and bank accounts with appropriate information, such as the account numbers, expiration dates and telephone numbers of the customer service department in a safe place -- not your wallet or purse.

If you need a password or personal identification number, don't use your birthdate, your middle name, the last digits of your Social Security number or anything else that could be easily figured out by thieves.

INTERNET PRECAUTIONS

Turn off your computer when not in use. Do not register for anything on the Internet without absolute assurance that the information will not be released to third parties for any reason. Turn off the "accept cookie" option with your Web browser. There are really only two well-known web browsers: Netscape and Microsoft Internet Explorer.

To turn off the "accept cookie" option with Netscape simply open "Options," go to "Network Preferences," then "Protocols," then tick "Show an Alert Before Accepting a Cookie."

To turn off the "accept cookie" option with Microsoft Internet Explorer open "View," then go to "Internet Options," then "Advanced," then scroll down to "Cookies," then tick "Prompt Before Accepting Cookies."

KNOW YOUR RIGHTS

One of the simplest routes to privacy is totally within your control. Do not furnish any more information than you have to.

People may ask about your assets, but you don't have to tell them. This can be especially important to remember should you face litigation. If a creditor is suing you, you are not required to tell them anything about your assets unless or until they have a judgement against you. Assets are relevant only insofar as they relate to your ability to pay, and this is no one's business until the case is essentially over.

Creditors may try to learn what you have during the discovery process of a court case, but it is your right to keep mum. They are trying to get something from you they are not entitled to, and if you are uninformed about your rights, you may wind up giving it to them.

The only exception to this is if you are being sued for punitive damages for wrongful conduct. The court may order you to disclose assets before the judgement so they can determine if you have enough to satisfy the punitive damage award. Also, if there has been a suspected fraudulent transfer of assets, this may be examined and even set aside at court order. But such an inquiry can only be about the assets in question -- not about anything else you may have.

ASSET TRANSFER?

What about fraudulent transfer of assets? This is when you place valuables in the name of someone else in order to avoid losing them in lawsuits. After all, what you don't own can't be taken from you. Getting rid of things is a good way to make yourself less of a target and is a perfectly legitimate component of your privacy strategy -- provided you handle it correctly. The key to any asset transfer is protecting you from accusation of fraudulent transfer. Laws related to fraudulent transfer are very important and you'll find an entire chapter devoted to this issue.

Placing assets offshore in trusts, corporations or other entities can be an important move towards greater personal privacy. Offshore transfers are generally beyond reasonable reach. This is an incredibly important principle.

TAX RETURNS

A key component of your privacy strategy is to become protective of information about your finances. One of the richest sources of information that can be used against you is your tax return. This document tells how much you have made and how much you have. Why share it with anyone when you do not have to?

Your tax returns are protected from involuntary disclosure to creditors. Tax returns are included among those things that might tend to incriminate, hence they are protected by the Fifth Amendment.

Judgement creditors can't make you reveal tax returns unless you waive your rights to keep them secret by offering or agreeing to reveal them or allow access to them by "disinterested parties." Those are people who do not have a "need to know." People such as your accountant, banker, spouse, lawyer, are those who have a need to know. To everyone else, it is your right to keep information such as tax returns off limits.

CLEAN UP YOUR DEBTS

To secure a loan, you may have furnished your tax return as evidence of your income. Make certain that lenders are aware you want to be notified if those records are subpoenaed. You can have an attorney quash the effort to learn about you through tax returns given to lenders.

If you have applied for a loan, chances are, in your effort to prove you have so many assets you don't need the loan, you may have revealed too much about your holdings or even exaggerated them. If you intend to transfer some of those assets out of your possession, it's best to ask to go back and "correct" your records.

Cash is your best friend because it cannot be traced. If you have a cash transaction over $10,000, never involve a bank. Divide the money into smaller amounts and process the cash on separate dates to avoid attracting attention.

SEAL YOUR FILES

If you have had a court case in which you were required to reveal information about your assets, it's best to ask the court to seal those files. Divorces or child support cases can force you to show and tell all about income, assets, liabilities, and that information can become public record unless you act to prevent it. Your court records can be read and copied but not removed from the building. If the records are sealed, you have protected your privacy.

THE CORPORATE VEIL

Your own corporation is a great way to preserve your privacy. We discuss corporations of various kinds at length in this book. If you own nothing, there is nothing to take from you. A wise goal in life is to own little, but control everything, and a corporation can help achieve this.

A friendly corporation could hold a mortgage on your home, for example, and your personal property such as a car or RV. You could even give this corporation a "blanket mortgage" on everything you own. This can insulate your assets from predatory litigation. For this strategy to be effective, the corporation may need to be owned by someone other than yourself.

If you have sensitive transactions, be sure to handle them through a corporation to stay at arm's length. Make sure the corporation has its own taxpayer identification number, to keep the transaction away from yourself, unless of course you're using an offshore corporation to handle certain transaction where reporting is not required. Give out your Social Security number as sparingly as possible. There is no law that actually requires you to have such a number, though you are prohibited from opening a U.S. bank account or working for an employer without one. But remember that this number is a way your movements and activities can be traced.

LIQUIDITY BUYS PRIVACY

Bank accounts are great because you can always access your money when you need it. That's liquidity. But bank accounts are problematic because they do not offer privacy. Until 1982, Americans were allowed to own "bearer bonds," which were securities not registered to any individual -- they could be transferred like cash. As of that date, however, they have been outlawed, and the ones still existing, when they are redeemed, elicit a Form 1099-B to the IRS from the brokerage firm. If you could acquire some of these securities, you could send them abroad for safekeeping and redemption -- but beware. Sending more than $10,000 outside the U.S., without reporting it to U.S. customs, is a felony.

If you are willing to pay in the coin of liquidity, however, you can purchase anonymity. By that I mean that you can have a substantial portion of your wealth in semi-liquid assets, such as collectibles, including rare coins, stamps, gemstones, art. They are easily transported, are a good store of wealth and are usually liquid enough for most purposes. Often they also offer some appreciation, but best of all, they are totally private. There is no bank reporting how much of these things you have in your possession, or where you have put them, or to whom you have given them.

If you want even more privacy, you can buy and sell these things through your own privately held corporation. The problem with them is security -- they are easily stolen.

Gold is often considered the best private investment. It is redeemable virtually everywhere for the local currency, and it is untraceable. It is the ultimate currency for protecting privacy. Gold can come in the form of coins, jewelry or even bullion. You can buy it many places with no record of the transaction.

Collectible coins can have higher value. There are thousands of international coin dealers who could help you turn coins into local currency. Diamond is the same. Unfortunately, both rare coins and diamond are usually bought retail and sold wholesale, so you can take a beating in the short term. The other disadvantage of coins is that gold and coin dealers must report large or unusual transactions to the government -- so keep purchases to several hundred dollars per transaction.

Stamps can be a good store of value and can appreciate, but require knowledgeable buyers to reclaim your value. There are other collectibles that are good, anonymous ways to transport wealth, such as baseball cards, autographs, some photographs, artwork, and rare comic books. If it is possible to do business using these means of conveyance without attracting attention, make it your practice to do so.

One way to store wealth anonymously is to rent a number of safety deposit boxes registered to corporations or trusts. Then buy gold bullion in small quantities and stash it away. Make sure all ends of the transaction -- including rental of the boxes -- is done in cash to avoid a paper trail making the connection. Incidentally, bank vaults are less secure than private vaults or secure home safes.

Silver may be especially attractive these days. It is relatively cheap compared to gold, especially as it relates to historical ratios, and its highly divisible for local exchange. On an individual level almost anyone will accept pure silver medallions or small silver ingots on private transactions. The novelty feature alone seems to interest an unusually high amount of average folks.

And, of course, there is always barter. Can I slip in a plug here for my recent book entitled *Barter & The Future of Money*?

WIRE TRANSFERS

Wire transfers can raise red flags when sent offshore. Under a regulation that took effect in January 1996, when a wire transfer is issued, the originator and the beneficiary must both be identified and this information must travel with the transfer. Experts have great concern that foreign banks, which will not be bound by these regulations, will not include the identity of the originator because of bank secrecy laws within their countries. Trying to track all of these wire transfers is a bureaucrat's nightmare. On the average business day, about 80,000 separate transactions totaling nearly $500 billion pass through the wire room at Citibank alone!

HOW MUCH IS ENOUGH?

How much privacy do you need? How far are you willing to go to protect yourself? As we said in the beginning of this chapter, you can achieve a great deal of privacy through sticking with "standard business practices." But there are those who want to go underground and have made a study of how to do it.

For you, we offer this select bibliography of some current writing on privacy:

How to Legally Obtain a Second Citizenship and Passport — and Why You Want To, by Adam Starchild

International rules regarding dual citizenship vary from country to country. If you are French, for example, and want a second citizenship, you must proceed according to French law. But it can be done, and this book tells how. It also discusses the pros and cons of dual nationality and nationalities that are for sale. Also, it highlights the best second nationalities for Americans and how to get them.

Reborn In The USA: Personal Privacy Through a New Identity, by Trent Sands

The second edition (1991) is said to be the best and most complete guide to building a new identity. The book features control of information about you in computer data bases.

Understanding U.S. Identity Documents, by John Q. Newman

This book is described as a reference for anyone concerned with their official identity and how it is maintained and manipulated. It deals with the most important documents for establishing an identity, such as birth certificates, Social Security cards, drivers licenses and passports. It shows how each document is generated and used, and explains the strengths and weaknesses of the agencies issuing them.

How To Disappear Completely and Never Be Found, by Doug Richmond

This book is for the individual who wants to completely drop out, telling how those who are searching for you might be looking and how to evade the pursuit. It tells how to plan for your disappearance, how to arrange a new identity, how to make it appear you have left the country when you haven't and even how to make it appear that you are dead. It tells how to find a job, establish credit and find a place to live and how to avoid creating a paper trail.

The Heavy Duty New Identity, by John Q. Newman

This is for people really on the run. It tells the down side of starting anew — the problems of mental stress, making sure all the bases are covered, avoiding traps and discovery and bonding with your new identity.

Reborn Overseas: Identity Building in Europe, Australia and New Zealand, by Trent Sands

With an identity in any European nation, you can live and work in any of the twelve. And you can penetrate that system without leaving the U.S. Or, you can do the same in Australia or New Zealand. The book shows how to get all the documents you need to become another nationality.

Reborn in Canada: Personal Privacy Through a New Identity, Expanded Second Edition, by Trent Sands

Canada is the easiest foreign country for the U.S. citizen to adapt to. This book explains how the identity systems in Canada differ from the U.S. You can even have a Canadian identity in your original American name, with no connection to your American past.

New I.D. In America: How to Create a Foolproof New Identity, by Anonymous

This is a step-by-step book on creating a new identity, from birth certificate, drivers license, passport, Social Security, credit cards. The author is a private investigator who has spent a career locating missing persons and helping others disappear.

SCRAM: Relocating Under a New Identity, by James S. Martin, attorney at law.

THE OFFSHORE ADVANTAGE

Many people would love to make a fresh start in a new location, under a new name. He answers questions such as whether to divorce before leaving, or declare bankruptcy first. The author discusses how the Justice Department creates new identities for criminals.

The Paper Trail: Personal and Financial Privacy in the Nineties, by M.L. Shannon

This book tells how to get a new ID and create a past to back it up; how to disappear and never be found— even by skip tracers. It details secret ways to communicate that can't he traced. It even tells how to make false trails to throw off pursuers.

All of these books can be ordered through Loompanics Unlimited, P.O. Box 1197, Port Townsend, WA 98368.

∞ Chapter 14 ∞

NEVIS, THE NEW FINANCIAL MECCA

".... they (the British) are weary of the War and would
get out if they knew how. They had not then received the
certain news of the loss of St. Christopher (St. Kitts-Nevis),
which will probably render them still more disposed to peace."

Benjamin Franklin
March 3, 1782

BACKGROUND

Nevis and its sister country St. Kitts form the Independent Federation of St. Kitts and Nevis. They are located in the Leeward Islands approximately 1,200 miles southeast of Miami, Florida. Although an independent two-island nation, they retain many traditions of the British, who settled and developed them. St. Kitts was the first British Colony in the Caribbean, founded in 1623. Nevis was considered "the richest jewel" of the Caribbean and St. Kitts was known as the Mother Colony and "cradle" of the Caribbean.

Admiral Horatio Nelson, arguably Britain's finest naval commander of all time, married a Nevisian, made Nevis the center of British naval operations in the Western Hemisphere, and considered it the most lovely place he'd ever lived. Alexander Hamilton, the first Secretary of the Treasury of the United States of America, and a signer of the Declaration of Independence and participant in the drafting of the U.S. Constitution, was born in Charlestown, the current capital of Nevis.

On Nevis, the scenery encompasses green hills, exotic gardens, secluded coves and pink sands. The beautiful islands of St. Kitts and Nevis represent the idyllic view most of us have of what constitutes a tropical island paradise. The climate is nearly perfect for people, as well as luxuriant tropical vegetation.

The island is encircled by miles of beaches facing on to aquamarine and turquoise seas. The natural beauty of Nevis is breathtaking. Tourism is a major revenue source and the Nevis Four Seasons Resort has recently been rated Number One of the Top One Hundred Resorts for the entire world.

Nevis was sighted by Christopher Columbus in 1493, and settled by the British in 1623. Even today, cricket is a favorite pastime, the motorists drive on the left, and the official language is English. Formerly one of the West Indies Associated States, it became an independent state within the British Commonwealth in 1983. Nevis is a democracy based on the British parliamentary system and has an elected local assembly.

The legal system is based on English common law, served by a high court of justice and a court of appeals. A Nevis offshore company is known as an International Business Corporation ("IBC") and although formed in a British Commonwealth country, corporate structure is based on the USA State of Delaware model.

The East Caribbean dollar is the official currency, although U.S. dollars are accepted anywhere. The East Caribbean dollar is fixed to the United States dollar at EC $2.70 per US $1.00 and therefore a stable rate of exchange has been in force for many years. Nevis banks allow for accounts to be held in either U.S. or Caribbean dollars.

Nevis offers excellent communication facilities, with direct dialing to Europe, the U.S. and Canada, in addition to facsimile, telex, and telegraph services.

Nevis offshore companies are exempt from Nevis taxes on all income, dividends or distributions not earned on the island.

THE NEVIS BUSINESS CORPORATION ORDINANCE

A Nevis offshore company, known universally as an International Business Corporation ("IBC"), is tax exempt on all income not earned on the island. An IBC need not file annual returns. Corporate records may be kept anywhere in the world, and annual general meetings or meetings of the Board of Directors are not required to be held in Nevis. An IBC has a number of other very attractive advantages:

1. There are no income taxes, social security taxes, capital gain taxes, withholding taxes, stamp, or duty taxes.
2. There are no gift, death, estate, dividend, distribution, or inheritance taxes.
3. No minimum authorized capital; bearer shares permitted.
4. A business license is not required.
5. Officers, directors, and members are not identified.

6. Plaintiff bringing civil suit must post U.S .$25,000 bond.

7. Statute of limitations for civil suits is one year.

The registration process is simple and can be accomplished with little effort. A Company may be incorporated to conduct any lawful business and there is no need to enumerate the particular objects for which the company is incorporated. An IBC registered in Nevis is re-quired to maintain a registered agent at all times. The Ministry of Fi-nance licenses trust companies and Registered Agents. A Nevis IBC is required to maintain a registered office in Nevis. This requirement is easily satisfied as the legislation permits the office of the registered agent to act as the office of the company.

Any person interested in forming an offshore company in Nevis need only provide the name of the corporation to a licensed trust com-pany. The trust company will form the company and function as it's registered agent and provide a local office address. Nevis American Trust Company Limited can arrange for your IBC by simply faxing them at 869-469-1614. If you want to discuss various offshore options I suggest you call Offshore Corporate Services at 604-684-2622.

The Nevis Business Corporation Ordinance Act was enacted in 1984 and is modeled in large part on USA Delaware corporate statutes. The legislation is contemporary and user-friendly. It is routinely up-dated to ensure that it remains progressive and avant-garde.

A particularly progressive feature of Nevis legislation is that it allows for the transfer of a corporation's legal domicile from any coun-try in the world into that of Nevis within 24 hours. By the same token, a Nevis corporation may be transferred out of Nevis and into any other jurisdiction in the world permitting this procedure.

NEVIS INTERNATIONAL EXEMPT TRUST ORDINANCE

A trust is a legal relationship, as opposed to a legal entity, whereby the creator or settler of the trust provides assets and names a trustee to manage and safeguard these assets for the benefit of person(s) who are called the beneficiaries, and who are the only persons entitled to gain from the trust or in whose favor a power to distribute trust property may be exercised.

The use of trusts has rapidly expanded as both corporations and individuals apply this mechanism to fuel and facilitate a wide range of activities and as an offshoot of this, the global community is moving into an era where the use of offshore trusts is becoming increasingly imaginative and prolific. In recognition of this trend, and of the contribution that international trusts would make to the offshore financial sector, the Nevis Island Assembly passed the Nevis International Exempt Trust Ordinance in 1994. This Ordinance governs the establishment and operation of international trusts and is an amalgamation of the more progressive International Trust legislation of various jurisdictions combined with innovative provisions of a totally unique nature.

An international trust, in order to qualify as such, must have certain characteristics. These requirements are easy to satisfy and basically they stipulate that at least one of the trustees must either be an offshore company incorporated in the jurisdiction, or a trust company doing business in Nevis. And, that the settler and the beneficiaries must at all times be non-resident and that the trust property must not include land situated in the jurisdiction.

Where an offshore company is a trustee of an international trust, its registered office in Nevis may also be the trust's registered office. This provision was designed to link all parts of the offshore sector, thus ensuring the smooth interaction and working of the offshore industry.

It is possible to create an international trust with only one trustee; and the settler or trustee of the trust may also be named as beneficiary. Registration of international trusts is also made easy in that there are a minimum of requirements. Essentially, these are the names of the trust and of the registered office of the trust. A Certificate certifies that the trust, upon registration, will be an international trust, and states the prescribed fee.

The confidentiality and the privacy of international trusts are ensured by legislation. For instance, even though a trust register is maintained, it is not a public document generally available for inspection; the only exception being where a trustee of a specific trust gives written authorization to a person allowing the inspection of the entry of that trust on the register.

Additionally, the Ordinance provides that all non-criminal judicial proceedings relating to the trust shall be heard in private and that no details may be published without leave of the court. Nevis American Trust Company Limited can provide you with the necessary documents to establish your International Exempt Trust, they may be reached via fax at 869-469-1614. If you wish to discuss trusts with a knowledgeable Nevis American Trust associate contact Offshore Corporate Services at 604-684-2622.

THE NEVIS LIMITED LIABILITY COMPANY ORDINANCE

With the enactment of the Nevis Limited Liability Company Ordinance 1995, the island of Nevis boasts the most state-of-the-art LLC Legislation in the world. This legislation is aimed at solving many of the problems that perturb lawyers and business people using, or hoping to use LLCs.

The Nevis LLC is a business entity that provides an alternative to those who might consider using corporations or partnerships. It is analogous to limited liability companies springing up throughout the U.S., to limited life companies elsewhere in the Caribbean, to GmbH's in Germany, to SARL's in France and to Limitada's in Latin America.

The owners of the Nevis LLC are referred to as members, who may be thought of in the same way as one thinks of partners in a partnership or shareholders in a corporation. Their precise characterization will depend on the nature of the LLC's management. The management might be vested in all of its members, who would have many of the characteristics of partners in a general partnership. Alternatively, the company might be run by designated managers, who may come from the ranks of the members or might be hired from the outside, making the company appear to be like a limited partnership or a corporation with general partners or officers and directors. In the latter case the members will be more like passive investors similar to limited partners or shareholders.

A Nevis LLC is formed by filing articles of organization with the Registrar of Offshore Companies. The company's operations and the rights among the members are defined through an operating agreement. A foreign LLC (or like entity), may easily convert to a Nevis LLC by simply going through the conversion procedure (no more difficult than filing articles of organization): other foreign entities, such as corporations, may convert after transferring their domicile under equally simple processes.

Only the company is liable for its debts. No member, except those who may have affirmatively guaranteed company debts has liability for any company obligations.

The United States Internal Revenue Service has indicated that limited liability companies generally may be taxed either as corporations, with potential corporate level tax, or as partnerships, with income and losses flowing through to the members without any incidence of tax effects at the entity level. The Nevis LLC Ordinance permits planners to structure their Nevis LLC in any manner that suits their situation.

169

Hence, if partnership tax treatment is desired, the Nevis LLC could be structured to lack continuity of life, free transferability, centralized management, and even limited liability (only two need be avoided.) The latest IRS pronouncements have been taken into consideration, including Rev. Proc. 95-10 and the self-employment tax proposed regulation, in order to assure the utility of LLCs in U.S. business planning.

The Nevis LLC can be used for any business venture or professional practice anywhere in the world outside Nevis, including international financing arrangements to gather funds internationally for U.S. or non-U.S. operations, real estate holding in the U.S. or elsewhere, manufacturing concerns and operational or investment vehicles for offshore trusts. Those structuring the popular MIPS financing arrangements will find the Nevis LLC more appropriate for their needs than LLCs formed in any other jurisdiction. This is particularly true in light of recent U.S. Internal Revenue Service pronouncements and because of the conversion provisions in the statue which allow existing MIPS LLCs to be transferred from their current domicile to Nevis with little cost or trouble.

One concern among those employing LLCs in estate planning is the valuation issue under Internal Revenue Code section 2704(b). The Nevis LLC Ordinance prohibits members from "putting" their interests to the Company unless the members agree otherwise, thereby assuring a going-concern valuation rather than a liquidation valuation for gift tax purposes.

While most U.S. LLC statutes protect company assets from its members' creditors through the limitation of creditors to a charging order, the Nevis LLC Ordinance further specifies that this is the exclusive remedy available to the creditor and also gives the company the power to redeem the creditors' interest.

The proposed self-employment tax regulation may subject members of LLCs to self-employment tax unless, among other things, they were a limited partner in a limited partnership in the same jurisdiction. With enactment of the Nevis Limited Partnership Ordinance in the very near future, and the permissibility for professionals to use Nevis LLC and limited partnerships, it may be possible under the present formulation of the proposed regulation to qualify all members for the exclusion from the self employment tax, including those in professional firms.

∽ Chapter 15 ∽

THE NEVADA OPTION

"Over and over again courts have said that there is nothing sinister in so arranging one's affairs as to keep taxes as low as possible. Everybody does so, rich or poor; and all do right, for nobody owes any public duty to pay more than the law demands: taxes are enforced exactions, not voluntary contributions. To demand more in the name of morals is mere cant."

Judge Learned Hand
Supreme Court Justice

THE NEVADA OPTION

If you've ever been to Nevada, you have no doubt quickly sensed something in the air. It isn't necessarily the sound of coins jingling into the pan of a slot machine. It isn't the sound of buccaneers fighting it out on pirate ships in front of a casino. It isn't the sound of people on street corners handing out advertising for prostitutes.

What's in the air is the freedom that makes all these things possible. Nevada is perhaps unique in the United States as a place where the frontier spirit of freedom still holds full sway. That spirit of freedom carries through to personal economics as well. And you can enjoy the economic freedom Nevada offers -- and never even go there.

Nevada, among other pluses, has no state income tax. The state doesn't need income tax because the revenues from the casinos carry half the tax load. Many taxes you find common elsewhere in the U.S. do not exist in Nevada. There is also the mentality that what a person earns a person ought to be able to keep. It's a mindset that I share and I bet you do, too. Nevada also respects privacy --- more about that later.

The Nevada option is really quite simple and is perfectly legal and ethical, although when you first hear how it works it seems as though something must be wrong. Let me assure you, the only thing wrong about what you are about to read is that you haven't yet done it yourself and reaped the savings.

If you believe that your state income tax is simply out of control and you'd like a way to legally reduce its impact on your business, read on.

THE SECRET

This is the principle in a nutshell: you transfer profits from a high-tax jurisdiction to a jurisdiction where the taxes are lower or nonexistent. The rest of this chapter explains more about applying it to Nevada, while much of the rest of the book explains how to apply it offshore.

The Nevada option works like this: first we will assume that you have a business that generates income in the state where you currently reside, and that your home state has some form of state income tax. The Nevada strategy calls for you to form a corporation in Nevada. With the help of a skilled professional, you so arrange your finances that your home state business continually owes money to your Nevada corporation -- so much so that it shows little or no profit. The profits show up in your Nevada corporation where there is no state income tax.

Presto! You have just saved an amount equal to the state income tax that would have been due from your home state business, minus the costs of maintaining the Nevada corporation. I have simplified the process for the sake of explanation, but to do it right, so that your "corporate veil" cannot be pierced, does take the input and assistance of someone knowledgeable in these matters. Tens of thousands of people throughout the United States have enacted this simple strategy.

WHY NEVADA?

The Nevada Option is a consequence of decisions made by the Founding Fathers of the United States. They decided that individual states should have the right of taxation – the citizens of each state have the right to tax themselves as they see fit. And each state sees things differently. Nevada has chosen to permit gambling. The result is an "industry without smokestacks" that brings billions of dollars into the state. Nevada gets half its revenue from taxing casino income.

This means there is no need for personal or corporate income taxes. Nor are there taxes that are common elsewhere, such as franchise taxes, franchise on income, special intangible taxes, capital stock taxes, chain store taxes, admissions taxes, stock transfer, state inheritance taxes, and gift taxes.

The variety of taxation methods between states is part of what makes life interesting in the U.S. For example, on the West Coast, Oregon has a long-standing taboo against sales taxes. Every now and then some politician gets the bright idea of asking the voters to approve a sales tax. Not only does it never pass, but it is also usually the kiss of death for that politician.

Neighboring states like Washington and California, on the other hand, have high sales taxes -- well over 8 percent in some parts of Washington. Not surprisingly, residents of border towns in that state do much of their retail shopping in Oregon, and skip paying the tax. It is illegal to do this without paying a "use tax" to the state of Washington, but state revenue officers glumly throw up their hands and acknowledge the problem. Nevadans are no different with their sales tax of as much as 7 percent.

Oregon benefits with one of the hottest retail markets in the country as wealth crosses state lines from all directions in the quest to avoid paying sales tax. It may seem like Oregon has an unfair advantage over its neighbors, but the price of forgoing a sales tax is a high state income tax -- 9 percent -- as well as some of the highest property taxes in the country.

Oregon's high income tax is surpassed by California's personal income tax of 9.8 percent. The beneficiary is Nevada, where there is none. If people will cross state lines to avoid paying 8 percent on the purchase of a television, how much more will they cross state lines to incorporate and save 10 percent of their company's net earnings?

A CURRENT EXAMPLE

Recently our firm helped an individual who had liquidated an asset and come into quite a bit of cash -- about 1.5 million. Had she paid state income taxes in California it would have cost her about $150,000 right out of the chute. With her Nevada corporation in place, all of that wealth remained in her own hands. That is to say, in the hands of her Nevada corporation.

Nevada is not the first domestic corporate shelter. Delaware had been the home to scores of major corporations — mainly because corporate directors had more control there than the shareholders. But Nevada and Wyoming both improved on Delaware's laws, and made the rules more favorable to both large and small corporations. The most recent incorporation rush started in Nevada on March 13, 1987, when new laws were approved protecting corporate directors and officers from personal liability for acts committed on behalf of the corporation or by the corporation. These laws have made Nevada the "incorporation capital of the country."

PRIVACY

For some, the most appealing aspect of incorporating in Nevada is the respect for privacy. Nevada does not keep the identity of shareholders in the public record. In other words, who owns a corporation is no one's business but the owner. If someone is pursuing your assets and they suspect you might own a related Nevada corporation, they're going to have more hurdles in discovery than in most states. A record search, for example, generally ends up in a dead end.

Nevada requires that corporations have at least one officer and one director -- but it can be the same individual. There are professionals in Nevada who will function as the officer/director of your company. They are essentially a nominee and will do as instructed, provided that their instructions do not violate the laws under which they operate. These services are usually a part of some kind of "Corporation Headquarters Package," that also includes a telephone number, someone to answer the phone, a fax number, a mailing address, a bank account, and a trained individual who acts as the director/officer of your corporation.

Nevada nominee officers and directors are frequently lawyers who specialize in such matters. Your nominee does not even have to know who the shareholders of the corporation are. This individual need only know from whom he or she takes instructions, and where the list of shareholders is kept. And he lets go of that information only on court order. Incidentally, the shareholder list can be maintained in another country altogether. Can you imagine how frustrated some predatory lawyer in your home state is going to be when trying to connect you with your Nevada corporation. Not only can you save income tax from your home state, you can also built a firewall of privacy to protect assets.

In addition to the full service corporate headquarters providers, there are companies that offer only resident agents and mail forwarding services. The total annual costs for these services range from a low of about $85 per year to a maximum of about $3,000; the latter of which includes an on site office package.

OTHER ADVANTAGES

Nevada has other advantages over Delaware. Delaware has been too eager to share with the federal government information about you that Nevada considers private. Delaware also charges a franchise tax in addition to a state income tax. Nevada, on the other hand, not only has no state income tax (there is a constitutional ban on such a thing), and no corporate income tax, there is no franchise tax either. Even though the franchise tax in Delaware is slight, it still means annual disclosures, including dates of stockholder meetings, places of business outside the state, and revelation of the number and value of shares issued. Nevada asks for none of this.

In fact, as a matter of policy, the state of Nevada involves itself as little as possible in business and corporate transactions. Shares in a corporation can be sold or transferred with no state taxes. Unlike some states that tax a corporation according to the number of shares issued, Nevada has no tax on corporate shares. Neither is there a succession tax, which is a type of inheritance tax some states require. And stockholders and directors need neither live in Nevada nor hold their meetings in the state. You could hold such a meeting in your own home or take a tax-deductible trip to Hawaii to do so. Your corporate records can be kept anywhere -- your home, India -- you decide.

Nevada has nothing to say about what kinds of stock your corporation issues -- preferred, common or whatever. Nevada and Wyoming also allow "bearer shares." This means shares of corporations can change hands with no names attached to them -- the transactions are anonymous. Neither does Nevada have an inventory tax, a unitary tax, a state inheritance tax or personal income taxes. The lack of inventory tax alone has made Reno one of the warehouse and distributions centers of the West Coast. Inventory taxes in California have driven scores of distribution businesses across the border for financial shelter.

Directors can change the By Laws of the corporation without interference from the state. And, there is no initial or minimum capital required to start a corporation. A Nevada corporation can buy shares of its own stock and hold them, transfer them, or sell them. The corporation can use the stock to buy or lease real estate or acquire options for them. Stock can be used to pay for labor or services, and whatever the directors decide these things are worth is essentially beyond anyone's question.

Nevada does not require tax reports, and it does not share the information it does gather with other states or the federal government -- not even with the IRS. Nevada is the only state that does not share information with the IRS, and it makes them mad. As a matter of fact, the last reported effort of the IRS to get such information from the state was in 1991. The fed tried to get information from Nevada's Department of Taxation, Department of Motor Vehicles, Employment Security, Gaming and Control Board, as well as the Secretary of State's office. They soon learned that for them in Nevada, it's "no dice." If the IRS wants information, the burden of proof is on them to prove they need it -- they can't simply go fishing. Nevada has even backed off joining a consortium of states to share information with one another because it could be a way for the IRS to gain access to information about Nevada corporations indirectly.

Although the State of Nevada has denied sharing information with outside government agencies, the IRS pulled a raid on a major, and very reputable, Nevada Resident Agent firm in 1997, seizing over 30,000 corporate records. Without any notice whatsoever, forty revenue agents bearing arms sealed off the building of Laughlin & Associates. A federal marshal presented a sealed subpoena and they proceeded to haul off 70 file cabinets and the contents of every drawer of every desk in the facility. No explanation was given for the search and seizure other than a commitment that the records would be returned in ten days. Several months later all the files had still not been returned. As of late 1998, no charges had been brought against Laughlin, or to their knowledge, any of their over 30,000 clients. The federal government had once again circumvented local law by simply breaking it.

CAUTION

You should select a nominee director/officer wisely, because Nevada will protect these individuals better than any other state would. Delaware has a longer statute of limitations to sue a person acting in this capacity when improper dividends have been paid. Be alert that articles of incorporation in Nevada may eliminate or limit the personal liability a nominee officer/director for claims resulting from breach of their fiduciary duty. This is true in just about all cases other than those involving the improper payment of dividends. The right of director indemnification is an absolute right in Nevada, while it is at the discretion of the court in Delaware and virtually all the other states.

Of course as the controlling stockholder, you can fire a nominee any time you want — but an unethical operator might be able to do damage before you found out about it. What it all means is, be careful who you trust with your assets. This is where the help of an experienced, impartial expert in choosing the corporate nominee director/officer is critical. Contracts can be written in such away that the officer/director can make no move without your approval, but it takes knowledge to gain this fail-safe protection.

On the plus side, if you choose to serve your own corporation in some capacity and you are in a position to incur liability, there are creative ways you may indemnify yourself. You could issue yourself insurance in the form of trust funds, self-insurance or give yourself a security interest or lien on assets the corporation holds. Be aware that unless prevented, a nominee corporate officer could indemnify himself by placing a lien on the assets of your corporation, and the authority to do this is absolute. In most other states this is illegal, but not in Nevada. Unless there is fraud, the decision of the board of directors regarding money is final, and is neither void nor voidable.

This is why the contract with your corporate officer/director must contain key provisions, giving you power to preempt or void any such decision, and here is where expert counsel is crucial once again.

HOW IT WORKS

It really is quite simple. It is so simple, in fact that tens of thousands of people do it. To review: you have a corporation in your home state that generates, say, $150,000 per year in profits. If you paid taxes in a high rate jurisdiction like California, $15,000 of that would go to the state every year.

Instead, you spend $85 for a corporate charter in Nevada, $695 prevailing rate on a one-time basis to get set up with your Nevada corporation, and $3,000 per year for your Nevada headquarters package.

Then, you arrange to have your high-tax corporation forever in debt to your low-tax Nevada corporation. Your Nevada corporation could buy shares in your local corporation, or could lend it money. You never pay off that debt, and it accrues a high interest rate on the balance. The Nevada corporation could take a mortgage on your home, your car, your boat or airplane, so that you no longer appear to have any equity in them. You can keep title, but drain out the equity of an asset, so that it is not attractive to someone seeking to sue you. You can encumber property with trust deeds transferring the equity to your Nevada corporation. You make a public filing, typically a UCC-1, that shows the equity in the property has been pledged to the Nevada corporation to secure a previous loan. You have thus restructured ownership of both possessions and cash flow such that they are held by the Nevada entity.

These possessions become somewhat judgment proof -- at least from any judgement rendered for litigation with your home state corporation. And, of course, you've saved almost 10 percent on your company profits.

In order for your Nevada corporation to avoid being dragged into court in your home state -- let alone submitting itself to its laws and taxes -- it must avoid conducting business in your home state. There are a number of criteria that must be met for your Nevada corporation to give you the protection you seek.

You need to have a bank account for your corporation, through which you conduct your major business, such as buying and selling and paying for contract services. Having the bank account allows you to conduct the rest of the activities that legitimize your Nevada corporate shield.

You need to have an actual business office address in Nevada, which is provided by your corporate office package. One excellent proof that you have this is a canceled check from your Nevada corporation for rent. This is why there are services to provide such addresses -- a post office box is not really sufficient.

You also need a telephone listing at that address. You can prove that with a monthly telephone bill and canceled checks paying for it. You should plan on securing a business license in the city where your address is located. You also need someone at the office to answer the phone and take messages. All of these services are provided with an appropriate headquarters package.

Nevada requires that you file a one-page list of officers and directors each year on the anniversary date of your incorporation. This list must include their name(s), post office address and the name and address of your resident agent. Nevada requires a fee of $85 to file this list every year -- but that is the extent of the state's fees. Any other expense is administrative to fulfill other requirements.

HOW CAN THIS BE?

Does all this sound too good to be true? Well, it is true. And it is because of the nature of corporate law. It is so true that many celebrities, such as Michael Jackson, Madonna, Chevy Chase, Rodney Dangerfield, etc., funnel their earnings through Nevada. Corporations are considered legal although artificial "persons" with most of the same rights as a natural person. Corporations can buy, own, and sell property. They can sue other corporations or natural persons or be sued by either. A corporation is an entity in itself with its own identity, separate from yours. When it enters into contracts, the corporate officers or shareholders are not obliged by the terms, only the corporation.

If it is sued, the corporate shareholders are not personally responsible for the liability. It is a thing that is apart from you -- it is not you -- even though you may control it and enjoy great benefits from it. For example, the corporation could accumulate debts that benefit you, and then go bankrupt, leaving your estate out of the settlement. (Please don't misunderstand. I'm not suggesting this as a strategy — just pointing out the implications.)

A Nevada corporation can help you in a potential bankruptcy situation. Say, for example, your businesses are generally doing very well, but you have one company that is doing so poorly it is dragging down the rest. You can incorporate that company separately, and then file bankruptcy for it, leaving the rest of your operations intact. If it is an income property, the lender will be restrained from foreclosure until you have the opportunity to sell or refinance the property, or come up with a reorganization plan to handle the loan.

If you have a Nevada corporation, you can push the bankruptcy far away from your solvent operations. The Nevada corporation can become the holding company for all the stock of your troubled corporation. Since the holding company is headquartered in Nevada, the subsidiary can file bankruptcy there. It won't be as embarrassing in your home state, and your lender -- if the bankruptcy is a property -- will have a harder time contesting the bankruptcy.

An example of applying this principle is a New York City taxi company that has 100 cabs. It has filed 50 corporations in Nevada - one for every two cabs. If they ever get sued, two cabs is the limit of assets that can be taken. An Alaska oil company did the same thing with each of its oil wells, and a ski lodge the same with each of its chair lifts. If anything goes wrong on any part of these operations, the financial consequences are limited.

All these protections are what's known as the "corporate veil." Those who benefit from the corporation are protected by it. As I mentioned earlier, the keys to preserving this corporate veil are maintaining the bank account, business address, business license, telephone number and personnel. If these standards are upheld, the corporation is entitled to the benefits and advantages due a corporation.

OFFSHORE ASSET PROTECTION

The ultimate in security for assets is to take the principles used in Nevada and apply them overseas. That is, move equity from your domestic holdings and place them in a carefully selected foreign country, through the vehicle of an offshore asset protection trust or International Business Corporation, ("IBC".) Business vehicles such as these can separate legal ownership from beneficial value. In other words, although you benefit from your assets, you no longer legally own them. It is as the old wisdom goes -- control everything but own nothing. If you ever get hauled into court you can state with a clear conscience that the corporation that you may have some control over is not owned by you.

To do this, you shift assets of your Nevada corporation through a lien or mortgage. Or, you simply issue all the stock in your Nevada corporation to an offshore trust, corporation, or LLC. This places ownership of sensitive assets farther and farther away from grasping hands and predatory lawyers. Your separation from the offshore legal structure may be guaranteed by a variety of international agreements, such as the Hague Convention, laws regarding the sovereignty of nations and trust laws.

SUMMARY

By now it should be clear to you that if you HAVE anything, or you have more than one income source, you should have at least one Nevada corporation and perhaps several. In the back of this book in the Appendices section you'll discover a Nevada Corporation Order Form. The cost to purchase a pre-formed Nevada corporation is relatively modest. You can fax, mail, or phone-in your purchase request.

As you activate your Nevada Corporation with IRS by securing a tax identification number, be certain to declare a fiscal year date ending different from that of the calendar year. This action will allow you future flexibility in shifting income between your corporation and yourself for any given year. A good date you may want to consider is having your fiscal year end January 31st.

Why is the fiscal year date important? Well, as you may know, an individual filing a joint return can earn up to $40,100 and still only be subject to 15% federal income tax. And, your personal corporation is only assessed 15% up to the first $50,000 of net income annually. This means, with some planning you and your corporation can earn up to $90,000 collectively and only be subject to a maximum of 15% federal income tax. By keeping your company qualified in Nevada you eliminate state income tax altogether. And, remember that many normal purchases you might want to make, such as computers, etc., are simply not tax deductible to you as an individual, whereas if purchased through your corporation the entire amount may come right off the top of your taxable income.

Using additional Nevada corporations correctly, you can shift income progressively forward into different fiscal periods delaying tax due dates for years and then settling up by spreading earned income over several corporations thereby not exceeding the lowest federal tax bracket of 15%. Oh, and let's not forget that during those years of LEGAL tax settlement DELAYS, you could be earning interest or investment income ON all that money. Of course if you don't mind paying a punitive 39.6% income tax, PLUS FICA taxes, PLUS Medicare, PLUS State income taxes, the aggregate which generally exceeds half your earned income, then you're still going to want to invoke privacy and asset protection strategies if you intend to protect what's left.

∞ Chapter 16 ∞

OFFSHORE DIRECTORY

"....The offshore financial market has many advantages for rational economic operations. The reasonable expectation, when one learns that an entity is engaged offshore, is that it is there for honest economic reasons, buttressed by whatever advantages privacy holds. The major categories for offshore use are to profit from higher interest rates when lending, to enjoy lower interest rates when borrowing, to escape taxation, to enjoy greater business flexibility by avoiding regulation in an efficient market, to enjoy the protection of confidentiality when engaged in activities, which if known to others in advance might hazard business success or profit margins, and, through the confidentiality mechanisms, to hedge and enjoy other risk-allaying methods through offshore diversification, liquidity, forward speculations and the like."

US Congress Staff Report

BACKGROUND

There are a significant number of tax havens available around the world depending largely upon where you are now resident. For example, within the USA the States of Nevada, Delaware, etc. are frequently referred to as "tax havens" simply because they are more private with incorporation information and they have no state income tax. There are agent companies in both of these states which provide interesting legal techniques for residents of other states to significantly reduce future state income taxes. Some of these are worthy of serious consideration, such as the "Daddy Warbucks verses Red Ink" incorporation strategy proposed by Laughlin & Associates of Carson City, Nevada.

The focus of the Offshore Directory is to profile corporate and trust domiciles that in the author's opinion represent valid options for the kind of strategies referred to in this book. I have specifically left out some of the better known countries as locations for incorporation simply because they no longer make sense to me. Not included are countries such as Austria, Luxembourg, Liberia, The Netherlands, and Switzerland. —— With the exception of Liberia, these locations provide excellent banking facilities and trust management services, but are not recommended areas for incorporation or individual tax planning.

It is my belief that non-English speaking countries will not be of significant interest to the majority of readers and with the exception of Liechtenstein, Costa Rica, and Panama, these domiciles are not included herein.

As to my recommendation regarding the "best" offshore jurisdiction, that is a question that should be posed on a relative basis. To attempt such an answer requires one understand the individual needs of the person asking the question. Each jurisdiction has something to offer or it would not be successful in developing itself as an offshore financial service center. Some jurisdictions have laws that are better crafted for various legal structures. Others have better infrastructure and a larger number of offshore financial professionals.

Clearly Switzerland, Holland, and the Caymans are much better at handling large sums of money expeditiously than say the British Virgin Islands, Anguilla, or Nevis. However, the latter three ——all Caribbean locations — are a good deal more flexible and less expensive for filing and maintaining LLC's, corporations, international exempt trusts, and the like.

Holland no longer provides near the quality of privacy it once did, and Switzerland and the Caymans have both recently made considerable concessions to the U.S. in this area. All things considered, Nevis and the British Virgins, in that order, are my first choices when working with individuals and private companies based in the U.S. or Canada. And for that reason, an entire chapter was dedicated to Nevis and a more lengthy description of the British Virgin Islands is included in this directory. The primary drawback to the British Virgin Islands has been the recent signing of a mutual legal assistance treaty between this jurisdiction and the United States.

It should be pointed out that Canadians have a wonderful option in Barbados where they may pay a very low income tax rate on business done through a corporation in that jurisdiction and then repatriate the funds to their home country.

THE OFFSHORE ADVANTAGE

A word of caution —— if you're seeking an offshore subsidiary to a public company there are a host of other considerations that require careful review.

Prime Offshore Havens

Anguilla	Isle of Man
Bahamas	Jersey
Barbados	Liechtenstein
Belize	Marshall Islands
Bermuda	Netherlands Antilles
British Virgin Islands	Nevis
Cayman Islands	Panama
Cook Islands	St. Vincent
Gibraltar	Turks & Caicos
Guernsey	Vanuatu
Ireland	Western Samoa

ANGUILLA

Location
Anguilla is located about 150 miles east of Puerto Rico and is close to the Virgin Islands. It is a mere six miles north of St Martin.

Overview
Anguilla was formerly part of the Federation of St Kitts and Nevis but separated from the alliance in 1981. Today it remains a British territory with a similar constitutional status to Bermuda, the Cayman Islands, and the British Virgin Islands. In April 1993, the Mokoro Report identified the financial services sector as a principal adjunct to Anguilla's tourist-based economy. Adopting that Report, the Anguilla and British governments embarked upon a thorough review and rewriting of the island's financial services legislation. The extensive legislation enacted in January of 1995 was the result. Anguilla has carefully crafted an image of a "high end" tourist destination. The capital is known as "The Valley," the official language is English and the adult literacy rate is 92%.

Advantages
Ease of formation and limited reporting requirements. Recent, cutting edge legislation, adequate confidentiality guarantees, flexible corporate, partnership, and LLC structures. Zero tax jurisdiction, no foreign exchange restrictions.

Disadvantages
Fairly recent entry to the offshore financial services sector. Recent signing of a Mutual Legal Assistance Treaty with the U.S. and Great Britain

Company Status
International Business Company

Corporate Legislation Source
The Companies Ordinance 1994
International Business Companies Ordinance 1995

Company Name
Prior approval required. Some restrictions apply, such as "Bank," "Insurance," "Trust," etc.

Minimum Number Of Shareholders
One

Are Bearer Shares Available?
Yes

Minimum Directors
One

Minimum Shareholders
One

Is a registered office and/or a registered agent required?
No/Yes

What information is available on the public file?
Articles of Incorporation, Registered Agent

What Documents must be kept with the Registered Agent?
Knowledge of where the list of shareholders is kept

Is an annual return required?
No

BAHAMAS

Location
The Bahamas comprise approximately 700 islands and some 2,000 cays spread over 100,000 square miles of ocean. Nassau, the capital, is located about 90 miles from Miami, Florida, on New Providence Island. The city of Freeport is located on Grand Bahamas island only about 50 miles offshore of Florida.

Overview
The Bahamas primary source of gross revenue is tourism, which represents about 52% of the economy. The second largest source of revenue comes from trust and bank service fees on the approximately 250 billion in Eurodollars held by Bahamian banks and corporations.

The Bahamas has an excellent legal system based on British common law. The Bahamas has been an independent country within the British Commonwealth since 1973.

There is an abundance of bankers, lawyers, accountants, and investment related corporations.

Advantages
One of the newest Caribbean jurisdictions that, as a result, has benefitted from mistakes that others have made by implementing highly flexible legislation which allows operation of the company's affairs in the way most desired by the beneficial owner. The Bahamas is a cost-effective option. Once incorporated a Bahamian IBC is guaranteed exemption from Bahamian taxes for twenty years.

Disadvantages

Because of lack of public registers, ownership can be difficult to prove. Not recommended for high profile trading operations. The Bahamas seems to be under extra scrutiny by IRS. Recent signing of a mutual legal assistance treaty with the United States and Great Britain.

Company Status

International Business Company

Corporate legislation source

Common Law - International Business Companies Act 1989 (No2 of 1990)

Company name

Certain words are prohibited, e.g., "Assurance," "Bank," "Building Society," etc. Names must end with an appropriate suffix, such as "Incorporated," "Societe Anonyme," "Limited," etc.

Minimum number of shareholders:

One

Are bearer shares available?

Yes

Minimum Directors:

One. The director(s) may be located anywhere in the world with no restriction.

Minimum Officers:

One. The officer(s) may be located anywhere in the world.

Is a registered office and/or a registered agent required?

Yes / Yes

What information is available on the public file?
Memorandum & Articles of Association, Registered Office & Registered Agent

What documents must be kept at the Registered Office?
Copies of the Register of Members and Register of Directors (if maintained) together with an impression of the seal.

Is an annual return required?
No

BARBADOS

Location
Barbados is an eastern Caribbean island located in the Lesser Antilles. Barbados rates tops for beauty, resources, and infrastructure. It is located near Jamaica, Haiti, and the South American coast. The weather ranges from 78 to 80 degrees F. Barbados is one of the world's most densely populated countries. It's capital and port city are Bridgetown.

Overview
Barbados is a politically stable, economically diversified country. Its primary industries are agriculture, tourism, offshore financial services and manufacturing. This island nation is home to the second oldest parliament outside of England. Barbados gained its independence as a self-governing state within the British Commonwealth in 1966. The governor general is appointed by the British monarch. The house of assembly consists of 27 locally elected members.

Advantages
A stable, well managed, democratic jurisdiction with a well developed legal system. Low tax rate, growing double tax treaty network with limited filing requirements.

Disadvantages
Details of shareholders are submitted to the Ministry of Finance when applying for an IBC license. Audited accounts are required where total assets or revenue exceed US$500,000. One meeting of the

Directors and one of the Shareholders is required within the first eighteen months of incorporation and thereafter within any fifteen month period.

Company Status
International Business Company

Corporate legislation source
The Companies Act 1982 (based on Canada Business Corporations Act) International Business Companies Act 1991

Company name
Certain words are prohibited, e.g. "Assurance," "Bank," "Building Society," etc. Names must end with an appropriate suffix such as "Incorporated," "Societe Anonyme," "Limited," etc. Additional consent or approval is required for the use of certain words, eg "Bank," "Insurance," etc. There is also a decided preference by the Registrar of Companies for not approving names using words such as "International," "Global," etc.

Minimum number of shareholders:
One

Are bearer shares available?
No

Minimum Directors:
One. The director(s) may be located anywhere in the world with no restriction.

Minimum Officers:
One. The officer(s) may be located anywhere in the world.

Is a registered office and/or a registered agent required?
Yes / No

What information is available on the public file?
Memorandum & Articles of Association, Registered Office & Registered Agent

What documents must be kept at the Registered Office?
Statutory records and registers

Is an annual return required?
No

BELIZE

Location

Belize is located on the Caribbean seaboard of Central America. It is located approximately 150 miles due south of Cancun, Mexico, directly east of Guatemala, and north of Honduras. It has pleasant weather much of the year but summers can be very hot. Belize is the starting point of the second largest barrier reef in the world which runs parallel to the Yucatan Peninsula due north to the island of Cozumel.

Overview

Tourism has become a priority. Mayan ecological tours have become numerous. The sugar industry is in decline. The government has aggressively passed laws to attract offshore financial activity. Belizian commercial law is based on the English law model. The court system is similar to that in England.

Belize has a long history of democracy, peace, and stability. It is a member of the British Commonwealth, the United Nations and the Non-Aligned Movement. Belize boasts a two party system that occasionally trade power without significant incident. Both political parties encourage overseas investment.

Advantages

It is one of the newest Caribbean jurisdictions that has benefitted from mistakes other jurisdictions have made. They have implemented highly flexible legislation which allows operation of the company's affairs in the way most desired by a beneficial owner.

Disadvantages

Because of the lack of public registers, ownership can be difficult to prove. (This may also be considered an advantage.) Although the country does have privacy and confidentiality legislation in place, there are those within the financial services sector who do not seem to take it seriously. This attitude seems to be changing and Belize may eventually come of age in this regard.

Company Status
International Business Company

Corporate legislation source
The International Business Companies Act of 1990

Company name
Certain words are prohibited, ie: "Royal," "Imperial," "Bank," "Insurance," etc..

Minimum number of shareholders:
One

Are bearer shares available?
Yes

Minimum Directors:
One. The director(s) may be located anywhere in the world with no restriction.

Minimum Officers:
One. The officer(s) may be located anywhere in the world.

Is a registered office and/or a registered agent required?
Yes / Yes

What information is available on the public file?
Memorandum & Articles of Association, Registered Office & Registered Agent

What documents must be kept at the Registered Office?
Copies of the Register of Members and Register of Directors (if maintained) together with an impression of the seal

Is an annual return required?
No

BERMUDA

Location

The islands of Bermuda are located approximately 600 miles off the east coast of the United States roughly due east of North Carolina. There are seven main islands, all connected by bridges. Bermuda enjoys semi-tropical temperatures.

Overview

Bermuda is the reinsurance capital of the world with something over 4,400 captive insurance companies chartered here. Bermuda is a prestigious offshore business hub with an upscale clientele. Bermuda law is based on British common law. It is a fully independent British Commonwealth member. The Queen of England appoints the governor. The country is administered by an appointed Upper House and an elected Lower House. The governor heads up the cabinet.

Advantages

Highly respected jurisdiction. Well known captive insurance jurisdiction. Excellent professional infrastructure of lawyers, accountants, brokers, and financial advisors.

Disadvantages

Expensive. Incorporation period takes weeks rather than days or hours. Minimum capital requirements. Annual fees to the government are twice to three times higher than it's Caribbean counterparts. A Board majority must be present in Bermuda.

Corporate legislation source

Companies Act of 1981.

Company name

Certain words are prohibited: "Bank," "Insurance," etc.. Names must end with an appropriate suffix such as "Incorporated,'" "Limited'," and "Ltd."

Minimum number of shareholders:

One

Are bearer shares available?
No

Minimum Directors:
Two. The director(s) may be located anywhere in the world but a quorum must be present in Bermuda.

Minimum Officers:
One. The officer(s) may be located anywhere in the world.

Is a registered office and/or a registered agent required?
Yes / No

What information is available on the public file?
Share Register

What documents must be kept at the Registered Office?
Copies of the Register of Members and Register of Directors
Minutes of Board of Directors and Shareholders Meetings

Is an annual return required?
No

BRITISH VIRGIN ISLANDS

Location
The British Virgin Islands are located directly northwest of the American Virgin Islands, a US territory. The distance between St. Thomas (American Virgins) and it's nearest British counterpart is less than twelve miles. Puerto Rico is 60 miles to the west. This dazzling little country consists of 60 small islands and cays having a total land mass of 59 square miles. The capital is Road Town, Tortola Island.

The British Virgin Islands are commonly referred to as the BVI's, and they comprise a group of four major and thirty-two minor islands in the Eastern Caribbean. Together with the United States Virgin Islands, they form a part of the Greater Antilles rising up from the Puerto Rican shelf about 200 feet below the sea surface.

Most Virgin Islanders are the descendants of slaves who worked colonial plantations. More recent immigrants to the islands have come from Puerto Rico, the United States, Venezuela, and the Lesser Antilles. Education and health standards are among the highest in the Caribbean. Christopher Columbus landed in this area in 1493. The British took over the islands they now hold in 1666, and in the same year the Danes occupied Saint Thomas, which is the largest town in the U.S. Virgin Islands. At the closest point, the U.S. Virgins and the British Virgins are only about 3 miles apart.

The climate is subtropical with daytime temperatures ranging from 85F to 93F. The population hovers around 18,000, 34% live in the vicinity of Road Town, which is the capital and primary commercial center. The BVI coastal zone consists of a number of beautiful beaches, cliffs, coral reefs, and seagrass beds, and serves as the primary tourist attraction.

The BVI has a typical British ministerial system of government headed by a Governor and an Executive Council of Ministers. They are a self governing crown colony of the United Kingdom. The Governor and the Attorney General make up the Executive branch of government, a Legislative Council makes the laws and is democratically elected every four years. BVI boasts a high literacy rate of 98.7%. The U.S. dollar is the local currency, and there are no exchange controls.

In 1984 BVI passed the International Business Corporation ACT of 1984 and launched itself into the financial services industry. This legislation proved extremely beneficial to government revenues and the Banks & Trust Company's Act of 1990, The Company Management Act of 1990, the Trustee Ordinance Amendment Act of 1993, the Insurance Act of 1994, and the Mutual Funds Act of 1996 followed it. Clearly this jurisdiction is dead set on being a competitive force in the growing offshore financial services marketplace.

The BVI has become world renowned for the simple and rapid formation of International Business Corporations, commonly known as IBCs. This particular financial service product produces eighty million in annual revenues. Over the few years since its inception, the international financial services sector has grown dramatically. By the close of 1984 there were only 235 IBCs formed. By the end of 1996 that number had increased to over 200,000. Citizens from all over the world are deeply committed to BVI corporations.

Financials services have continued to grow, with fifteen hundred BVI mutual funds representing investments in excess of US $55 Billion developed in an eighteen month period since the formation of mutual fund legislation. By the close of 1996 there were something over 180 insurance companies based in BVI.

The BVI strategy is to diversify its services by continuing to develop new products. Limited Liability Companies (LLCs) have become a popular vehicle in many parts of the world — beginning in the State of Wyoming and spreading like wild fire — and now BVI is bringing this product on line. It is likely that as complicated tax environments of countries like the U.S. become even more Draconian, two- and three-tiered corporate structures will accelerate the demand for these kinds of products.

Not to be caught resting on their laurels, the BVI government has opened up an office in Hong Kong as a step towards expanding their business activities. They are now expanding copyright and trademark legislation and upgrading their shipping registry. The offshore sector provides significant revenue to the BVI government and is the single largest contributor to its revenue base carrying 45% of the entire government overhead.

According to the BVI government, the IBC came about as a consequence of the disappearance of the double taxation agreement between the U.S., UK, and BVI. The flexibility of the IBC makes it attractive to residents of countries throughout the world. And, interestingly enough, more buyers of the ubiquitous IBC come from Europe than the States. However, recent legislation involving Limited Liability Companies and partnerships are clearly aimed at the upward mobile U.S. middle class.

The BVI has a fully automated Companies Registry that permits Trust Companies registered with the country to check company names and pay annual license fees via modem remotely. Granting direct access to the entire registry system to competent trust companies has allowed the jurisdiction to keep up with the pace of accelerating demand.

The BVI Trademark Act has provided another venue for generating revenue streams for government. Currently there appears to be a strong demand for the Registration of Trademarks in order that companies may protect global business activities. The constant threat of piracy of intellectual properties and the need for authors to protect their international copyrights have given impetus to BVI providing a suitable place for registering marks and copyrights. Registration in BVI provides recognition by the International Trademark Standards as well as in the Caribbean territory and the United Kingdom. There have been several thousand trade mark registrations filed with the BVI Trademark Registry.

Overview
The BVI's are world famous for their superb beaches, boating, and diving. Confidentiality is considered very important. This is a rapidly growing financial center with over 100 Billion Eurodollars under management. The legal system is based on English common law. The BVI's are a stable, self-governed British crown colony under the 1967 constitution.

Advantages
The flexibility of the legislation allows a company incorporated in the BVI's to operate with the absolute minimum of government interference. This is a highly popular domicile with over 200,000 IBC corporations having been filed since 1984. Annual fees are relatively low.

Disadvantages
The lack of public registers can make proof of ownership difficult. Banking infrastructure is light but growing. Recently BVI has reduced customer anonimity. In a series of recent initiatives, the BVI launched a major program to introduce far reaching anticrime legislation. The introduction of a new *Code of Conduct* marked the launch of this program.

The Code sets out general guidelines for the conduct of offshore practitioners and is designed to enhance regulatory vigilance. It was ratified by the Government and the Association of Registered Agents. Under the Code, BVI-licensed service providers are required to ensure that all business refered to them by overseas professionals has been subject to a rigouress "due diligence" and "know your client" principals.

The BVI Government is introducing due diligence audit requirements to reinforce the Code of Conduct. And, the BVI Governement is in the final stages of implementing the *Proceeds of Criminal Conduct Bill* which criminalizes ALL acts of money laundering, going beyond the *Criminal Justice (International Cooperation) Act* and the *Mutual legal Assistance Treaty* signed with the U.S. Government.

Company Status
International Business Company (IBC)

Corporate legislation source
Common Law - International Business Companies Act 1984 - as amended

Company name
Certain words are prohibited, ie: "Bank," "Insurance," "Trust."
Names must end with an appropriate suffix such as "Incorporated,"
"Limited," "Ltd," etc..

Minimum number of shareholders:
One

Are bearer shares available?
Yes

Minimum Directors:
One. The director(s) may be located anywhere in the world with no restriction.

Minimum Officers:
One. The officer(s) may be located anywhere in the world.

Is a registered office and/or a registered agent required?
Yes / Yes

What information is available on the public file?
Memorandum & Articles of Association, Registered Office & Registered Agent

What documents must be kept at the Registered Office?
Copies of the Register of Members and Register of
Directors (if maintained) together with an impression of
the seal.

Is an annual return required?
No

CAYMAN ISLANDS

Location
The Cayman Islands are situated approximately 450 miles south of Florida. They are south of Jamaica, east of Cozumel and Cancun, Mexico, and west of the majority of the Caribbean islands. The Caymans are tropical with comfortable dry winters and moderately hot summers. The three islands that comprise the Cayman's total 102 square miles of land. The capital is George Town, Grand Cayman.

Overview
The Caymans are a traditional British tax haven. The government is very supportive of the tax haven industry because it is a major factor in its economic development. Known world round for its phenomenal scuba diving, it is even better known for its tax shelter status. Cayman law is based on English common law. The Caymans are a pure tax haven with no direct taxation being levied on either residents, domestic corporations, or IBC corporations. There is no capital gains, inheritance or gift tax. However, the Caymans have signed an exchange of information agreement with the United States.

Advantages
One of the most well established of the Caribbean jurisdictions. Sophisticated legal and banking infrastructures. Flexible approach to legislative alterations.

Disadvantages
Relatively expensive compared to other Caribbean jurisdictions. Recently signed mutual legal assistance treaty.

Company Status
Non-Resident or Exempt

Corporate legislation source
The Companies Law 1960, as amended.

Company name

Certain words are prohibited, i.e., "Bank," "Insurance," "Trust." Names must end with an appropriate suffix, such as "Incorporated," "Ltd." "Limited," etc.

Minimum number of shareholders:

One

Are bearer shares available?

Yes

Minimum Directors:

One. The director(s) may be located anywhere in the world with no restriction.

Minimum Officers:

One. The officer(s) may be located anywhere in the world.

Is a registered office and/or a registered agent required?

Yes / No

What information is available on the public file?

Memorandum & Articles of Association, Registered Office & Registered Agent

What documents must be kept at the Registered Office?

Copies of the Register of Members and Register of Directors, mortgages and charges.

Is an annual return required?

Yes

COOK ISLANDS

Location

The Cook Islands are located in the South Pacific ocean. Tahiti is east of the Cooks and the Samoa's and Tonga are to the west. The main island is Rarotonga.

Overview

New Zealand is the dominant influence in the Cook Islands. New Zealand dollars comprise the primary currency and there are no exchange controls. The government has firmly continued its support for making the Cook Islands into a true financial center. Although small in population and on the other side of the world from a U.S. point of view, the Cooks boast good telecommunications and direct dialing is available from most countries. The legal system is based on English common law. The islands were ceded by Britain to New Zealand in 1901. They became fully self-governing in 1965.

Advantages

Very flexible share holding and debt structuring methods are available here. No taxes of any kind are a part of the offshore company. There appears to be a high level of confidentiality. Laws that impose penal sanctions on any person who discloses information derived from an inspection of the records of an international company guarantee anonymity in the Cook Islands.

Disadvantages

Presently suffering from bad publicity surrounding the Island's default on loans from Nauru and the rescheduling of loans from other banks.

Company Status

International Company

Corporate legislation source

International Companies Act 1981-82 as amended.

Company name

Approval required. The words "Bank," "Trust," or "Insurance," are restricted to special license holders.

Minimum number of shareholders:

One

Are bearer shares available?

Yes

Minimum Directors:
One. The director(s) may be located anywhere in the world with no restriction.

Minimum Officers:
One. At least one joint secretary must be resident in the Cook Islands.

Is a registered office and/or a registered agent required?
Yes / No

What information is available on the public file?
Name and registered office

What documents must be kept at the Registered Office?
Copies of the Register of Members and Register of Directors, secretary, and charges.

Is an annual return required?
Yes

GIBRALTAR

Location
Gibraltar is a peninsula on the southern tip of Spain. It is directly across the mouth of the Mediterranean from Morocco, Africa. Gibraltar is geographically part of Europe but only a short jet-boat ride away from Africa.

Overview
Gibraltar enjoys special status within the European Community. It is exempted from customs tariff, the value-added tax, and the common agricultural policy. Gibraltar is politically stable. The government actively promotes Gibraltar as a first-class international financial center. The court system is based on English common law. There is an abundance of professional and banking services.

Advantages
The first European jurisdiction to provide exempt company status which allows a business to be controlled and managed from Gibraltar and still enjoy preferential tax status. Probably the most cost effective

European jurisdiction. The exempt certificate gives a 25 year guarantee of exemption from Gibraltarian taxes.

Disadvantages
As a full member of the EC, pressure will likely be applied at some future date to coerce Gibraltar into changing their tax structure.

Company Status
Non resident Exempt

Corporate legislation source
UK Common Law 1929 Act introduced locally as "The Companies Ordinance."

Company name
Prior approval not required. Some words are sensitive such as "Bank," "Trust," "Royal," "Holdings," "International," "Insurance," etc. Names must end with "Limited."

Minimum number of shareholders:
One

Are bearer shares available?
Technically yes, but under Gibraltar law they are impractical.

Minimum Directors:
One. Must be a resident.

Minimum Officers:
One. Must be resident.

Is a registered office and/or a registered agent required?
Yes / No

What information is available on the public file?
Memorandum & Articles of Association, Registered Office, Directors, Shareholders, Annual Return, Mortgages, and Charges.

What documents must be kept at the Registered Office?
Copies of the Register of Members and Register of Directors, Mortgages and Charges

Is an annual return required?
Yes

GUERNSEY

Location
Located in the English Channel off the northwest coast of France, Guernsey is the second largest of these British Islands. The capital is St. Peter Port. The island of Guernsey consists of Guernsey Island and the Lihou, Herm and Jethou Islands. The Bailiwick of Guernsey consists of the island of Guernsey, Alderney and the Fief of Sark. The climate is warmer than that of the south coast of England.

Overview
The economy of Guernsey is based on tourism, agriculture, and financial services. Farming is in some decline, the financial service sector is becoming increasingly important. The majority of Guernsey legislation is derived from English common law but there are significant differences, especially as it relates to inheritance and company law.

Advantages
Guernsey offers stability, a comparatively free economic climate, a penchant for confidentiality, and favorable tax laws for companies. Many of the world's most respected financial institutions are based here. Guernsey enjoys a high degree of respectability in the world's financial circles.

Disadvantages
Higher costs, a bit slower in responding to incorporation requests. Beneficial ownership must be disclosed to the authorities, together with intended trading activities of the Company prior to incorporation. Public disclosure of shareholders and directors is required.

Company Status
Exempt companies are only incorporated at Court sessions, twice weekly.

Company name
Prior approval is required. Certain words, ie: "Insurance," "Assurance," "Bank," "Trust," etc., require further approval. Names must end with the word "Limited."

Minimum number of shareholders:
Two

Are bearer shares available?
No

Minimum Directors:
One. The director(s) may be located anywhere in the world with no restriction.

Minimum Officers:
One. The officer(s) may be located anywhere in the world.

Is a registered office and/or a registered agent required?
Yes / No

What information is available on the public file?
Memorandum & Articles of Association, Registered Office, Share Capital, Shareholders, and Directors

What documents must be kept at the Registered Office?
Copies of the Register of Members and Register of Directors, Board and Shareholder Minutes

Is an annual return required?
Yes

IRELAND

Location
Ireland is located to the west of Great Britain and is separated from Great Britain by the Irish Sea. The climate is cool, rainy and damp. The capital and primary commercial center is Dublin.

Overview
Ireland is a member of the EC. The Republic of Ireland is a common-law jurisdiction. The legal system is similar to the United States, Australia, and England. The Republic of Ireland is a parliamentary democracy with a written constitution. Ireland is not a pure tax haven. However, where an Irish corporation is 100% foreign owned and does all of its business outside of Ireland, there are no taxes.

Advantages
Full EC membership gives the Irish Company a high international status.

Disadvantages
Audited accounts must be filed annually. Disclosure of beneficial ownership to the authorities is required unless the shares are held in trust. As an EC member pressure may be brought to bear on Ireland to change their taxation system to eliminate this type of company at some stage.

Company Status
Non-Resident Corporation not subject to tax in the Irish Republic on profits, but liable to stamp duty on transfer of shares.

Corporate legislation source
Common Law - Companies Act 1963 to 1990

Company name
Certain words are prohibited, ie: "Bank," "Trust," "Insurance," etc.. Names must end with "Limited," or "Teoranta."

Minimum number of shareholders:
One

Are bearer shares available?
No

Minimum Directors:
Two. The director(s) may be located anywhere in the world except in Ireland.

Minimum Officers:
One. The officer(s) may be located anywhere in the world.

Is a registered office and/or a registered agent required?
Yes / No

What information is available on the public file?
Memorandum & Articles of Association, Registered Office, List of Directors, Secretary, Shareholders List, Annual Return, Annual Accounts, Mortgages, Charges

What documents must be kept at the Registered Office?
Register of Directors, Register of Members, Secretaries, Mortgages, Charges

Is an annual return required?
Yes

ISLE OF MAN

Location
The Isle of Man is located on the Irish Sea, close to England, Scotland and Ireland. The capital is Douglas. The population is approximately 70,000.

Overview
The Isle of Man's economy has until most recently been based on agriculture and tourism. More emphasis is now placed on industrial investment and its financial center activities. The Isle of Man is the only low-tax financial center in Europe that actively encourages new residents. There are over 50 banks, many international, that provide discreet effective service. The Isle of Man boasts an excellent com-

pliment of professionals including lawyers, accountants, top flight banking services, insurance, and brokers of all kinds.

Advantages
Different tax statuses allow clients to obtain the correct corporate structure dependent on their needs. Sophisticated infrastructure and high respectability. No stamp duty, estate duty or capital gains tax.

Disadvantages
Can be expensive for non-trading operations. Annual fees are twice that of other flexible jurisdictions such as Bahamas, BVI's, Nevis, or Anguilla. Some corporate taxes may be assessed.

Company Status
International or Exempt, not Resident or Non Resident

Corporate legislation source
The Companies Acts of 1931 to 1993

Company name
Prior approval of names are required.   Certain words are restricted, i.e., "International," "Bank," "Trust," "Holdings," "Group," "Royal." Names must end with "Limited," or "Public Limited Company."

Minimum number of shareholders:
One - but two are usual.

Are bearer shares available?
Yes

Minimum Directors:
Two. At least one must be a resident.

Minimum Officers:
One. Must be a resident that is qualified to be an officer.

Is a registered office and/or a registered agent required?
Yes / No

What information is available on the public file?
Memorandum & Articles of Association, Registered Office, List of Directors, List of Shareholders, Annual Returns, Mortgages, Charges

What documents must be kept at the Registered Office?
Copies of the Register of Members and Register of Directors, Secretaries, Mortgages, Charges, and the Corporate Seal

Is an annual return required?
Yes

JERSEY

Location

Jersey is located off the northwest coast of France near the Cherbourg peninsula. Jersey is the largest of the Channel Islands. Jersey is approximately 100 miles south of England and 14 miles from France. The capital is St. Helier. The population is approximately 83,000.

Overview

The financial services sector is the primary source of income for this island nation, followed by tourism. Jersey considers itself a tax haven and Amendments to the Income Tax Law effective 1989 add to Jersey's overall appeal. There are no laws on bank secrecy or privacy of information, however Jersey banks will restrict the identification of an account holder to senior bank officers and will provide numbered banks accounts upon request.

Advantages

A highly respected offshore financial center. Jersey has a reputation for seeking elite offshore business. Highly sophisticated infrastructure of trust companies, banking services, accountants, lawyers, and other financial related services.

Disadvantages

Relatively expensive jurisdiction as compared with other more convenient jurisdictions. Disclosure of beneficial ownership to the authorities, but not to the public. References may be required prior to incorporation.

Company Status
Exempt company is taxed at approximately $1,000 per year

Corporate legislation source
Companies (Jersey) Law 1991

Company name
Names must be approved in advance. Certain words are considered sensitive: "Royal," "International," "Bank," etc. Names must end with "Limited," or "Ltd."

Minimum number of shareholders:
Two

Are bearer shares available?
No

Minimum Directors:
One. The director(s) may be located anywhere in the world with no restriction.

Minimum Officers:
One. The officer(s) may be located anywhere in the world.

Is a registered office and/or a registered agent required?
Yes / No

What information is available on the public file?
Registered Office, Shareholders, Annual Return, Articles of Incorporation

What documents must be kept at the Registered Office?
Copies of the Register of Members, Register of Directors, list of Secretaries Minutes of General Meetings of the Directors — available to shareholder/members only

Is an annual return required?
Yes

LIECHTENSTEIN

Location
Liechtenstein is located between Switzerland and Austria. The capital is Vaduz. The population is approximately 29,000.

Overview
Liechtenstein is a highly developed, industrialized nation with a healthy economy. Liechtenstein has a firm belief in the free enterprise system and the concepts of personal privacy. Its banks are considered very confidential and tax matters are believed to be a private matter.

Advantages
Liechtenstein levies no income taxes against any company that is domiciled there if the corporation does not earn income from within the country. Flexible and liberal company law with its own trust law. Political stability and bank secrecy law. It is possible to not disclose the beneficial ownership of an account to the bank.

Disadvantages
Can be expensive for non-trading businesses or ones with small assets.

Company Status
Exempt taxed at flat minimum

Corporate legislation source
With the inclusion of EEA regulations company law has been modified. There is little to no effect on offshore companies as to book-keeping.

Company name
Certain words are prohibited: "Bank," "Insurance," "Liechtenstein," etc.. Names must end with "Aktiengesellschaft," "Limited," or "Anstalt."

Minimum number of shareholders:
One

Are bearer shares available?
Yes - usually bearer shares

Minimum Directors:
One. At least one director must meet professional standards. Currently only Liechtenstein residents qualify. Other director(s) may be located anywhere in the world with no restriction.

Minimum Officers:
One. The officer(s) may be located anywhere in the world.

Is a registered office and/or a registered agent required?
For an exempt corporation, yes and yes.

What information is available on the public file?
Corporate name, domicile, corporate body, date of registration, board members, signatory rights of board members, purpose of the company, legal representation, share capital, modifications of public information

What documents must be kept at the Registered Office?
Memorandum of association, articles of association, correspondence necessary for registration, confirmation that the minimum capital for formation is deposited with a bank, company limited by shares, subscription forms

Is an annual return required?
Not for exempt companies. Trusts are also exempt, however there are requirements for some reporting on trading activities and a 4% tax applied on dividends.

MARSHALL ISLANDS

Location

The Republic of the Marshall Islands is located about 2,200 miles southwest of Hawaii in the Pacific Ocean. From 1947 to 1990 the islands were part of the U.S. administered Trust Territory of the Pacific Islands. The Marshall Islands are divided into two parallel chains separated by about 125 miles. The Marshalls have a tropical climate. The capital is Dalap-Uliga-Darritt on Majuro Atoll.

Overview

The Marshall Islands are heavily dependent on aid from the United States. The islands have a serious balance of trade deficit and have embraced international banking as a mechanism to improve their economy. Tourism and banking are of primary economic importance. The Marshalls became internally self governing in 1979, signed a free association agreement with the U.S. in 1983, it was approved by Congress in 1986. The Marshall Islands became a member of the UN in 1991.

Advantages

Corporate law based on New York and Delaware statutes. Allows for British or US corporate management structures. Corporate law is one of the most modern in the world.

Disadvantages

A relatively new offshore jurisdiction with little experience and slight infrastructure. Heavily dependent on U.S. government. Time zone difficulties.

Company Status

Non Resident Corporation

Corporate legislation source

Marshall Islands Business Corporation Act 1990

Company name

Any name not already being used by another corporation. May use any suffix except the following: "Bank," "Foundation," "Chartered," "Partnership," "Establishment," "Insurance," and "Trust."

Minimum number of shareholders:
One

Are bearer shares available?
Yes

Minimum Directors:
One. The director(s) may be located anywhere in the world with no restriction.

Minimum Officers:
One. The officer(s) may be located anywhere in the world.

Is a registered office and/or a registered agent required?
No / Yes

What information is available on the public file?
Registered agents address, Articles of Incorporation, Amendments, Voluntary filings, Dissolution

What documents must be kept at the Registered Office?
None

Is an annual return required?
No

NETHERLANDS ANTILLES

Location

The Antilles is part of the Caribbean Leeward Islands and the Windward Islands. These two sets of islands are approximately 500 miles apart. The Windward Islands are east of Puerto Rico and the Leeward Islands are north of Venezuela. The capital is Willemstad. The population is approximately 195,000.

THE OFFSHORE ADVANTAGE

Overview

The Antilles has a legal system based on the Dutch system of the Netherlands. Although Dutch is the official language, English is widely used and prevalent in business activities. Over the past three decades offshore banking has become a booming business in the Antilles. No tax is paid on the income of companies that collect capital gains, royalties, and dividends. Holding companies pay up to a 3 percent tax on net income. An income tax exemption may be given for as many as 11 years if the new company can demonstrate how it will contribute to economy of the Antilles.

Advantages

A zero tax rate on net profits arising from offshore business activities. No withholding tax on dividends and benefits payable by offshore entities. No estate, duty, or inheritance tax is payable on the inheritance of shares in an offshore entity. No capital gains tax.

Disadvantages

No access to Double Taxation Agreements. Dutch is the primary language, confidentiality is suspect.

Company Status

Non Resident for tax purposes.

Corporate legislation source

International Companies Act 1994

Company name

Prior approval required. Many words are sensitive, ie: "Assurance," "Bank," "Insurance," "Chartered," etc.

Minimum number of shareholders:

One

Are bearer shares available?

Yes

Minimum Directors:

One. The director(s) may be located anywhere in the world with no restriction.

Minimum Officers:
One. The officer(s) may be located anywhere in the world.

Is a registered office and/or a registered agent required?
Yes / Yes

What information is available on the public file?
None

What documents must be kept at the Registered Office?
Copies of the Register of Members and Register of Directors, other documents as seem reasonable. All documents can be kept at the "agent's" office rather than the "registered" office.

Is an annual return required?
No

NEVIS

Location
Nevis and its sister country St. Kitts form a single national federation. Nevis-St. Kitts are only two miles a part at the closest point. These two island nations are located in the Leeward Islands approximately 1,200 miles southeast of Miami. The climate is nearly perfect and the island itself is a natural garden of tropical vegetation. The capital of the federation is Basseterre located on St Kitts. The commercial center of Nevis is Georgetown. The population of Nevis is 10,000; St. Kitts 38,000.

Overview
Nevis offers a very attractive program for offshore investors. There are no taxes levied in Nevis on income or the distribution of dividends for revenue earned off island. The legal system of the island is based upon English common law. The St. Kitts-Nevis federation is an active member of the British Commonwealth. It is not necessary to file the names of directors, shareholders, or officers with the public register. Excellent communications facilities offer direct dialing from the U.S., Canada, and Europe. English is the official and commercial language of the island. Nevis enjoys a literacy rate of 96%, greater than the

U.S. and one of the highest in the Western Hemisphere. An independent study has ranked the Federation of St. Kitts and Nevis as one of the ten freest nations in the world for seven years running.

Advantages
Total tax exemption is provided by law for IBC companies. Legislation is based on U.S. Delaware Law, with English conventions permitted. There are no reporting requirements, no filing requirements, and extremely flexible structures.

Disadvantages
Proof of beneficial ownership or management is difficult for lack of public disclosure requirement, however the law does provide for the voluntary disclosure of information.

Company Status
Non-resident domestic companies

Corporate legislation source
Nevis Business Corporation Ordinance 1984 as amended May 1995. Nevis International Exempt Trust Ordinance as amended 1994. Nevis Limited Liability Company Ordinance 1995.

Company name
Name cannot be in conflict with a Nevis pre-existing company. The words "Bank" and "Insurance," or derivatives are prohibited. Corporate suffix required, ie: "Limited," "Ltd," "Inc.," "Corp.," "Corporation."

Minimum number of shareholders:
One

Are bearer shares available?
Yes

Minimum Directors:
One. The director(s) may be located anywhere in the world with no restriction. There must be a director for each shareholder to a maximum required directors of three.

Minimum Officers:
One. The officer(s) may be located anywhere in the world.

Is a registered office and/or a registered agent required?
No / Yes

What information is available on the public file?
Registered Agent's address, and Articles of Incorporation

What documents must be kept at the Registered Office?
Discretionary - documents may be kept anywhere in the world.

Is an annual return required?
No

PANAMA

Location
The Republic of Panama is located between Costa Rica on the north and Colombia on the south. Panama forms the narrowest and lowest portion of the isthmus that links North and South America; Central America. The capital is Panama City. Although the official language is Spanish, most professionals also speak English. The climate is characterized by humidity and heavy rains.

Overview
Panama is notable for its tax and business advantages, notwithstanding the U.S. invasion in 1991. Panama claims to have formed over 600,000 "foreign corporations." Privacy is guaranteed with both bearer shares and numbered bank accounts held in the currency of the depositor's choice. Since the United States invasion the democracy process seems to be working.

Advantages
A very well established jurisdiction that has developed a good reputation over a number of years. No exchange controls, no taxes, and no required financial or other annual reports by corporations doing business exclusively outside Panama. The legal infrastructure is well developed and the professionals within Panama have marketed the jurisdiction aggressively and actively over an extended period.

Disadvantages
One of the few non-English offshore jurisdictions. Some concern over political stability.

Company Status
Exempt Non-Resident Corporation

Corporate legislation source
Civil Law; Law Number 32 of 1927 on Corporations and others

Company name
The name of the corporation may be in any language and must end with an appropriate suffix, i.e. "Corporation," "SA, " "Inc.," etc.

Minimum number of shareholders:
Two subscribers, but after incorporation one shareholder is acceptable.

Are bearer shares available?
Yes

Minimum Directors:
Three. The directors are not restricted to location.

Minimum Officers:
One. The officer(s) may be located anywhere in the world.

Is a registered office and/or a registered agent required?
No / Yes

What information is available on the public file?
Deed of Incorporation, Name and Addresses of Directors, Registered Agent

What documents must be kept at the Registered Office?
The company must maintain a minute book and stock register, both of which may be maintained in any part of the world.

Is an annual return required?
No

TURKS & CAICOS

Location
The Turks and Caicos are north of Haiti and the Dominican Republic and are at the bottom of the Bahamas chain. The capital is Grand Turk. The population is less than 10,000.

Overview
The Turks and Caicos New Company Act of 1982 developed a foreign investment program that was really the first in the area and which set the standard for the later BVI and Bahamas legislation. Due to a lack of effective marketing, the Turks and Caicos is under utilized.

Advantages
Very quick formation process. Very flexible corporate structure which allows a T&C company to be almost totally dependent upon the requirements of the client. A twenty year guarantee of exemption from future taxes can be obtained.

Disadvantages
Does not have as high a profile as many of its Caribbean cousins. Light professional infrastructure. Signed a Mutual Legal Assistance Treaty with the U.S.

Company Status
International Business Company

Corporate legislation source
Companies Ordinance 1981 as amended

Company name
Prior approval required. The name may be in any language and need not end with "Limited," etc.

Minimum number of shareholders:
One

Are bearer shares available?
Yes

Minimum Directors:
One. The director(s) may be located anywhere in the world with no restriction.

Minimum Officers:
One. The officer(s) may be located anywhere in the world.

Is a registered office and/or a registered agent required?
Yes / No

What information is available on the public file?
Articles of Incorporation, Registered Office

What documents must be kept at the Registered Office?
No register of members or directors need be maintained. The company should have a seal.

Is an annual return required?
No

VANUATU

Location

Vanuatu (formerly New Hebrides) is a group of about 12 islands and 60 islets extending for about 500 miles in the southwestern Pacific. Vanuatu is located about 1,000 miles northeast of Australia. The capital is Vila, located on the island of Efate.

Overview

Vanuatu's economy is based on agriculture and tourism. Vanuatu has no taxation and is developing an international banking center. The independent republic government is a parliamentary democracy with a judicial, legislative and executive branch headed by an elected president. Vanuatu was the first South Pacific island nation to establish diplomatic relations with Libya and the former Soviet Union.

Advantages
Modern, flexible International Companies Act. Good time zone for
the Far East. Suitable distancing from both Europe and the States,
which is considered beneficial by some. No income or corporate
taxes or estate duties. Twenty year guarantee of no taxes for international companies.

Disadvantages
A small "telephone window" for needed contact due to the time
differentials with North America.

Company Status
All companies untaxed.

Corporate legislation source
UK Common Law. Companies Act 1986. International Companies
Act 1992.

Company name
Can be in any language, any script, with any common ending.

Minimum number of shareholders:
One

Are bearer shares available?
Yes

Minimum Directors:
One. The director(s) may be located anywhere in the world with no
restriction.

Minimum Officers:
One. The officer(s) may be located anywhere in the world.

Is a registered office and/or a registered agent required?
Yes / Yes

What information is available on the public file?
Memorandum & Articles of Association, Registered Office & Registered Agent

What documents must be kept at the Registered Office?
Company name, Registered Office, Registered Agent, Share Capital, Restrictions, Incorporator

Is an annual return required?
No

WESTERN SAMOA

Location
Western Samoa is comprised of two large islands and seven smaller ones. Western Samoa along with nearby American Samoa comprise the Polynesian Samoa Archipelago about 1,700 miles northeast of New Zealand. The capital is Apia, located on Upola. The population is about 165,000.

Overview
Western Samoa has a long history of political, social, and economic stability. Anonymity is guaranteed by law. Western Samoa has been a fully independent nation since 1962. Parliamentary elections are held every three years. Corporations may be directors in international corporations.

Advantages
No international offshore company pays taxes. There is no obligation to appoint a resident director. Privacy is guaranteed by law.

Disadvantages
Very distant from European and American time zones. Very basic infrastructure.

Company Status
International Company

Corporate legislation source
International Companies Act 1987

Company name
Prior approval required. Names can be in any language.

Minimum number of shareholders:
One

Are bearer shares available?
Yes

Minimum Directors:
One. The director(s) may be located anywhere in the world with no restriction.

Minimum Officers:
One. The officer(s) may be located anywhere in the world.

Is a registered office and/or a registered agent required?
Yes / Yes

What information is available on the public file?
Memorandum & Articles of Association, Registered Office & Registered Agent and other voluntary filings

What documents must be kept at the Registered Office?
Copies of the Register of Members and Register of Directors

Is an annual return required?
No

EPILOGUE

Summing It Up

THE WHY & THE HOW

The cover of *The Offshore Advantage* includes the phrase ***Privacy, Asset Protection, Tax Shelters, Offshore Banking & Investing ..... WHY & HOW.***

The first section of the *Offshore Advantage*, comprising chapters 1 through 6, is entitled *"The Problem;"* these chapters deal head-on with the forces that motivate an ever-increasing number of Americans to access offshore options.

The second section of this book, chapters 7 through 11, entitled *"Decisive Information"* provides specific and pertinent intelligence on the "WHY" and the "HOW" of the *offshore advantage*.

Chapters 12 through 16 are gathered under *"The Solution"* where pragmatic action items for using the *offshore advantage* and specific information on tax shelter jurisdictions are contained.

The fourth and last section is the *Appendices* and it is crammed with important support information including the *1998 Offshore Tax Guide*, which is a summary for professionals, regarding current U.S. tax rules involving offshore legal structures.

PLANNING

Throughout recorded history people have sought ways to protect what they've worked hard to create and accumulate. Protection is sometimes required from those that would lull you into believing that they are in fact your protector, such as the tax collector, the bureaucracy, and your home legal system. Modern times require a multitude of strategies to deal with the current complicity of threats.

Many asset protection tools have become common place. The corporation is one of the most common such strategies. A corporation is in reality a "legal fiction;" an entity constructed of paper documents, which has most of the rights and powers of a living person. A corporation can buy and sell, own and control assets of every description, sue or be sued.

Even if a single individual is the sole owner of his or her own corporation, simply conducting business through a corporation (or limited liability company) can effect considerable asset protection. The corporate entity is now so commonplace that most people have forgotten that corporations were originally formed *solely* for asset protection reasons. Where the corporation was formed, what information is in the public record, and the corporation's legal home jurisdiction, can be extremely important. These simple facts frequently constitute the basis of a quality asset protection and tax planning strategy.

If you are properly incorporated, it is absolutely imperative that you respect the corporate entity as if it were a separate individual. One must be careful to follow the formalities of the law to ensure that the corporate shield will not be pierced. A lawsuit against a corporation may succeed against corporate assets, but a creditor will not be able to consume your personal assets and bank accounts - even if you are the sole shareholder of the corporation, provided corporate formalities have been adequately maintained.

Seeking out a well informed professional advisor is an integral part of developing a well-designed strategy. He or she will likely review with you some rather "esoteric" legal structures, in addition to domestic and offshore corporations, that are just as legal and ethical as those that are more commonly known. You will need to develop new privacy habits and be cautious with whom you discuss your overall strategy. Many people mistakenly believe that tax avoidance and asset protection tools that are not well known by the majority of people are somehow less effective or less legal. This is simply not true. Why is it we instantly believe it's perfectly legal for the Rockefeller's to use offshore structures but highly suspect if it's our next door neighbor?

You may be familiar with a number of legal devices but are not familiar with their asset protection and privacy value. Some structures, such as offshore asset protection trusts, seem almost mystical and are generally assumed by most to be used only by the ultra wealthy. The fact that the very rich have been using these structures for centuries attests that they are superb and effective asset protection tools that preserve wealth. And, although widely used by the super-rich, these structures are as simple as the corporate form and can be used by the common citizen.

Legal and financial planners have engaged in asset protection planning for many years. Lawyers regularly advise their clients to take advantage of limited liability vehicles. America, more than any other country has developed into an extremely litigious society, which in turn has given rise to asset protection planning for the general citizenry that was previously reserved for only the best informed of the world's society.

Setting up an offshore structure can be the most practical and cost effective insurance you will ever acquire to protect your hard-earned estate. It will definitely provide you enhanced privacy and access to greater investment returns, and you may be able to enjoy the added benefit of significant tax deferral or even legal tax avoidance.

LITIGATION EXPLOSION

Dramatic journalism, radio and television, and a high concentration of government subsidized citizens who tend to comprise the jury system have given impetus to larger and larger awards. These awards are often comprised of actual reparations, with huge sums in punitive damages. Our society has grown to expect large punitive damage awards far outweighing the actual damage to the plaintiff. Litigation, and government at large, is spinning out of control.

Plaintiffs and their attorneys target the wealthy, or at least those that have assets to seize, as well as professionals and business owners, who might not be considered wealthy, but are simply "better odds" for collection than other defendants. The bureaucracy targets the same group in an effort to increase revenues.

FLEXIBLE PERSONALIZED STRUCTURE

An experienced asset protection attorney or consultant will have dozens of domestic and offshore core-strategies that may be used in creating a personalized program to evoke high quality protection for client's assets and simultaneously achieve specific estate planning goals.

There is no panacea for asset protection and tax deferral structuring. A mechanism that will give you superior asset protection may not provide privacy or have sufficient tax advantages. There is no one "perfect" structure. An experienced asset protection planner will therefore recommend a program or strategy that may incorporate several, or even many, different devices that meet the particular needs, circumstances, and desires of a client.

To be successful, a plan will require that a specialist in this field review carefully all of your relevant circumstances and fully understand your particular goals. He or she must be thoroughly informed as to your potential or actual legal exposures at the time the strategies are to be implemented in order to avoid fraudulent conveyances. You must tell your asset protection attorney everything pertinent to possible claims outstanding.

The number of structures necessary to accomplish your particular needs varies according to your particular circumstances. A cookie-cutter approach where one size fits all, is rarely a legitimate approach.

BUSINESSES NEED SPECIAL REVIEW

Your real property and business holdings require special attention in setting up a sound asset protection strategy. These type of holdings generate liabilities that potentially effect the company's operation, as well as effecting non business assets. In comparison, assets such as stocks, bonds, furniture, and artwork, do not generate liability that might allow judgement-seeking creditors to reach your other assets.

The choice of the entity you use for your business operation may have subtle but profound effects on you, your assets, and your overall asset protection system. Your asset protection counselor will be principally concerned with (1) limiting the reach of business-generated liability, and (2) limiting your non-business creditors from attacking business assets or personal assets. Your strategic plan must also consider the tax ramifications of these asset protection choices. Remember that there is no cure-all. This requires a balancing and weighing of the benefits of any particular device, and its effect on the overall asset protection structure.

REVIEW OF ASSET PROTECTION DEVICES

The business form you use is an important aspect of your asset protection strategy. Trusts comprise another valuable asset protection device. Not only are trusts effective for asset protection in-and-of-themselves, they usually work well in conjunction with other devices in comprising the entire strategy.

As an example, you may decide that the most appropriate business form for you is a corporation. Thus protecting your personal assets from business creditors. However, the corporation's stock is a valuable asset that a personal creditor could take to satisfy a judgment. Therefore, the stock of your corporation could be placed within a trust to protect business's assets from your personal creditors.

There are various types of trusts, such as: revocable trusts, irrevocable trusts, discretionary trusts, spendthrift trusts, support trusts, charitable remainder trusts, capital gains by-pass trusts, real estate privacy trusts, living trusts, Rabbi trusts, and an interesting domestic trust developed by a U.S. attorney friend of mine named Paul Young, which he calls a "Complex Trust." Various trust types, both domestic and international, may be used as devices to invoke asset protection, privacy, and tax timing strategies. Offshore Asset Protection Trusts are as "bullet proof" a device as you will find, but recent legislation has interfered with their use as an effective tax avoidance mechanism.

JURISDICTIONS

There are a considerable number of tax haven and asset protection jurisdictions, and each of them has their pros and cons. For example, some jurisdictions do not have treaties with the United States. Others have express laws not recognizing foreign (U.S.) civil judgements. Some jurisdictions have shorter statutes of limitations than others, less expensive set-up or maintenance costs, better business infrastructures, etc. Your counselor will evaluate your personal circumstances in determining which jurisdiction might be the best for you. **While costs may be slightly higher for offshore corporate structures and trusts than their domestic counterparts, when properly employed and established, they provide, by far, the best asset protection and tax deferral opportunities available to U.S. citizens.**

OFFSHORE BANKING

Offshore banking is often employed for privacy and asset protection reasons and there are a variety of issues and concerns regarding this course of action, but on the whole offshore banks are at least as secure as U.S. banks. The United States, in its drive to curb the drug trade and other criminal activities, has also curbed personal and financial privacy right out of existence. The way you hold your money, your accounts and your assets, will determine whether the "Bank Secrecy Act" or the "Money Laundering Control Act" will apply to your overall strategy.

There are many legal and ethical devices that can and should be used to protect the assets of those in every income bracket. If you have a home, a bank account, investments, corporate securities, valuable family heirlooms, or you feel that you just cannot afford to start all over again, then your assets are at risk in today's litigious and over taxed society and should be protected.

If you have questions are comments please feel free to call us in Portland, Oregon at 503-645-9553, in Vancouver, Canada at 604-684-2622, or in Nevis, West Indies at 869-469-1606.

JAMAICA · PORT ANTONIO · HISPANIOLA · PEDERNALES · OVIEDO · BANI · SAONA

LIZA LA MAR · BLACK RIVER · KINGSTON

A N T I L L E S

ibbean Sea

N

Aruba

ORANJESTAD

Curacao

PUERTO ESTRELLA

PUEBLO NUEVO WILLEMSTAD

KRALENDIJK · Bo

COJORO · PUNTA CARDON · PUERTO

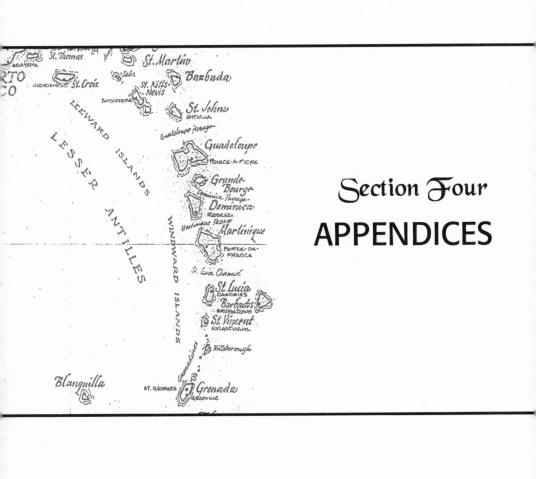

Section Four
APPENDICES

INTRODUCTION
TO THE APPENDICES

This book is focused on privacy, asset protection, and legal tax shelter, both domestically and offshore. And by now it should be clear to you that if you HAVE anything, or you have more than one income source, you should have at least one Nevada corporation and perhaps several.

As you activate your Nevada Corporation with the IRS by securing a tax identification number, be certain to declare a fiscal year date ending different from that of the calendar year. This action will allow you future flexibility in shifting income between your corporation and yourself for any given year. A good date you may want to consider is having your fiscal year end January 31st.

Why is the fiscal year date important? An individual filing a joint return can earn up to $40,100 and still only be subject to 15% federal income tax. And, your "C" corporation is only assessed 15% up to the first $50,000 of net income annually. This means that with some careful planning you and your corporation can earn up to $90,000 collectively and only be subject to a maximum of 15% federal income tax. And, by keeping your company qualified in Nevada you eliminate state income tax altogether!

Your circumstances may well warrant participation with an offshore corporation or limited liability company, and you may find it advantageous to invoke a domestic or international exempt trust in concert with an offshore corporation. However, it is my opinion that regardless of whether or not you intend to enter the offshore world, in most cases you are still well advised to have at least one Nevada corporation. There are many advantages to offshore strategies, including guaranteed privacy, premier asset protection, various tax shelter options, and higher and safer investment returns. But, before you launch into the offshore world or if you would like a recommendation for a Nevada agent, you may want to call us at 604-684-2622 in Vancouver, Canada; 503-645-9553 in Portland, Oregon; or 869-466-8642 in St Kitts, West Indies.

In this section you will find trust company contact information and a list of various law firms that specialize in offshore work which you may want to contact. There is also an application from one of the offshore trust companies, with which I work and recommend.

In our consulting activities at Offshore Corporate Services, we have worked with high net worth and high-income individuals where they have been able to legitimately reduce taxes on surplus income by up to 95%. Yes, it's true and absolutely legal, although the norm is considerably less and the expenses to achieve this kind of reduction must be carefully considered.

A comment about a related matter not addressed in this book — If you have not set up a Living Trust, then do so. A living trust should be established to prevent your heirs from suffering with the complicated and very expensive issues related to probate after your death. A living trust does not provide YOU with improved privacy, although it can keep particulars about your estate out of the newspaper as required by probate. A living trust does not provide YOU with asset protection although it can provide your heirs with critical protection regarding your estate. And, a living trust does not provide YOU with any real tax advantages, but again it can do so for your heirs.

As you take the steps to implement strategies to take back your privacy, invoke real world asset protection mechanisms, reduce your taxes where possible, and simply MAKE and KEEP a great deal more money, do not forget your heirs. This means you need to address some basic estate planning issues. Interestingly enough, one little understood value to having a Nevada and/or Offshore corporation is simply that a corporation never dies, it just elects a new president! Having two classes of stock in your corporations could allow for your future heirs to own the vast majority of the stock immediately, thus eliminating future problems with probate and punitive estate taxes. Perhaps 98% of the shares could be non-voting stock held by your children or grandchildren, with only about 2% of such a family-style company actually held in your name. The 2% of the total issued shares would represent the only VOTING class of stock and therefore keep 100% control of your business assets and activities within your power until you wish to make a change or they are passed on in your will.

Appendix A

DISCLAIMER AND
RESERVATION OF RIGHTS

DISCLAIMER.

The Offshore Tax Guide is a summary of the Internal Revenue Code as it relates to the treatment of various offshore legal entities, their structure, intent, and other information pertinent to their taxation. It is provided with the understanding that the authors and publishers are not engaged in rendering legal, accounting, or other professional advice to the reader. We strongly recommend that before relying on any of the information contained herein, competent professional legal advice and opinions should be obtained.

This summary contains information on the laws and regulations of the United States government and its agencies that is very technical in nature and which is subject to change at any time. Therefore, the authors and publishers make no guarantee as to the accuracy of this information insofar as it is applied to any particular individual or situation. The information contained in this summary is believed to be accurate in the opinion of the authors at the time this summary was completed.

The authors and publishers specifically disclaim any liability, loss or risk, personal or otherwise, incurred as a consequence directly or indirectly of the use and application of any of the information in this summary. In no event will the author, the publisher, their successors, or any resellers of this information be liable to the purchaser for any amount greater than the purchase price of these materials.

RESERVATION OF RIGHTS.

You have a right to non-exclusive use of these materials for your own educational purposes. *Your right to use these materials is non-transferable.* You agree that you will not copy or reproduce any of the information contained herein, in any form whatsoever, and that you will not sell, lease, loan, or otherwise make these materials available to third parties or permit anyone else to do the same.

Appendix B

Summary of U.S. Tax Rules Involving International Corporations, LLCs, Partnerships, and Trusts

INTRODUCTION

A variety of mechanisms imposing current U.S. tax on income earned through a foreign corporation have been reflected in the Code. Today the principal anti-deferral regimes set forth in the Code are the controlled foreign corporation rules of subpart F (951-964) and the passive foreign investment company rules (291-1297). Additional anti-deferral regimes set forth in the Code are the foreign personal holding company rules (551-558); the personal holding company rules (541-547); the accumulated earnings tax (531-537); and the foreign investment company and electing foreign investment company rules (1246-1247). The anti-deferral regimes included in the Code overlap such that a given taxpayer may be subject to multiple sets of anti-deferral rules.

However, some relief from overlapping rules is also available and is described below. In addition to those code sections which are intended to prevent the use of foreign corporations for tax deferral or avoidance purposes, this summary also explains the rules for favorable tax treatment available to corporations that meet the requirements of a Foreign Sales Corporation or Interest Charge Domestic International Sales Corporation.

An overview of the rules for foreign grantor trusts is provided, and the requirements for filing informational returns, tax returns, and disclosure statements are explained.

PART I: OWNERSHIP IN FOREIGN ENTITIES

I. Controlled Foreign Corporation laws: __ 951-964

A. *Who is taxed*: the shareholders in a foreign corporation that meets the tests below.

1. U.S._shareholders are defined as any shareholder or group of shareholders who are U.S. citizens or residents who—individually or together—own more than 50% of the total combined voting power OR more than 50% of the total value of a foreign corporation. 957(a)

a) a U.S. shareholder is any U.S. person who owns at least 10% of the total combined voting power of the outstanding stock. 957(c), 951(b).

b) rules of constructive ownership of stock apply to a foreign corporation in determining whether the corporation is a CFC. The rules of constructive ownership of stock are set forth in 958 and 318(a). Under these rules, stock is considered owned by you if your spouse, children, or an entity you control, such as a corporation, trust, or partnership owns it. Stock is also considered owned by you if it is held by any other party or agent for your benefit and upon your instructions.

2. Examples of foreign corporations that are **NOT** CFC's:

a) Eleven unrelated U.S. persons each own 9.09 % of the shares.

b) One U.S. person owns 50% and 6 (or more) other U.S. persons own equal portions of the remaining 50% (assuming they are all unrelated parties). In this case, the 50% shareholder is the only U.S. shareholder of the group, because he is the only one who owns 10% or more of the shares. The corporation is therefore not a CFC because U.S. shareholders do not own more than 50% of the shares.

3. Timing issues: although a corporation is a CFC on any day that it meets the ownership requirements set forth above, a U.S. shareholder is are not required to declare the income of the corporation on his or her personal tax return unless the corporation qualified as a CFC for at least 30 consecutive days during the tax year. 951(a)(1)

B. *How taxed*: the U.S. shareholders of a CFC are taxed as if the CFC were a pass-through entity. Each U.S. shareholder includes in his or her personal income the sum of two major components. These include the shareholder's pro rata share of Subpart F income (explained below) and any earnings of the CFC from investment in U.S. property (also explained below).

1. Subpart F income: generally, it is foreign base company income, which includes:

a) Foreign personal holding company income. (954(a)(1) and (c) This is generally passive income such as interest, dividends, rents, royalties, and gains from sales of stock, commodity transactions, foreign currency gains, etc.

b) Foreign base company sales income (see 954(a)(2) and (d)

c) Foreign base company services income (see 954(a)(3) and (e)

d) Air & sea transportation income

2. Investment earnings from U.S. property: this includes earnings from tangible property located in the US; any security issued by a US payor, or the right to use intellectual property in the US. 956(b)(1)

C. *Exceptions*: since the purpose of the CFC rules is to cut down on the use of foreign corporations as tax deferral structures, Congress created several exceptions for foreign corporations that are conducting legitimate international business activities. These exceptions are intended to give relief to foreign corporations that generate subpart F income in the ordinary course of business (e.g. interest from bank accounts or financing sales).

1. De minimis rule: the CFC rules will not apply to any corporation that has gross foreign base company income which is less than the smaller of 5% of the CFC's gross income, or $1 million. 954(b)(3)(B)

2. 90% foreign tax rule: income that would otherwise be taxable as Subpart F income is exempt from the CFC rules if it is subject to an effective rate of foreign income tax which is greater than 90% of the maximum U.S. corporate tax rate.

II. Accumulated Earnings Tax: 531-537

A. *Who is taxed*: any corporation, domestic or foreign, which has earnings from U.S. sources, if earnings have been allowed to accumulate beyond the reasonable needs of the business. T. Reg. 1.532-1(c)

B. *How taxed*: the corporation is assessed a tax of up to 28% at the corporate level on the amount of earnings that the IRS deems should be distributed as a dividend.

C. *What income is taxed*: any profits of whatever kind. The tax is assessed against the corporation itself, not the shareholders. This tax rarely comes into force against foreign corporations that are not operating in the U.S. Most foreign corporations with U.S. shareholders that operate outside of the U.S. will not be subject to the enforcement mechanisms of the U.S. government. And if a foreign corporation has U.S. shareholders, it usually is taxed by the CFC rules. If the CFC rules apply, there is no accumulated earnings tax applied (since earnings are taxed as if they were actually distributed).

III. Personal Holding Company Tax: 541-547

A. *Who is taxed*: a corporation with 5 or less individuals who own directly or indirectly more than 50% of the stock, and 60% or more of the gross income of the corporation is personal holding company income.

1. Tax not applicable if nonresident aliens own all the stock. 542(c)(7)

2. If U.S. shareholders own less than 10% of the stock, then only that percentage of undistributed personal holding company income is taxed. 545(a)

B. *How taxed*: the corporation is assessed a 28% - 39% tax on any undistributed personal holding company income.

C. *What income is taxed*: only undistributed personal holding company income that is derived from _U.S. sources as defined by the code. _ 882(b).

1. Personal Holding Company Income: is essentially passive, investment-type income, including dividends, interest royalties, annuities, and rents. 543 Exceptions exist.

* Where the Personal Holding Company Tax applies, there is no accumulated earnings tax. 532(b)(1)

** Where the Foreign Personal Holding Company Tax applies, the tax under this section does not apply. 542(c)(5)

IV. Foreign Personal Holding Company Tax: 551-558

A. *Who is taxed*: like the CFC rules, the FPHC rules impose a tax directly on the U.S. shareholders of a foreign corporation if:

    1. at least 50% of the stock (by vote or value) is owned by 5 or less US residents or citizens; and

    2. at least 60% of the corporation's income is foreign personal holding company income. 552(a)

        As with the CFC rules, an U.S. shareholder includes a U.S. corporation, trust, partnership, LLC or estate. 551(a) Although the rules of this situation will overlap with the CFC and personal holding company rules, there are some situations in which the CFC rules or the personal holding company rules may not apply. The FPHC rules were developed to plug such a loophole. Example: the CFC rules do not apply to a shareholder owning less than 10% of a CFC. But the FPHC rules apply to any U.S. shareholder as long as the 50% and 60% tests above are met.

B. *How taxed*: the US shareholders include as gross income their share of the foreign personal holding company income that remained undistributed in the corporation. 551(a)

C. *What income it taxed*: only undistributed personal holding company income.

    1. <u>Personal Holding Company Income</u>: is essentially passive, investment-type income. It also includes gains from the sale of stock (non-foreign personal holding company income does not include gains from sale of stock). 553(a)(2)

        * The corporate level Personal Holding Company tax does not apply if the tax under this section applies.

        **If the CFC tax applies, the tax under this section does NOT apply. Apply CFC rules instead. _ 951(d).

V. Passive Foreign Investment Company Provisions: 1291-1297

A. *Who is taxed*: any US shareholder of a PFIC, regardless of that shareholders individual ownership level, and regardless of overall US ownership level.

    1. *A corporation is a PFIC if*:

        a) at least 75% of the corporation's gross income is passive income; or

        b) the average percentage of its assets which provide passive income or which are held for the production of passive income is at least 50%. 1296(a)(1) 1296(a)(2) *Exceptions exist*

B. *How taxed*: two methods of taxation possible:

    1. <u>Qualified Electing Fund</u> (QEF): if a fund provides information to the shareholder necessary to determine the income and identity of the shareholders, then the US owners are taxed currently on their pro rata portions of the company's actual income, subject to an election to defer payment of tax (plus an interest charge) until a distribution is made or a disposition of stock occurs.

2. Non QEF: a US owner completes a current year inclusion estimate and defers payment of taxes, (plus interest) until a distribution is made or a disposition of stock occurs. 1291 The owner is taxed at his highest statutory rate during the time he held the stock.

C. What income is taxed: the corporation's actual income.

D. What is passive income: a group of Code sections are utilized to define the type of income that is considered passive. Generally, it includes dividends and deemed dividends, most kinds of taxable interest, certain royalty payments, annuity payments, and some rents. 1296(b) defines passive income as income that falls within the definition of foreign personal holding company income as defined in 954(c), except that passive income does not include:

1. Banking business income: income derived in the active conduct of a banking business, either as a U.S. banking company, or a foreign corporation which obtains an advance ruling from the IRS and proves compliance with Regulations. 1296(b)(2)(A); Reg. 1.552-4,5; Proposed regulations 1.1296-4(c) and (d) sets forth three requirements to meet the banking business income exception for foreign banks:
   (i) the foreign bank must be licensed or authorized to accept deposits from the residents of the country in which it is incorporated, and to conduct one or more banking activities there (but, this requirement is not satisfied if the principal purpose of obtaining a banking license is to qualify for the banking business income exception to the PFIC rules);
   (ii) the corporation must regularly accept deposits from customers that are residents of the country of incorporation, and deposits must be substantial; and
   (iii) the corporation must make loans to customers in the ordinary course of its business.
2. Insurance business income: income derived in the active conduct of an insurance business by a corporation, which is predominantly engaged in the insurance business. 1296(b)(2)(B)
3. Interest, Dividend, Rent, or Royalty income: if the income is received from a related person (as defined in 954(d)(3)), and to the extent such income is properly allocable to income of such related person which is not passive income. 1296(b)(2)(C)
   a) related person: means an individual, corporation, partnership, trust, or estate which controls or is controlled by the PFIC; or which is controlled by the same persons who control the PFIC. Control means ownership of over 50% of total value or voting stock. 954(d)(3)
4. Securities business income: income of a corporation which is registered as a securities broker or dealer with the SEC, or which meets the requirements of proposed regulation 1.1296-6; 1296(b)(3). Proposed regulations 1.1296-6 provides that income earned by an active securities dealer or broker is non-passive and exempt from PFIC taxation if either of two tests are met:

(i) the corporation is registered with the Securities & Exchange Commission as a broker/dealer;
(ii) if unregistered with the SEC, meets both of the following tests:
   (A) is licensed and authorized in the country of incorporation to conduct one or more securities activities with residents of that country, and is subject to regularly enforced securities regulations of that country;
   (B) regularly purchases securities or sells securities to customers in the ordinary course of its business, or enters into or terminates positions in securities with customers.

E. Passive Income Categories: as explained above, the PFIC rules define passive income as income which would be foreign personal holding company income under 954(c). 954(c) and related regulations define foreign personal holding company income as:

1. <u>Dividends & interest</u> (954(c)(1)(A)): except for:
   a) dividends and interest that are received from a related person which (i) is a corporation created or organized under the laws of the same foreign country as the PFIC, and (ii) has a substantial part of its assets used in its trade or business located in such same foreign country. This exception does not apply to dividends with respect to any stock which is attributable to earnings and profits of the distributing corporation accumulated during any period during which the person receiving such dividend did not hold such stock either directly, or through a chain of one or more subsidiaries, each of which meet the 2 criteria (i and ii) above.

2. <u>Royalties, rents & annuities</u> (954(c)(1)(A)): except for:
   a) rents and royalties received from a corporation which is a related person, for the use of property within the same country as the PFIC resides.
   b) rents and royalties derived in the active conduct of a trade or business received from a non-related person. Reg.1.954-2T (b)(5)
   (A) active trade or business rental income: see list of types of activities that are considered active in Reg. 1.954-2T(c).
   (B) active trade or business royalty income: see list of types of activities that are considered active in Reg. 1.954-2T(d).

Although 954(c) outlines what is and is not passive (FPHC) income, keep in mind that the exceptions to what is considered passive income in 1296(b)(2) (as discussed in section D above) trump the rules for passive income outlined in 954(c) and regulations thereto if there is any conflict.

** Note: In the literature on passive income and FPHC-type income, there is some confusion on what is considered passive income to a PFIC because the PFIC rules refer to 954(c), which deals with controlled foreign corporations. 954(c) defines what constitutes foreign personal holding company income and gives exceptions. However, the definition of passive, FPHC income is slightly different under 1296 & 954(c) and the regulations to 954 than the definitions of FPHC income under the rules for FPHCs, found in 551-558. In other words, the rules for what is passive FPHC income (with exceptions) are different in 954(c) than in 553 and 543. But both groups of code and regulations use the exact same terms: namely, foreign personal holding company income. They are not the same, however.

F. Overlap with CFC rules: The Taxpayer Relief Act of 1997 eliminates the overlap between the CFC rules and the rules under this section. In general, if a foreign corporation is a CFC and also a PFIC, a shareholder required to include income under the CFC rules will not be required to comply with the rules for PFICs. (Effective January 1, 1998).

VI.   Foreign Sales Corporations: 921-927

A. Government Sanctioned Tax Breaks: in an effort to stimulate U.S. exports without violating the rules of the World Trade Organization (formerly the GATT), Congress created the foreign sales corporation (FSC) tax rules to replace their first attempt at encouraging exports—the Domestic International Sales Corporation (DISC) rules (see section VII below for more on DISC rules). Under the new rules, qualifying corporations will be exempt from U.S. tax on a portion of their taxable income. The exemption is from 15% - 32% of the combined taxable income earned by the FSC and its related suppliers from qualified exports. 923
B. Requirements to Qualify as a FSC: a FSC is a corporation that has met all of the following tests:

1. *Qualifying foreign jurisdiction*: it must be organized under the laws of a foreign country that meets the exchange of information requirements of U.S. law, or, be formed in one of the following U.S. possessions: Guam, American Samoa, the Northern Mariana Islands, the U.S. Virgin Islands. 922(a)(1)(A) Many of the offshore tax havens will not meet this test, but some will. The key is whether there is an agreement between the U.S. government and the foreign country that provides for exchange of information regarding the tax and financial dealings of resident corporations. One of the most popular sites for incorporation of FSCs is the U.S. Virgin Islands.
2. *25 shareholder maximum*: it must have no more than 25 shareholders at any time during the tax year. 922(a)(1)(B)
3. *No preferred stock*: it must not have preferred stock outstanding at any time during the tax year. 922(a)(1)(C)
4. *Foreign office & books*: the corporation must maintain an office in a qualifying foreign country or U.S. possession with proper books of accounting, and also proper books and records at a permanent site in the U.S. 922(a)(1)(D)
5. *Foreign director*: at all times there must be at least one director on the board of directors who is not a U.S. resident. 922(a)(1)(E)
6. *No DISC relations*: it must not be a member, at any time during the tax year, of a controlled group of corporations that includes a DISC 922(a)(1)(F)

7. *Timely election*: it must have made a proper election to be taxed as a qualifying FSC within the time periods allowed by the regulations. 922(a)(2); 927(f)

C. What Income is Exempt? A qualifying FSC that has foreign trading gross receipts will qualify for an exemption from U.S. tax on a portion of its exempt foreign trade income (from 15% - 32%). In order to qualify as exempt foreign trade income, there are two additional requirements:

1. *Foreign Management:* except for a small FSC (discussed below), a FSC must have certain management functions and activities occur outside of the U.S. These include the following:

a) meetings of the board of directors and shareholders;

b) disbursement of cash dividends, outside legal and accounting fees, salaries of officers, and salaries or fees of directors out of the principal bank account;

c) maintaining the principal bank account at all times during the year. 924(b)(1)(A); 924(c)

2. Foreign Economic Processes: except for a small FSC (see below), a FSC must, either directly or by a contract, conduct the following economic processes outside of the U.S.:

a) solicitation (other than advertising), and negotiation of the sale of goods or services which are intended to qualify as foreign trading gross receipts;

b) incur direct costs attributable to the transaction equal to either at least 50% of the total direct costs attributable to the transaction in five specified categories of sales-related activities, or 85% of the direct costs attributable to any two of the five categories. 924(b)(1)(B); 924(d)

D. Overlap with CFC rules: most of the income earned by a FSC will be subpart F income under the CFC rules. However, in general, most of the income of a FSC is not subject to the CFC rules.

E. Small FSC's: 922(b) and 924(b) provide that any otherwise qualifying FSC with exempt foreign trade income receipts of $5 million or less does not have to meet the foreign management and foreign economic process requirements explained in section C. above. But taxpayers cannot use multiple small FSC's to avoid this limitation. _924(b)(2)(B)

VII. Interest Charge Domestic International Sales Corporations:

A. *Basic rules*: as explained above, the FSC rules were adopted by Congress in response to charges by GATT members that the old Domestic International Sales Corporation (DISC) rules were an unfair subsidy of American industry. Although the DISC rules were largely replaced by the FSC rules, one vestige of the old DISC rules remains. This is the Interest Charge Domestic International Sales Corporation (IC-DISC). The primary feature of the IC-DISC is that it allows domestic U.S. corporations with significant export sales to defer tax on up to $10 million of qualified export income, provided its shareholders pay an interest charge on the tax that would otherwise be due if the deferred income were distributed. 995. A corporation can elect IC-DISC tax status by meeting the following tests:

1. It must be an eligible U.S. corporation;
2. At least 95% of its gross receipts must be qualified export receipts;
3. At least 95% of its gross assets must be qualified export assets;
4. It must have only one class of stock, and the par value of its outstanding stock must be at least $2,500 on each day of the tax year;
5. It must elect IC-DISC status and the election must be in effect for the tax year;
6. It must not be a member of a controlled group that also includes a FSC;
7. It must keep separate books and records. 992(a).

VIII., Sales of Appreciated Foreign Stock: 1246-1248. Because some CFC's avoid taxation by earning income that falls outside of subpart F, 1248 was implemented. For example, in the absence of this section, a U.S. shareholder could avoid the ordinary income tax treatment that would occur if a CFC with no subpart F income made a dividend to the shareholder by simply selling the appreciated stock of the CFC to a foreign party. The U.S. shareholder would thereby only recognize a capital gain. In order to prevent this result, 1248 mandates that gain on the sale of CFC stock that would otherwise be treated as capital gain must be reported by the U.S. taxpayer as ordinary income to the extent of the CFC's earnings and profits (except for any portions of income of the CFC that did fall under Subpart F in the past).

A. *Who is taxed*: any U.S. person owning at least 10% of a CFC (either directly or indirectly, or by virtue of the constructive ownership rules applicable to CFC's).

1. Timing of sale: 1248 will apply to the sale of stock in a CFC if the foreign corporation was a CFC at any time during the preceding 5 years. The classification of the corporation at the time of sale is immaterial.

B. *How taxed:* the selling shareholder reports the gain on sale of the stock as if it were a dividend. 1248(a)

C. *What income is taxed*: only that portion of the gain recognized by the selling shareholder which is attributable to earnings and profits generated during years which the shareholder held the stock. 1248(a) (c)

D. *Section 1246 Foreign Investment Company Stock*: in cases where 1248 does not apply because a U.S. shareholder holds less than a 10% interest in a CFC, 1246 will apply to achieve the same result, preventing the selling shareholder from receiving capital gains treatment on the disposition of their stock. 1246 only applies if:

1. 50% or more of the CFC_s stock is owned by _U.S. persons (as defined under same principles as for CFC's); and
a) the CFC is registered as a management company; or
b) the CFC is engaged primarily in the business of investing or trading in securities, commodities, or any interest in such. 1246(b).

IX. Foreign Grantor Trusts: 671-679

A. *Who is taxed*: any grantor or transferor of property to any foreign trust that has any U.S. beneficiary. The basic effect of the grantor trust rules is that if the owner of property transferred to a trust retains an economic interest in, or control over the trust, the owner is treated for income tax purposes as the owner of the trust property. This means there is no true distinction between the trust and the grantor-owner for tax purposes. The result is that all transactions by the trust are treated as transactions of the owner. All expenses and income of the trust belong to and must be reported by the grantor, and tax deductions and losses arising from transactions between the owner and the trust would be ignored. See Revenue Ruling 85-13; IRS Notice 97-24.

1. *What is a foreign trust*: new rules provided in the 1996 Small Business Job Protection Act clarify whether a trust is considered foreign or domestic. The new rules provide that a trust will be considered a United States person if:
   a) a court within the United States is able to exercise primary supervision over the administration of the trust, and
   b) one or more U.S. fiduciaries have the authority to control all substantial decisions of the trust. 7701(a)(30)(E) 7701(a)(31)(B) provides that the term foreign trust means any trust other than one that meets the tests above. Trusts formed and existing before December 31, 1996 are still determined to be foreign or domestic under the old rules for determining residence, which were much more complicated and required a consideration of a long list of factors.

2. *Who is a grantor*: the IRS interprets Code sections 672-679 to mean that the following persons are considered grantors under the rules:
   a) any person who creates and funds a trust;
   b) any person who directly or indirectly makes a gratuitous transfer of money or property to a trust;
   c) any person who acquires an interest in a trust in a nongratuitous transfer from a person who is a grantor of a trust;
   d) an investor who acquires an interest in a fixed investment trust from a grantor of the trust. IRS Notice 97-34, 1997-25 Internal Revenue Bulletin; 672-679.

3. *Who is a beneficiary*: the same Notice, 97-34, also gives the IRS position that a beneficiary of a trust includes any person that could possibly benefit (directly or indirectly) from the trust at any time (including any person who could benefit if the trust were amended), whether or not the person is named in the trust instrument as a beneficiary and whether or not the person can receive a distribution from the trust in the current year. 679(c).

B. *How taxed*:
1. *U.S. Beneficiaries & Grantors*: a U.S. person who transfers property to a foreign trust that has a beneficiary who is a U.S. citizen or resident is taxed on any income that the transferred property generates during the year. This tax applies regardless of whether the transferor is a beneficiary or grantor of the

trust. (see 672(f)) Furthermore, there would be no taxable exchange of property with the trust, and the tax basis of property transferred to the trust would not be stepped-up for depreciation purposes.

a) An exception to this rule exists if fair market value is received in exchange for the asset transferred, and where the transferor recognizes the full amount of gain on the transfer. 679(a)(2)(B)

2. *Principal Purpose test for Transfer*: a gratuitous transfer under 679 includes any direct or indirect transfer that is structured with a principal purpose of avoiding the application of 679 or 6048 (see Notice 97-34, 1997-25 IRB p.23).

3. *Look through rules*: a foreign trust shall be treated as having a U.S. beneficiary unless (1) under the trust terms, no part of the income or corpus of the trust may be paid or accumulated to or for the benefit of a U.S. person, and (2) if the trust were terminated during the year, no part of the income or corpus could be paid to or for the benefit of a U.S. person. 679(c)(1)

4. *Other legal entities*: a foreign trust is treated as having a U.S. beneficiary if an amount is paid or accumulated to or for the benefit of a foreign corporation (if more than 50% of the corporation is owned by U.S. shareholders), a trust that has a U.S. beneficiary, a partnership that has a U.S. partner, or U.S. beneficiary of an estate. 679 (c)(2)

PART II: OUTBOUND TRANSACTIONS & REPORTING OBLIGATIONS

I. Reporting Required for US Citizens Holding Shares of Foreign Corporations:

A. 10% Rule and Officers/Directors in CFC's and FPHC's: 6038 and 6035 generally require every U.S. citizen or resident who is an officer, director, or who owns at least 10 percent of the stock of a foreign corporation that is a CFC or a FPHC to file Form 5471 annually.

B. Miscellaneous ownership rules: 6046 mandates the filing of information returns by certain U.S. persons with respect to a foreign corporation upon the occurrence of certain events. U.S. persons required to file these information returns are those who:

1. acquire 5% (changes to 10% on 1/1/98 under Taxpayer Relief Act of 1997) or more of the value of the stock of a foreign corporation,

2. become U.S. persons while owning that percentage of the stock of a foreign corporation, and

3. U.S. citizens and residents who are officers or directors of foreign corporations with such U.S. ownership.

C. Penalties: A failure to file the required information return under section 6038 may result in monetary penalties or reduction of foreign tax credit benefits. A failure to file the required information returns under sections 6035 or 6046 may result in monetary penalties.

II.. Recognition of Gain upon Transfers to Foreign Entities 1491-1494

A. The Old Rule—Excise Tax: Before the 1997 Taxpayer Relief Act was passed, 1491 required that a 35% excise tax be paid on any transfer of property with built-in gain to any foreign trust, corporation, estate, or partnership. Sections 1491 and 1494 were repealed by the Act.

B. The New General Rule: Effective January 1, 1998, a transferor of any asset with built-in gain to any foreign trust, corporation, estate, partnership, or LLC must immediately recognize the gain in the year transferred.

C. Reporting Obligation: the transferor of such an asset is required to report any such transfer. Failure to report results in a penalty of 35%. Reporting is not required under this section if the transfer is to a foreign trust and the transferor reports under 6048.

III. Reporting of Transfers of Money and Other Property to Foreign Trusts:

A. Section 6048(a): any US person who directly or indirectly transfers money or other property (with no gain built-in) to a foreign trust must report the transfer.
    1. *Principal Purpose test for Transfer*: a gratuitous transfer under 679 includes any direct or indirect transfer that is structured with a principal purpose of avoiding the application of 679 or 6048 (see Notice 97-34, 1997-25 IRB p.23).

B. Failure to report: results in a 35% penalty tax on the transfer under 6677(a).

C. Loans & Other Qualified Obligations Received from Trusts: Congress was concerned that taxpayers might use trust obligations to avoid taxes under 679 and reporting under 6048 (see Notice 97-34, 1997-25 IRB p.23-24). Therefore, they enacted the following rules:
    1. The obligation is nontaxable (under the 679(a)(2)(b) exception for transfers for FMV where gain is recognized by transferor) if the obligation is a qualified obligation
        a) Qualified obligations must: (1) be in writing; (2) not exceed 5 year term; (3) payments made in U.S. dollars; (4) interest yield must not be less than 100% of federal rate and not greater than 130%; (5) the transferor reports the status of the obligation including principal and interest payments on Form 3520 for each year the obligation is outstanding. Annuity contracts cannot be considered qualified obligations.

IV. Reporting of Distributions & Loans received from Foreign Trusts: 6048(c)

A. Distributions Received by a U.S. Taxpayer: generally, any U.S. person who receives a distribution, either directly or indirectly, from a foreign trust after August 20, 1996 must report on form 3520 the name of the trust, aggregate amount of distributions received during the year, etc. Again, failure to report results in a 35% penalty tax on the gross amount of the distribution.

1. *Distribution* includes gratuitous transfers of money or property, and includes distributions of trust corpus as well as trust income.

a) *Received* includes actual or constructive receipts. For example, if a U.S. beneficiary uses a credit card and the charges are paid or otherwise satisfied by a foreign trust or guaranteed or secured by the assets of a foreign trust, the amount charged on the card will be treated as a distribution to the U.S. beneficiary and must be reported under this section. Checks written on a foreign trust accounts are also treated as distributions received.

B. Loans to U.S. Grantors and U.S. Beneficiaries: 643(i) provides that (with some exceptions) if a foreign trust directly or indirectly makes a loan of cash or securities to a U.S. grantor or a U.S. beneficiary (or anyone related to them) of the trust, the amount of the loan will be treated as a distribution to that grantor or beneficiary.

V. Annual Income Tax Return for Foreign Trusts: 6048

A. Section 6048: requires that any U.S. person treated as the owner of a foreign trust for the taxable year must file a return for the trust setting forth all trust activities, trust operations, income, expenses, etc.

VI. U.S. Recipients of Large Foreign Gifts: 6039F

A. Reporting Requirements: this new section of the code requires U.S. recipients of foreign gifts to report the receipt of gifts in the following categories:
1. *Gifts from foreign individuals & estates*: a US person is required to report gifts from these parties only if in excess of $100,000 per year.
2. *Gifts from foreign corporations or partnerships*: must be reported if the aggregate amount of purported gifts from all such entities exceeds $10,000 per year.

B. How reported: the recipient must report the gifts by filing form 3520 annually. Failure to file the report results in a penalty equal to 5% of the value of the gift for each month the gift goes unreported, but cannot exceed 25%. In addition, the IRS has the option to determine how the gift should be treated for tax purposes. 6039F

C. Special Rule for Foreign Trusts: Any gift received from a foreign trust is deemed to be a distribution, and is reportable under 6048(c) and not 6039F

PART III: MISCELLANEOUS SPECIAL RULES

A. U.S. Possessions: There are a variety of special rules in place for various U.S. possessions. Because of the vast number of special exceptions, this guide will not cover them all here. The only way to be sure all possibilities have been thoroughly investigated and considered is to obtain the assistance of a qualified international tax attorney. In general, the rules are designed to create favorable conditions for investment, trade, or local economic development. Since 1986, the possessions that qualify for special treatment are:

Puerto Rico
U.S. Virgin Islands
Guam
Midway Island
Federated States of Micronesia
Paloa
American Samoa
Wake Island
Johnston Island
The Northern Meridians
The Marshall Islands

Any time that one is considering doing business in these possessions or with residents of these possessions there may be opportunities for tax savings that should be fully considered.

B. *Tax Havens*: the federal government maintains a list of tax havens that is used as a guide by IRS agents investigating U.S. persons and entities. Any time that an IRS agent discovers activities or transactions with people or entities located in a tax haven jurisdiction, a heightened level of scrutiny is applied to the review, and the agent must check for a number of potential violations or suspicious activities. The Internal Revenue Manual lists the following 30 jurisdictions as tax havens:

Antigua	Liberia
Austria	Liechtenstein
Bahamas	Luxembourg
Bahrain	Monaco
Barbados	Nauru
Belize	Netherlands
Bermuda	Netherlands Antilles
British Virgin Islands	Mananotu
Cayman Islands	Panama
Channel Islands	Singapore
Gibraltar	St. Kitts
Grenada	St. Vincent
Hong Kong	Switzerland
Ireland	Turks and Caicos Islands
Isle of Man	

Appendix C
ARTICLES OF FREE ENTERPRISE

- We believe that all men and women are created equal, and that all are endowed by their creator with certain inalienable rights that government has no right to withhold.

- We believe in each individual's right to life, liberty, and the pursuit of happiness.

- We believe in free agency, which is the right and power to choose for oneself.

- We believe that the right to own and control personal property is fundamental to the concepts of personal liberty and true freedom. And, that without the individual's right to own and control personal property, freedom cannot exist.

- We believe it is the sovereign right of an individual to accumulate wealth, and to preserve and protect it for future generations to come.

- We believe it is the right of the individual to engage in legal commerce with whom, and wherever, he or she might wish.

- We believe each individual has the right to enjoy personal and financial privacy according to their wants and needs.

- We believe it is moral and appropriate that an individual may so structure their affairs as to pay the least amount of taxes allowable under law.

- We believe in each individual's right to pursue aggressive and unrestrained enterprise, and that it may best be developed through a secure, reliable, confidential, and tax friendly jurisdiction.

- We believe that undergirding and overarching every business function must be the fundamental concept best described as "conscience over contract," meaning that it is every corporation and business person's responsibility to conduct their affairs such that they are both legal and ethical and that the highest standard of business morality is expected of all participants at all times.

Appendix D
Protect your Assets from Litigation
Stop the invasion of your Privacy
Reduce your Taxes

Privacy, asset protection and tax minimization are issues that become more poignant with each day as predatory lawyers and an invasive government strive to take what you've worked hard to earn and accumulate.

Offshore Corporate Services (Canada) Ltd. ("OCS") is a wholly owned subsidiary of Nevis American Trust Company Limited, a licensed, chartered trust company based in Nevis, West Indies with private banking, securities and mutual fund subsidiaries.

OCS specializes in the formation and administration of International Business Corporations for the benefit of undisclosed third parties.

OCS provides U.S., Canada, Nevis, Gibraltar, Ireland, Cayman, British Virgin Island, Isle of Man, Bahamian and other international structures designed to protect client's assets, ensure privacy, reduce risks taxes and costs. Gain access to offshore High Yield, Tax Free Funds! For your information, outlined below is a typical Offshore Corporate Package:

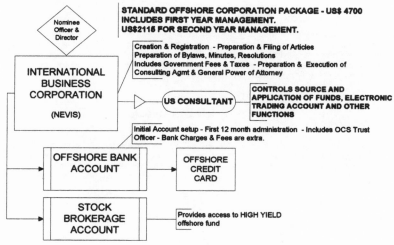

Appendix E

OFFSHORE CORPORATE SERVICES (CANADA), LTD.

CONFIDENTIAL PURCHASE ORDER

1. THE APPLICANT   **REFERRAL NO. 21313**

FULL NAME (First, Middle, Last)

ADDRESS

CITY   STATE/PROVINCE   ZIP/POSTAL CODE

OFFICE PHONE   HOME PHONE   CELL PHONE

VOICE MAIL/PAGER   FAX   E-MAIL

Copy and submit two copies of photo ID along with your notarized signature

2. CORPORATE ("IBC") NAME

CLIENT'S CHOICE OF NAME (S) -- If left blank a pre-formed corporation will be assigned

3. CORPORATE STRUCTURE

CHECK THE TYPE OF STRUCTURED IBC PACKAGE BELOW – REFER TO CURRENT PRICE SCHEDULE

☐ Basic IBC   ☐ Standard IBC   ☐ Two Tiered IBC Structure   ☐ Other

Applicant is ordering a Nevis IBC package with nominee director/officer which he/she shall be permitted to operate as a "business consultant." Venue and governing law is with Nevis. Any dispute with Offshore Corporate Services, (Canada) Ltd. ("OCS"), Nevis American Trust Company Limited, and/or any other Sovereign Crest affiliate, shall be submitted to arbitration in Charlestown, Nevis. OCS is not engaged in rendering legal, accounting, or tax advice.

_____
Applicant(s) Signature(s)

4. BANK ACCOUNT

Please open a Private Demand Deposit Account with *Exchange Bank & Trust Inc* in the name of the Nevis corporation ordered above, and execute as my nominee all required bank documentation. Please administer this bank account as needed to maintain the corporation and its accounts in good standing and in accordance with my written instructions as will be forthcoming from time to time.

_____
Applicant(s) Signature(s)

Continued …/2

Main Street, Charlestown, Nevis, WI, Phone 869.469.1606 – Fax 869.469.1614
777 Hornby, 20th Floor, Vancouver, BC Canada V6Z 1S4, Phone 604.684.2622 – Fax 604.684.2633

252

5. BENEFICIARY

FULL NAME (First, Middle, Last)

ADDRESS

CITY	STATE/PROVINCE	ZIP/POSTAL CODE

PHONE	FAX	E-MAIL

6. DOWN PAYMENT - CREDIT CARD INFORMATION

☐ VISA ☐ MASTERCARD ☐ AMERCIAN EXPRESS

CARD HOLDER NAME

CARD HOLDER NUMBER	EXPIRATION DATE

☐ I HEREBY AUTHORIZE NEVIS AMERICAN TRUST COMPANY LIMITED, OR A SUBSIDIARY, TO CHARGE MY CREDIT CARD DETAILED ABOVE, THE SUM OF TWO THOUSAND DOLLARS ($2,000.00) AS A DOWN PAYMENT FOR THE CORPORATE STRUCTURE I HAVE ORDERED HEREIN. I UNDERSTAND THAT THE BALANCE OF PAYMENT WILL BE WITHDRAWN FROM THE OPENING DEPOSIT MADE TO THE BANK ACCOUNT TO BE ESTABLISHED FOR THE CORPORATION, WHICH IS A PART OF THIS AGREEMENT. I FURTHER AUTHORIZE NEVIS AMERICAN TRUST TO DEBIT MY CREDIT CARD FOR FEES ASSOCIATED WITH THE NEW CORPORATION, OR ITS ACCOUNTS, AS SET FORTH IN THE CURRENT FEE SCHEDULE IN THE EVENT THE MANAGED CORPORATE BANK ACCOUNT HAS INSUFFICIENT FUNDS TO COVER SAID COSTS.

- or -

☐ I HEREBY AUTHORIZE NEVIS AMERICAN TRUST COMPANY LIMITED, OR A SUBSIDIARY, TO CHARGE MY CREDIT CARD DETAILED ABOVE FOR THE FULL PRICE OF THE CORPORATE STRUCTURE I HAVE ORDERED HEREIN. . I FURTHER AUTHORIZE NEVIS AMERICAN TRUST TO DEBIT MY CREDIT CARD FOR FEES ASSOCIATED WITH THE NEW CORPORATION OR ITS ACCOUNTS AS SET FORTH IN THE CURRENT FEE SCHEDULE IN THE EVENT THE MANAGED CORPORATE BANK ACCOUNT HAS INSUFFICIENT FUNDS TO COVER SAID COSTS.

_____
Authorized Signature   date

Completing the Confidential Purchase Order

1. THE APPLICANT – PLEASE COMPLETE ALL FIELDS. DON'T FORGET TO PROVIDE TWO COPIES OF YOUR PHOTO IDENTIFICATION ALONG WITH A NOTORIZED COPY OF YOUR SIGNATURE.

2. CORPORATE NAME – CHOOSE A NAME FOR THE CORPORATION. IF LEFT BLANK, A PRE-FORMED CORPORATION WILL BE USED.

3. CORPORATE STRUCTURE – CHECK BOX BY APPROPRIATE STRUCTRE TYPE, THEN SIGN AS APPLICANT IN THIS SECTION.

4. BANK ACCOUNT – IF YOU WISH US TO OPEN AN *EXCHANGE BANK & TRUST INC.*, BANK ACCOUNT IN THE NAME OF THE CORPORATION, SIGN AS APPLICANT IN THIS SECTION.

5. BENEFICIARY – THIS SECTION SHOULD CONTAIN THE NAME OR TRUST WITH WHOM WE SHOULD SEEK COUNSEL REGARDING THE CORPORATION'S ACTIVITIES IN THE EVENT OF YOUR DEMISE OR INCAPACITY.

6. DOWN PAYMENT – A MINIMUM DOWN PAYMENT OF US$2000 IS REQUIRED TO PROCESS THIS APPLICATION OR YOU MAY PAY THE FULL AMOUNT IN ADVANCE. PLEASE COMPLETE THE CREDIT CARD INFORMATION AND CHECK THE APPROPRIATE PAYMENT OPTION BOX.

Offshore Corporate Services, (Canada), Ltd, and Nevis American Trust Company Limited, agree that they will keep notes of conversations, financial records, and all written correspondence with clients confidential. Other than mailing lists, all paper and electronic files are stored in St Kitts & Nevis, West Indies, protected by privacy statutes.

Main Street, Charlestown, Nevis, WI, Phone 869.469.1606 – Fax 869.469.1614
777 Hornby, 20ᵗʰ Floor, Vancouver, BC Canada V6Z 1S4, Phone 604.684.2622 – Fax 604.684.2633

Appendix F

U.S.A.

Asset Protection Lawyers

Dunn, Carney, Allen	Wallace Glausi	503-224-6440
Anglo-American International	Dane Hines	801-818-0433
Arnold Goldstein & Assoc	Arnold Goldstein	954-420-4990
Capital Asset Management	Michael Brette	909-693-1644
Richard Higgins & Associates	Richard Higgins	801-352-8200
Benjamin D Knaupp, PC	Ben Knaupp	503-350-0900
Ord & Norman	William Norman	310-282-9900
Potter & Day	Michael Potter	619-755-6672
The Global Group	Arnold Cornez	650-617-4585
The MacPherson Group	Donald MacPherson	602-866-9566

The U.S. attorney's listed above are a sampling of experts in the fields of Privacy, Asset Protection, and Tax Shelter. Most of the above are published on these subjects. Each of them have highly specialized strategies for achieving client anonomity and asset protection, and most lawyers adept in this arena will confirm that proper use of an offshore legal structure provides the highest quality results in these endeavors. On the other hand, to accomplish defensable tax deferral generally requires one or more personal visits with counsel and that he or she carefully craft a strategy that works for an individual's particular situation. For your personal protection, please note that in order to invoke the Client-Attorney Priveledge you must retain counsel, not just visit with them over the phone.

Offshore Corporate Services, (Canada), Ltd., ("OCS") is your connection to professional solutions for the opportunities and hazards of wealth. OCS is a multi-disciplined professional firm targeted to the unique needs of the wealthy and upward-mobile middle class. Our firm provides *International Management and Financial Services* with focus on **Privacy, Asset Protection, and Tax Shelter** issues. OCS is a wholly owned subsidiary of *Nevis American Trust Company Limited* a licensed, chartered trust company based in Nevis, West Indies with bank, securities, and investment fund subsidiaries. Nevis American Trust provides legal structures, nominee services, offshore banking, offshore credit cards and access to offshore investments. OCS is not engaged in rendering legal, accounting, or tax advice.

Appendix G

Confidential Consultation Agreement

This document represents an agreement for a private consultation with Offshore Corporate Services, (Canada) Ltd. The consultation will be rendered to: , hereinafter referred to as "Client." Client may be contacted at phone number: , and/or fax number   .

It is understood that the minimum cost for the initial consultation is US $1,000. Additional consultative work will be charged Client at the rate of $360 per hour for work performed by Terry L Neal, $175 per hour for work performed by staff.

The purpose of the initial consultation is to consider how Client may regain lost privacy, implement an effective asset protection strategy, and provide information on various international topics. It is clearly understood that Offshore Corporate Services, (Canada) Ltd., is not providing legal or accounting advice, and that before implementing strategies that may be the topic of this consultation that Client shall seek the advise of an independent, trained and competent, lawyer, accountant, or financial planner, in these regards.

This consultation is non-cancelable and the consultation fee of US $1,000 is non-refundable.

Parties to this Agreement commit that information exchanged during the course of consultation shall be considered ABSOLUTLEY CONFIDENTIAL and shall not be released to any person, agency, or legal structure, except upon written authorization of the other party. For purposes of this Agreement, facsimile signatures shall have full force and effect as original signatures.

Dated: _____

_____
Client

_____
For: OCS

Appendix H

BUSINESS TERMS AND ABBREVIATIONS

ADR. American Depositary Receipt.

ADR. An Advance Determination Ruling obtained upon application to the IRS. Used, for example, to determine if a multinational policy decision is tax compliant.

Adverse trustee. One who has a substantial, beneficial interest in the trust assets as well as the income or benefits derived from the trust. A trustee that is related to the creator by birth, marriage or in an employer/employee relationship. The term is generally found in the "business" trust or dual trust program.

Annuitant. The beneficiary or beneficiaries (in a last-to-die arrangement) of an annuity who receives a stream of payments pursuant to the terms of the annuity contract.

Annuity. A tax sheltering vehicle. An unsecured contract between the company and the annuitant(s) that grows deferred-free and is used to provide for one's later years. All income taxes are deferred until maturing of the annuity. Capital gains and income accumulate tax deferred. Results in a stream of payments made to the annuitant during his or her lifetime under the annuity agreement. Taxes are paid on the income, interest earned and the capital gains but only to the extent as and when they are received. Currently, there is no annual limit on purchases, but there is no tax credit for purchases. An annuity is not an insurance policy.

Anstalt. A Liechtenstein entity.

AP. Asset protection.

APT. See Asset Protection Trust.

Asset manager. A person appointed by a written contract between the IBC (or the exempt company) or the APT and that person to direct the investment program. It can be a fully discretionary account or limitations can be imposed by the contract under the terms of the APT or by the officers of the IBC. Fees to the asset manager can be based on performance achieved, trading commissions or a percentage of the valuation of the estate under his or her management.

Asset Protection Trust (APT). A special form of irrevocable trust, usually created (settled) offshore for the principal purposes of preserving and protecting part of one's wealth offshore against creditors. Title to the asset is transferred to a person named the trustee. Generally used for asset protection and usually tax neutral. Its ultimate function is to provide for the beneficiaries of the APT.

Authorized capital. With respect to a corporation or company (IBC), the sum value of the aggregate of par value of all shares which the company is authorized to issue. (Also see flight capital.)

Badges of Fraud. Conduct that raises a strong presumption that it was undertaken with the intent to delay, hinder or defraud a creditor.

Bank of International Settlements (BIS). Structured like America's Federal Reserve Bank, controlled by the Basel Committee of the G-10 nations' Central Banks, it sets standards for capital adequacy among the member central banks.

Beneficial interest or ownership. Not a direct interest, but rather through a nominee, holding legal title on behalf of the beneficial owner's equitable interest. Provides privacy and avoids use of one's own name for transactions.

Beneficiary. The person(s), company, trust or estate named by the grantor, settler or creator to receive the benefits of a trust in due course upon conditions, which the grantor established by way of a trust deed. An exception would be the fully discretionary trust. The beneficiary could be a charity, foundation and/or person(s) which or who are characterized by "classes" in terms of their order of entitlement_their hierarchy.

BIS. See Bank of International Settlements.

Board of Trustees. A board acting as a trustee of a trust or as advisors to the trustee depending upon the language of the trust indenture. Also see Committee of Advisors.

British public company. See PLC.

British West Indies (BWI). All of the Eastern Caribbean Islands, such as St Kitts & Nevis, Antigua, etc., and including the UK-dependent territories of Anguilla, the British Virgin Islands (BVI), the Cayman Islands, Montserrat and the Turks and Caicos Islands.

Business trust. A trust created for the primary purpose of operating or engaging in a business. It is a person under the Internal Revenue Code (IRC). It must have a business purpose and actually function as a business.

BWI. See British West Indies.

Capital. See authorized capital or flight capital.

CARICOM. Caribbean Common Market. Consists of 14 sister-member countries of the Caribbean community. Members include: Antigua and Barbuda, Bahamas, Barbados, Belize, Dominica, Grenada, Guyana, Jamaica, Montserrat, St. Kitts and Nevis, St. Lucia, St. Vincent, Surinam, Trinidad and Tobago. They have set as a goal that in 1997 there will be a single market allowing for the free movement of labor. Conspicuous by their absence are the Cayman Islands and the British Virgin Islands, two major players in international banking and finance.

Certified public accountant (CPA). A term used in the U.S. to designate a licensed qualified accountant, its international counterpart is the chartered accountant.

CFC. See controlled foreign corporation.

Committee of Advisors. Provides nonbinding advice to the trustee of a trust and/or the trust protector. Friendly towards settler but must still maintain independence. In cases where there is too close a relationship with the settler, the committee can be construed as an alter ego of the settler.

Committee of trust protectors. An alternative to utilizing merely one trust protector. Friendly towards settler, but must remain independent. See trust protector.

Common Law. The early English system of case law as opposed to statutory law.

Companies Act or Ordinance. Legislation enacted by a tax haven to provide for the incorporation, registration and operation of international business companies (IBCs). More commonly found in the Caribbean tax havens. For a typical example, read the Bahamas' International Business Company Act of 1989.

Company. A restricted corporation, i.e., an IBC or exempt company.

Contingent beneficial interest. An interest given to a beneficiary which is not fully vested by being discretionary. In theory, since they are inchoate interests, not truly gifting, they are unvested, they are not subject to an attachment by the beneficiary's creditor and are not reportable as an IRS form 709 gifting.

Controlled foreign corporation (CFC). An offshore company which, because of ownership or voting control of U.S. persons, is treated by the IRS as a U.S. tax reporting entity. IRC §951 and §957 collectively define the CFC as one in which a U.S. person owns 10 percent or more of a foreign corporation or in which 50 percent or more of the total voting stock is owned by U.S. shareholders collectively or 10 percent or more of the voting control is owned by U.S. persons.

CPA. See certified public accountant.

Creator. A person who creates a trust. Also see settler and grantor.

Current Account. An offshore, personal savings or checking account.

Custodian. A bank, financial institution or other entity that has the responsibility to manage or administer the custody or other safekeeping of assets for other persons or institutions.

Custodian trustee. A trustee that holds the trust assets in his or her name.

Declaration of trust. A document creating a trust; a trust deed.

Discretionary trust. A grantor trust in which the trustee has complete discretion as to who among the class of beneficiaries receives income and/or principal distributions. There are no limits upon the trustee or it would cease to be a discretionary trust. The letter of wishes could provide some "guidance" to the trustee without having any legal and binding effects. Provides flexibility to the trustee and the utmost privacy.

Donor. A transferor. One who transfers title to an asset by gifting.

EC. The European Commission of the European Union (EU).

Economic Recovery Act of 1981. See the Foreign Investor in Real Property Tax Act of 1980 (FIRPTA).

ECU. European Currency Unit.

EEC. European Economic Community.

EMU. European Monetary Unit.

Estate. Interests in real and/or personal property.

EU. European Union; replaced by the European Commission (EC).

Ex parte. An application for an injunction filed and heard without notice to the other side to protect assets.
Expat. An expatriate.

Family holding trust. A trust that is created specifically to hold the family's assets consisting of real and/or personal property.

Family limited partnership (FLP). A limited partnership created for family estate planning and some asset protection. It is family controlled by the general partners. A highly appreciated asset is transferred into the FLP to achieve a capital gains tax reduction. Usually, the parents are the general partners holding a 1 to 2 percent interest. The other family members are the limited partners holding the balance of the interest in the partnership.

Family protective trust. A UK term. See Asset Protection Trust (APT).

FIRPTA. See Foreign Investor in Real Property Tax Act of 1980.

Flight capital. Money that flows offshore and likely never returns. Flight is exacerbated by a lack of confidence as government grows without bounds, the cost of government grows out of control and the federal deficit grows (over $5 billion) without the ability of Washington to cap it; it is precipitated further by increasing concerns over invasion of personal privacy, rampant litigation and the threats of further confiscatory direct and indirect taxes.

FLP. See family limited partnership.

Foreign. May be utilized in a geographic, legal or tax sense. When used geographically, it is that which is situated outside of the U.S. or is characteristic of a country other than the U.S.

Foreign Investor in Real Property Tax Act of 1980 (FIRPTA).
Under FIRPTA and the Economic Recovery Act of 1981, unless an exemption is granted by the IRS, upon the sale of real property owned by offshore (foreign) persons, the agency, attorney or escrow officer handling the transaction is required to withhold capital gains taxes at the closing of the sale transaction. Unless withheld and submitted to the IRS, the party handling the sale transaction is personally liable for the taxes.

Foreign person. Any person, including a U.S. citizen, who resides outside the U.S. or is subject to the jurisdiction and laws of a country other than the U.S.

Foreign personal holding company (FPHC). Different than a controlled foreign corporation. Discuss with your CPA.

FPHC. See foreign personal holding company.

FPT. See family protective trust. Also see asset protection trust (APT).

Fraudulent conveyance. A transfer of an asset that violates the fraudulent conveyance statutes of the affected jurisdictions.

GmbH. A German form of a limited liability corporation. Gesellschaft mit beschrankte Haftung.

Grantor. A person who creates a trust or transfers real property to another entity. In a U.S. grantor trust, the person responsible for U.S. income taxes on the trust. May have a reversionary interest in a trust.

Grantor trust. A trust created by a grantor and taxed to that grantor (settlor).

High net worth (HNW) person. An individual with more than US500,000 in liquid assets to manage.

HNW. See high net worth person.

Homestead exemption. State or federal bankruptcy laws that protect one's residence from confiscation by a judgment creditor or loss in a personal bankruptcy.

IBC. A corporation. See international business company or exempt company.

IFC. See international financial and banking centre.

Inbound. Coming into the U.S.; onshore; such as funds being paid to a U.S. person from an offshore entity.

Incomplete gift. Where the settlor has reserved the right to add or delete beneficiaries to the trust, it is construed as an incomplete gift. See contingent beneficiary interest.

Independent trustee. A trustee who is independent of the settlor. Independence is generally defined as not being related to the settlor by blood, through marriage, by adoption or in an employer/employee relationship.

INTERFIPOL. International Fiscal Police. The tax crime counterpart to INTERPOL.

International business company (IBC). A corporation formed (incorporated) under a "Company Act" of a tax haven, but *not* authorized to do business within that country of incorporation; intended to be used for global operations. Owned by member(s)/shareholder(s). Has the usual corporate attributes.

International financial and banking centre (IFC). A country identified as being a tax haven.

International trust. A Cook Islands term for a special type of an Asset Protection Trust (APT). Governed by the laws of the Cook Islands.

INTERPOL. International Criminal Police Organization. The network of multinational law enforcement authorities established to exchange information regarding money laundering and other criminal activities. More than 125 member nations.

IRC. The U.S. Internal Revenue Code.

IRS. The U.S. Internal Revenue Service of the Treasury Department.

Layered trusts. Trusts placed in series where the beneficiary of the first trust is the second trust; used for privacy.

Layering. May be achieved with numerous combinations of entities. For example, 100 percent of the shares of an IBC being owned by the first trust, which has as its sole beneficiary a second trust.

LC. Another abbreviation for limited Liability Company. Also l.l.c. and l.c. are authorized in some states.

Letter of wishes. Guidance and a request to the trustee having no binding powers over the trustee. There may be multiple letters. They must be carefully drafted to avoid creating problems with the settlor or true settlor in the case of a grantor trust becoming a co-trustee. The trustee cannot be a "pawn" of the settlor or there is basis for the argument that there never was a complete renouncement of the assets. Sometimes referred to as a side letter.

Limited company. Not an international business company. May be a resident of the tax haven and is set up under a special company act with a simpler body of administrative laws.

Limited liability company (LLC and LC). Consists of member owners and a manager, at a minimum. Similar to a corporation that is taxed as a partnership or as an S-corporation. More specifically, it combines the more favorable characteristics of a corporation and a partnership. The LLC structure permits the complete pass-through of tax advantages and operational flexibility found in a partnership, operating in a corporate-style structure, with limited liability as provided by the state's laws. The LLC may be managed by members but need not be. It may be managed by a professional company manager. A caveat is in order: LLCs are in a state of embryonic evolution, without a clear body of case law and firm guidelines. They will generate much income for the legal community until they become an integral part of our tax, business and legal system.

Living trust. Revocable trust, for reduction of probate costs and to expedite sale of assets upon death of grantor. Provides no asset protection.

LLC. See limited liability company. Also seen in the form of L.L.C., l.l.c., L.C. (Utah) and l.c.

LLP. Limited liability partnership. A form of the LLC favored and used for professional associations, such as accountants and attorneys.

LLLP. Limited liability limited partnership. Intended to protect the general partners from liability. Previously, the general partner was a corporation to protect the principals from personal liability. Under the LLLP, an individual could be a general partner and have limited personal liability.

Ltd. An abbreviation for the word limited.

Mark. Abbreviation for German currency, the Deutche Mark.

Marital Partition Agreement. See Post Nupital Agreement.

Mavera injunction. A court injunction preventing the trustee for a trust from transferring trust assets pending the outcome of a law suit.

Member. An equity owner of a limited liability company ((LLC), limited liability partnership (LLP), limited liability limited partnership (LLLP) or a shareholder in an IBC.

Memorandum. The Memorandum of Association of an IBC, equivalent to articles of incorporation.

MLAT. See Mutual Legal Assistance Treaty.

Money laundering. Processes of placing "dirty money" into legitimate banks or business transactions to cleanse the money.

Mutual Legal Assistance Treaty (MLAT). An agreement among the U.S. and many Caribbean countries for the exchange of information for the enforcement of criminal laws. U.S. tax evasion is excluded as not being a crime to the offshore countries. Nevis has not executed the Treaty.

Non-grantor trust. Usually an APT created by a NRA person on behalf of the U.S. beneficiaries.

NRA. Nonresident (of the U.S.) alien. Not a U.S. person as defined under the Internal Revenue Code (IRC).

Offshore (OS). Offshore is an international term meaning not only out of your country (jurisdiction) but out of the tax reach of your country of residence or citizenship; synonymous with foreign, transnational, global, international, transworld and multi-national, though foreign is used more in reference to the IRS.

Offshore center. See international financial and banking centre (IFC). A more sophisticated tax haven.

OS. See offshore.

Outbound. Assets flowing offshore from the U.S.

Ownership. Ownership constitutes the holding or possession of limited liability company legal claim or title to an offshore asset.

Person. Any individual, branch, partnership, associated group, association, estate, trust, corporation, company, or other organization, agency or financial institution under the IRC.

PLC. A UK *public* limited company . Compare with the UK *private* limited company.

Portfolio manager. See asset manager.

Post Nupital Agreement. Also referred to as a Marital Partition Agreement. A legal document whereby a marial community agrees to divide its assets. Generally this type of agreement is used for asset protection and/or estate planning purposes.

Preferential transfer. A disposition of an asset that is unfair to other creditors of the transferor.

Pre-filing notice. Mailed by the IRS to parties (tax payers) who are believed to be participating in fraudulent trust programs. The notice requests that the receiver seek professional counsel before filing their next tax return.

Private banking. OS banking services for high net worth (HNW) persons.

Probate. The legal process for the distribution of the estate of a decedent.

Protector. See trust protector.

Pure equity trust. A special type of irrevocable trust marketed by promoters. The trust assets are obtained by an "exchange" of a certificate of beneficial interest in return for the assets, as opposed to traditional means, such as by gifting.

Pure trust. A contractual trust as opposed to a statutory trust, created under the Common Law. A pure trust is one in which there must be a minimum of three parties-the creator or settlor (never grantor), the trustee and the beneficiary-and each is a separate entity. A pure trust is claimed to be a lawful, irrevocable, separate legal entity.

Register. The register of international business companies (IBCs) and exempt companies maintained by the Registrar of a tax haven.

Registrar. The Registrar of Companies, a governmental body controlling the formation and renewal of companies created under their company act.

RICO. Racketeer, Influence and Corruption Organization Act of 1984.

Rule against perpetuities. A legal limit on remote vesting of assets in the beneficiaries. May be void *ab initio* (from the beginning), a fixed term or determined on a "wait and see" basis.

S.A. See Société Anonyme.

Securities. Shares and debt obligations of every kind, including options, warrants, and rights to acquire shares and debt obligations.

Settle. To create or establish an offshore trust. Done by the settlor (offshore term) or the grantor (U.S. and IRS term).

Settlor. One (the entity) who (which) creates or settles an offshore trust.

Side letter. Same as a letter of wishes.

SIPC. The Securities Industry Protection Corporation. Provides up to $500,000 insurance protection for your U.S. stock brokerage account.

Situs or site. The situs is the domicile or dominating or controlling jurisdiction of the trust. It may be changed to another jurisdiction, to be sited in another country or U.S. state.

Société Anonyme (SA). A limited liability corporation established under French Law. Requires a minimum of seven shareholders. In Spanish speaking countries, it is known as the Sociedad Anonima. Important characteristic of both is that the liability of the shareholder is limited *up to* the amount of their capital contribution.

Sparbuch. An Austrian numbered savings account.

Special custodian. An appointee of the trustee in an APT.

Special investment advisor. An appointee of the trustee in an APT.

Statute of Limitations. The deadline after which a party claiming to be injured by the settlor may (should) no longer file an action to recover his or her damages.

Statutory. That which is fixed by statutes, as opposed to Common Law.

Stiftung. A Liechtenstein form of private foundation.

SWIFT. Society for Worldwide InterBank Financial Telecommunications.

Symbols.
§ section number, singular.
§§ section numbers, plural.
(+) Favorable attribute; (++) very favorable, etc.
(-) Negative attribute; (—) very negative, etc.
~ Tilde-used as part of an Internet URL.

Tax haven. An international banking and financial center providing privacy and tax benefits.

Tax regimen. The local tax treatment of income tax, foreign source income, nonresident treatment and special tax concessions which, when combined, form complex issues.

TCI. Turks and Caicos Islands.

Tranch. A bond series issued for sale in a foreign country.

Transmogrifying. Conversion of nonexempt assets to exempt assets.

True settlor. The true grantor is not the true settlor, and his or her identity is kept quite private by the trustee. See grantor trust.

Trust. An entity created for the purpose of protecting and conserving assets for the benefit of a third party, the beneficiary. A contract affecting three parties, the settlor, the trustee and the beneficiary. A trust protector is optional but recommended, as well. In the trust, the settlor transfers asset ownership to the trustee on behalf of the beneficiaries.

Trust deed. An asset protection trust document or instrument.

Trust indenture. A trust instrument such as a trust deed creating an offshore trust.

Trust protector. A person appointed by the settlor to oversee the trust on behalf of the beneficiaries. In many jurisdictions, local trust laws define the concept of the trust protector. Has veto power over the trustee with respect to discretionary matters but no say with respect to issues unequivocally covered in the trust deed. Trust decisions are the trustee's alone. Has the power to remove the trustee and appoint trustees. Consults with the settlor, but the final decisions must be the protector's.

Trustee. A person totally independent of the settlor who has the fiduciary responsibility to the beneficiaries to manage the assets of the trust as a reasonable prudent business person would do in the same circumstances. Shall defer to the trust protector when required in the best interest of the trust. The trustee reporting requirements shall be defined at the onset and should include how often, to whom, how to respond to instructions or inquiries, global investment strategies, fees (flat and/or percentage of the valuation of the trust estate), anticipated future increases in fees, hourly rates for consulting services, seminars and client educational materials, etc. The trustee may have full discretionary powers of distributions to beneficiaries.

Trust settlement document. See trust deed.

UBO. Unincorporated business organization.

UO. Unincorporated business organization.

Uniform Partnership Act (UPA). One of the uniform type of laws adopted by some states or used as a baseline for other states.

United States (U.S.). Comprised of the 50 states, as well as the District of Columbia, the Commonwealth of Puerto Rico, the Commonwealth of the Northern Mariana Islands, American Samoa, Guam, the Midway Islands, the U.S. Virgin Islands and Wake Island.

UPA. See Uniform Partnership Act.

Upstreaming. The process of retaining earnings offshore through the billing process.

URL. Universal resource locator on the World Wide Web. A combination of letters, numbers and punctuation that comprise and "address" for a "home page."

U.S.C. United States Code (of statutes).

USD or US$. United States dollars.

U.S. person. Any person, including a foreign citizen, who resides in the United States or is subject to the jurisdiction of the U.S. tax system (regardless of where the person is situated worldwide).

Variable annuity. An annuity in which you select the investment program that suits your future needs. The ultimate payback is a function of how well your program performs during the intervening period before the maturity of the annuity.

Vetting. It is the process used by the offshore consultant for qualifying the prospective client to determine if he or she is a good candidate for offshore asset protection; as in to "vet" the prospective client.

Web. The World Wide Web (WWW) of the Internet.

World Bank. Formed to be the bank lender and technical advisor to the developing countries, utilizing funds and technical resources from the member nations (the depositors). The headquarters are in Washington D.C.

THE OFFSHORE ADVANTAGE

WWW. The World Wide Web of the Internet.